Halloween Horror Nights:
The Unofficial Story & Guide (2015)

By Christopher Ripley

Published by: Eskdale & Kent Publishing of Henwood House, Henwood, Ashford, Kent, TN24 8DH, England, United Kingdom.

Printed by: CreateSpace, a DBA of On-Demand Publishing, LLC, 4900 LaCross Road, North Charleston, SC 29406, United States of America.

Cover photos and artwork were created by Emily, with some photos by Susan Clark. The book was edited by Jenny Bentley.

ISBN-13: 978-1515170945

ISBN-10: 1515170942

DEDICATION

For Emily, Anne, Colin, Emma, George, Daisy, Mo, Mag & Trev

CONTENTS

ACKNOWLEDGMENTS

A special thank you to the team who have helped create this wonderful book and for all the assistance and support given by the various interviewees.

Terminology

Guest:
A member of the public who is attending the event.

House/Maze:
Haunted house attraction. A temporary built attraction that is built by Universal utilizing the experienced craftsmen and women of the resort. Typically the whole event takes more than 18 months to plan, design and build. It appears that Universal prefer the term 'maze' whereas the media and fans prefer the term 'house'.

Scareactor:
The term Universal uses to describe any actor trained and deployed within the event with the sole purpose of scaring the guests. This includes actors in both the houses and streets. I have seen Universal spell it 'Scaractor', 'Scuractor' and 'Scareactor', with the latter being the most widespread, therefore the most used within this book.

Scarezone:
An area within the park which is full of scareactors, typically with props and sets to build the story of each scarezone.

Soundstage:
A large building within the parks that has been built either for film/TV productions and Halloween Horror Nights.

Icon:
The main character of the event who is seen on all marketing and is chiefly portrayed within the event's narrative for that year.

Mascot:
A secondary character who is not the main icon but might be involved in the houses or marketing.

Art & Design:
The colloquial term for the department within Universal Orlando that is responsible for designing all the scares for the event.

Rat Lady:
A lady often encased within glass and covered by rats. She is seen at every event, sometimes within a house or

within a casket on wheels on the streets.

Roach Man: Same as the Rat Lady but with roaches and usually not mobile at the event.

Jello-Shot Girl/Guy: Man/Women employed within the park selling fake blood packs filled with a jello substance coloured red and containing alcohol, to mimic the look of blood. Usually dressed as vampires or demons with fake blood on them and pulling a stand with a flashing red beacon to denote their presence in a queue.

Blood Day: The day within the calendar prior to opening when the members of Art and Design go around each house with a bucket of fake blood and spray it onto the newly created sets.

CAD: Computer aided design, a computer program used to design the houses of the event, including virtual 3D walkthroughs.

IP: Intellectual Property, the term comes from the two different types of houses and scarezones at the event. Original houses are imaged in-house by Universal for the event, IPs are where deals are done to bring outside franchises to the event (such as movies or TV shows). Typically, original houses are favored by the fans and IPs are favored by the general public.

Building permits: Applications to build the temporary haunted houses are issued for approval by Universal Orlando to the City of Orlando.

Frequent Fear: A type of pass which allows the owner to attend the event on more than one night.

Gory Getaway: A vacation package which includes tickets to the event and a hotel stay.

Rush of Fear: The same as the frequent fear pass but typically held for guests attending the event in the first two weeks.

RIP Tour: A tour with a tour guide which takes guests to every house and every show in one night.

Express Pass: An extra add-on ticket which can be purchased to enable guests to get into houses more quickly by using a special queue line. The pass works on the basis that it is good for one use per house and can be used multiple times for any open rides.

Behind-the-screams: A tour that takes guests during the day around some of the houses to see how they were designed and built.

Stay and Scream: People who stay in either the Studios or Islands Park while the event is setting up. Sometimes special offers are given to guests wanting to do this.

For more information regarding ticket options, please see the official event website at Halloweenhorrornights.com

Opening Scaremonies: A show that is often presented on opening night of the event, which introduces the event's icon and narrative for the event's duration. It is not held every year.

Streetmosphere: A term created by theme park professionals that encompasses all entertainment types within the areas between the rides, including but not limited to: street performers, street shows, sets, lighting, soundtrack etc.

E-Ticket: A term originally created by Walt Disney to mean the most anticipated ride within a park. It has later been reworked to mean the most thrilling or largest ride within a park. Originally at Disneyland in the 1950s, guests would buy tickets to enter into the attractions, the tickets would be graded A to E, with E being for the most popular rides and therefore limited in quantity.

Boo-doors: Hatches and apertures within a set that scareactors use to appear from to scare guests.

Sprung Tents: A style of building whose appearance is that of a tent, however these buildings are not as temporary as a tent and are utilized solely for Halloween Horror Nights.

Scare-moving / scare propelling: A means of moving guests from one room to another by scaring them into moving forward.

Red Button: Hidden as 'Easter eggs' through select houses, they often trigger effects when pressed.

Hell Week: A week within the calendar when local and out-of-State schools all close for the holidays during the event, this often ties with South American and European guests (particularly British and German) who also have school closures around this week. This causes the event to be heavily packed with guests. It often occurs around mid to late October.

Chicken Runs: Pathways that are built within scarezones or to the side of scarezones to allow guests who do not want to be scared to move through. These have not always appeared throughout the events.

Introduction

If you've just picked this book up and have no idea what Halloween Horror Nights is, then allow me to explain. It is an annual event held at the Universal Studios Resort in Orlando and in other Universal locations around the world (though this book is mostly concerned with the events in Orlando). It is a separate after-hours hard ticketed event that is directly aimed at teenagers and adults.

The event has over the last 25 years morphed into probably the world's largest most detailed and experiential Halloween party. This rich history of the development of this beloved event is captured within this book, along with a guide towards the end that explains the best means for all attendees to get the best out of their trips.

So sit back, pull up a comfy chair and enjoy in reading the unofficial story of Halloween Horror Nights...

Where it all began… on the West Coast

The world's premier Halloween event in Florida has a very long and protracted history even before the actual original 'Fright Nights' took place, and our story doesn't even start in Orlando, it starts on the West coast at Universal Studios in Hollywood…

Since October 26th, 1973 local theme park and Southern California mainstay, Knott's Berry Farm had been running a small Halloween event that had been growing ever higher in popularity with the local residents. The event, 'Knott's Scary Farm' in 1981, appointed actor and song-parodist Weird Al Yankovic to become the event's icon or center of their marketing, with 1980s glamour-puss Elvira taking on the mantle the following year. Soon the event was bursting with guests and quickly became sold out. Upstate Universal Studios' parent company head Lew Wasserman was noticing the fleets of guests making their way home early from the park to make their way to Knott's Berry, which would simply not do. As early as 1985 plans had been made to create a series of 'Horror Nights' around the popular Halloween holiday to try and combat the perceived loss of trade resulting from the popular event held at Knott's Berry. The plans didn't take off in 1985 mostly due in part to increased studios requirements for shooting. Missing their window of 1985 did not deter the company though. When in the following year a bold decision was made to enable the event to take priority over any filming for the 1986 Halloween holiday season.

On October 8th the local press ran a publicized story[1] that the local studio were to run 'Horror Nights' where 15,000 "*frightniks*" were ready to part with $14.95 to a specially ticketed event to be run in the evenings after park close. The marketing for the event, which included newspaper adverts and radio commercials (Power 106 FM and others), promised guests the chance to spend an evening with Dracula, the Mummy, the Wolf Man, the Phantom of the Opera and even Norman Bates' dead mom! Over 70 costumed characters were promised to be roaming the expansive backlot along with allowing the studio tram tour to run at night, for the first time in Universal history (it happened first here in 1986 and not in 2015 as some believe!).

Universal had been the crowned home of horror since the 1920s where Lon Chaney Snr delighted audiences with 'The Hunchback of Notre Dame' and more successfully in 'The Phantom of the Opera' (the set still remained intact on Soundstage 28 on the backlot up until 2015 when it was demolished to make way for park expansion, though most of the surviving set pieces were retained for storage in the studios' expansive prop storage warehouse[2]). Building on Chaney's success the mantel was passed to British (by patronage) Boris Karloff and Hungarian born Bela Lugosi who terrified audiences with Frankenstein's Monster, The Mummy and Dracula movies with all sorts of combinations and sequels[3]. Lon Chaney Jnr joined the franchise in the 1940s with 'The Wolf Man' using detailed makeup, like his father before him, to both delight and terrify audiences in equal measures. This legacy of horror continued well into the 1960s when the ever-increasing series of self-reverential comedy parodies' (Abbott and Costello Meet the... series etc.) allowed for the regular succession of hits to come to a slow end. It was the renewed interest of the current 1980s generation, who had not grown up with attending the cinema of the past to see these monster hits, that allowed for a whole new plethora of monster related serials, merchandise, books and comics to feed into popular culture, once again putting the Universal Monsters center stage of the cultural lexicon.

A Universal spokesman announced to the local media outlets that the event would run from 7pm to midnight on both October 31st and November 1st 1986 respectively. They advised that the tickets would be sold on a first-come-first-served basis with a limit on ticket sales of just 7,500 per day. This event would be a one-of-a-kind event utilizing Universal's impressive back catalogue of monster heritage to its full strength, "We're getting set up to scare up the devil out of people" the spokesman for Universal said, "so please, do not bring your children", he continued.

The plan for the event was to utilize existing park assets such as the Bates Motel, which had recently been under increased popularity with the summer release of 'Psycho 3' that year. 'Psycho 2' (1983) which had been released a couple of years before had, at that time, been the longest awaited sequel in film history. The newly formed Psycho franchise was drawing on the new wave of new 'slasher' and monster movies that were becoming extremely popular. Since creating the genre by definition in 1960 with Sir Alfred Hitchcock's original masterpiece, 'Psycho', the niche genre a combination of a thriller and horror (usually with a knife toting psychopath in toe) had gone from strength to strength in the 1970s and 1980s with classics such as 'Friday 13th' (1980), 'A Nightmare on Elm Street' (1984) and 'Halloween' (1978) proving popular with audiences. Along with Courthouse Square dressed to look like a killing spree had occurred and the Court of Miracles made to look like a peasants' revolt. The Court of Miracles area had actually been used to shoot the original 'Dracula' with Bela Lugosi, 'The Wolf Man' and most famously 'The Hunchback of Notre

Dame' and the original 'Frankenstein'. This section of the park proved popular with horror filmmakers as the area was compact with many small streets representing vague areas of continental Europe; these were all put to good use when passing trams would be confronted by hordes of village folk chasing down the monster of choice for that hour.[4]

The event was humble in its beginnings. The aim was to allow the famous studio tram tour to be run at night for the first time ever, with a new tour guide script focused on horror and sci-fi sights of the backlot combined with costumed characters jumping out at every turn. Local posters and newspaper adverts promised that "They're here. Lurking in the shadows. Hiding behind corners. Stalking dark alleys. Those terrifying monsters who haunted our streets for 60 years have come back… to get you!" Whilst running the popular tram tour (or Terror Tram) and a few select attractions in the main theme park, the park also put on a concert to keep the event relevant and young in audience. Michigan based R&B band, 'Ready for the World' would perform especially for the event each night on stage at the park, performing such hits as "Oh Shelia" and "Love You Down" to delighted park guests. 'Ready for the World' were signed to MCA, the parent company of Universal Studios and were only too happy to play to local audiences.[5]

Using a MCA signed musical act, costumes from their own huge costume department, using actors from their own talent agency with park operational staff kept costs down in what would be a water test to the local economy to see if such an event would be successful. After the first night, the studio knew they had created a hit.

The event was a huge success. Quickly, the event sold out, due in part to the advent of the ability to call the park and pay over the phone with a credit card. Universal's excellent marketing department quickly distributed posters and radio commercials informing the local communities that the event was sold out but had decided to run one extra day on Sunday November 2nd with a slightly earlier start of 6.30pm. Posters of Jack-o-Lanterns were printed showing the popular holiday icon being destroyed from above via a chainsaw, a symbol that would be reused again years later. The posters advised to book now to avoid disappointment as if you don't it *"will haunt you forever!"*

However, despite the sell-out of tickets and orderly manner of the guests, the event was soon gripped by a very unfortunate tragedy. Late in the evening of November 1st Paul Rebalde, 20, of Woodland Hills stationed along the Terror Tram route in full zombie makeup was sadly killed. He was tasked with sitting within a parked tram along the route with scores of mannequins which all had similar makeup applied, allowing the guests the ability to believe they were all dummies. Rebalde's role was charged with jumping from the parked tram to scare guests passing by in another tram.[6]

Rebalde along with other actors had been theme park attendants who had been asked to work-on the Terror Tram's new cast of over 70 costumed characters that lined the route of the tram. Rebalde had been described in a LA Times article as "a thin, rusty-haired youth who was quick with a smile". They said he had worked in the theme park at several jobs. "He was one of the sweetest kids that worked up here," one fellow employee said. "He was the kind of guy that always walked around with a smile on his face. Everybody liked him." Rebalde was believed to have jumped from his stationery tram at around 8.30pm to scare one of the passing trams when he was believed to have become trapped between the third and fourth sections of the moving four-part tram. He was likely crushed to death and then sadly dragged some 100 feet. He was pronounced dead by local medics at around 9pm.

An investigation was quickly setup by Investigators from the Los Angeles County district attorney's environmental crimes and occupational safety division headed up by John F. Lynch. Joan Bullard, marketing and publicity director for Universal Studios, said "There was no indication that the tram had a problem or anything like that. The sheriff has told us that it was an unfortunate accident." She continued, "The tour's safety record is exemplary and that we (Universal) have never had an incident like this in our 22-year history. We're all very sad," she said. The Terror Tram was abandoned for the rest of the night and additional safety measures for the final extra night were put into place to protect both actors and guests; this mostly included the omission of any actors being allowed to 'jump or attack' any moving trams and that only stationary trams would be allowed for scaring purposes.

Rebalde had worked in the merchandising department for the Studios since the beginning of May of 1986. His role was defined by a spokesman for the park as being "very broad," but several studio workers interviewed at the time said that Rebalde's job included selling various merchandise to park guests and serving as an assistant manager of a stall that sold film near the famous front gates of the park.

A combination of expenditure required for park refurbishments and backlot availability due to feature film and television requirements, marred with the tragic consequences that occurred on November 1st, afforded for the event to be discontinued for the unforeseeable future. The recent addition of King Kong to the Tram Tour required further expenditure for maintenance purposes and various popular stage shows were being overhauled, 'The A-Team' stunt show was swopped out for a 'Miami Vice' themed show; this combined with a huge increase in shooting space required for TV shows such as 'Murder She Wrote' and 'Matlock'. MCA was keen for Universal Studios to be the new home of televisual serials, particularly in the niche genre of 'afternoon murder mystery', something that could be readily and repetitively syndicated (still to this day even).

Soon on the horizon MCA had a planned expansion for more child friendly areas of the park including 'Fievel's Playland'. Seeking to distance its image of a park that was built mostly for adults and teens the park's revised image of horror was downplayed for some years in part due to the tragic events that had occurred but also in reply to an ever growing Disneyland which was drawing ever larger crowds. Halloween Horror Nights or Horror Nights (as it was dubbed at the time) was not planned to return, indeed it simply did not fit with the park's revised family spirit but it would return one day.

Notes:

[1] Los Angeles Times, Oct 8th, 1986
[2] http://insideuniversal.net/
[3] Universal Studios Monsters: A Legacy of Horror Hardcover, 2009 by Michael Mallory
[4] Matthew Peterson Interview
[5] USH distributed posters and press adverts
[6] Los Angeles Times, Nov 2nd, 1986

A new player in town...

Back in Florida, Disney pretty much owned the holiday seasons, particularly Christmas. Every festive period the main park of the Magic Kingdom would put on their annual Disney Parks Christmas Day Parade. Airing on the ABC show would be a massive commercial for all things Disney in the Southern State and would highlight that Disney was the place to be for families. Starting in 1983 and continuing to this day, it has aired every Christmas with the exception of 1989 and 2000, where the latter year Disney chose to air a special on 'Tracking Santa' for Christmas Eve. Celebrities such as Regis Philbin and Joan Lunden were often on presenting duties during this time. Throughout this time the local buzz was all about coming to Disney and bringing your family.

In the late 1980s, the event at Disney was going from strength to strength. Disney Channel's extremely popular 'Ducktales' had premiered in 1987 and by this time Scrooge McDuck himself was headlining the event. Scrooge McDuck would go on to star in 'A Sparkling Christmas Spectacular', a song-and-dance show that would premiere Dec 20th with daily performances through to Dec 30th. Completing the line-up with McDuck and his nephews would be the appearance of Santa Goofy and a cast of over 300. The show then alternated with the "15 Years of Magic" show on the Cinderella Castle stage which was also popular at the time.

Not only did Disney throw televised parades with national coverage and bringing about characters from the new hit Disney Channel shows, it also started to test the market with special evening hard ticketed events. 'Mickey's Very Merry Christmas Party,' as it was then and still to this day, premiered in 1983 as a single one-time-only hard ticketed event. It sold out and the park reached capacity. The event was a huge hit but Disney being Disney, and not wanting to run before they walked, ran the event again the next year for one night and then again the following year for exactly one night, with each year selling out. It wasn't until 1989 that Disney pumped for two nights, again they sold out and then in 1990 three nights were offered and again all sold out. The Party offered a mixture of caroling, hot chocolate, cookies, a giant Christmas tree and sing-alongs. Disney was bringing the big guns out.

It was also around this time of the late 1980s and early 1990s that Disney started to experiment with success of these Christmas parties as to what else they might be able to offer. Senior management quickly happened on the idea of filling slower months of park attendances with specially ticketed events. It was at this time the first 'Flower & Garden Festival' premiered at EPCOT during the early spring downtime and the first 'Holidays Around the World' was held at the World Showcase in Epcot in the late Autumn. Mardi Gras celebrations were ramped up at Downtown Disney's Pleasure Island in the slow month of February with a weeklong 'St Valentines' special' appearing too. The popular 'International Food and Wine' Festival at Epcot and 'Mickey's-Not-So-Scary-Halloween' Party were both not presented to until the mid-1990s when Halloween Horror Nights at the Studios was in full swing.

Meanwhile, during this time Universal was having problems. Right at the beginning of the park's existence in 1990, they were having huge issues with their star performers. The biggest star and the most problematic was Big Bruce himself, Jaws. The sharks within the newly constructed ride just didn't work and the press liked to report this often. Jaws updates on the local media outlets were becoming a regular topic of discussion and a mighty embarrassment for the company. From day one there were the tell-tale signs. Rumors were abounding that Steven Spielberg, the director of the original smash-hit summer blockbuster got stuck along with his family on the actual opening day. Rumors aside, we do know from press reports that the ride was forcibly shut down on the actual opening day. Other attractions such as 'Earthquake' and 'Kongfrontation' were not fairing much better either, though their stories are less important when it comes to the development of Halloween Horror Nights.

Notes:

Various articles and relocations used for this chapter, including:

Orlando Sentinel June 10, 1990
Orlando Sentinel Aug 23, 1990
Orlando Sentinel Aug 27, 1990
Orlando Sentinel Dec 13, 1990
Orlando Sentinel Aug 22, 1990
Orlando Sentinel Apr 10, 1991
Orlando Sentinel Aug 28, 1990
Orlando Sentinel Sept 14, 1986
Orlando Sentinel Oct 24, 1995

'Jump-start-ing' the Shark

Though the Universal Studios park had opened June 7th, 1990 along with the Jaws ride, the ride was forcibly shut down by park management on the afternoon of the 7th and did not reopen until the 10th. The testing during this time found that the persistent breakdowns were a direct result of the variety of special effects that were required, combined with the state of the sharks submersed under the water for 90% of the day, every day. It was quickly becoming a logistical nightmare and a daily occurrence for disgruntled families being rescued from the ever halting tour boats. General Manager of the Studios at this time was Tom Williams who was providing the best disaster limitation he could, and was providing free tickets for extra days at the parks to complaining guests and any that had been caught on the broken-down ride. Celebrities such as Beau Bridges and Anthony Perkins were rumored to have been deployed by the park's management to save face. Bridges himself was documented to have greeted and spoken with guests about their experiences at the fledgling park in this first week.

Despite the handouts and celebrities, queues were forming quicker some days at the park's customer services than at some of the rides during this short period. Sadly, from the June 10th, the boats could physically move around the lake but they couldn't get the special effects to work consistently. Some of the Amity Island Skippers quipped that "look over there, that's where explosions should be happening", much to senior management's reprimands and annoyance. By June 9th a 1000 people had demanded a full refund for their tickets. Engineers from both the ride developer and the park were instructed to work around the clock, this was combined with a park attendance high of reaching near capacity on day one that was quickly cooling off as the passing days came. A park guest that week, 50-year-old George Lowke, of Laytonsville, Maryland was quoted as saying, "They weren't quite ready for us, I don't think, but we are having a good time. And we have a ticket to come back," though not all guests were quite that positive.

Finally the news came on Aug 23th, 1990 that the ride would shut down temporarily whilst adjustments were made. In fact it would be a major overhaul and the closure would last well over 2 years. The press took delight in letting their readers know that the park was at this time starting to struggle. The summer of 1990 was a worrying time for the new park. The initial few days of reaching full park capacity (rumored to be between 40,000 to 50,000 people) was past and the summer returned no such visitor numbers. The park reported that this was just a blip and where they had fixed the 'Earthquake' and 'King Kong' attractions, which were both running reasonably well, a quick fix for the toothy shark would be addressed and likely by the New Year the ride would probably be opened again; though in real terms it would be longer and the Park's management were seething at the developer of the ride for this.

The park president Steven Lew, quickly announced to the media that a lawsuit was imminently being filed by Universal in Orange County Circuit Court against the ride's developer for the issues suffered by the park because of the 'Jaws' ride. The developer had also built the 'Earthquake' attraction for the park but the faults with this ride were deemed enough for technical adjustments to be made 'Pro-bono' by the developer and would become sufficient long-term fixes, though this was not the case for 'Jaws'. By the end of August 1990 with struggling attendance figures and a headliner 'E-Ticket' attraction beyond repair, the park issued its 40 page suit which described at length the woes of the new ride but it did not specify the amount of damages the company was seeking to obtain from the developer. Naming both attractions respectively, it made the case that these rides not working directly attributed to the park's profits being directly below even the modest of park estimates. Namely the two rides were victims of poor workmanship, defective designs, bad planning with no eye on program whatsoever. When both the park's engineers and that of the developers could no longer fix the issues, the park hired external consultants to appraise the sheer scale of the faults that lay at the bottom of Amity Island's lagoon. "We are angry. We are disappointed," Lew Wasserman of the park's parent company MCA said at the time. "There are numerous design flaws in 'Jaws'. The ride works for a few hours and then must be taken down for repairs." A lot of the local staff knew that as this issue had hit Lew's desk then the problem was a huge one for the company.

Attendance was diving and Universal had to make cut backs, quickly many of the originally employed staff were let-go and the law suit for the attraction was issued. The park then had to readdress all of the extensive marketing that had been produced that featured the headlining 'Jaws' ride. It was an embarrassing time for the company as 3D bill boards along the Interstate 4 were taken down, TV commercials were re-edited and recalls to vacation brochures quickly begun. During this time the ride's developers responded, off the record in the first instance, by informing the press that a lot of their company's issues were from direct result of the company losing their president during the rides' planning stage. A spokesman for the developer was reportedly said to have remarked that the issues were due to the complexity of mixing live special effects timed to meet large mechanical maneuvers in a body of water which led, to the project over-running in the design stage which ultimately affected the construction phase of the project. The ride was very optimistic from day one he was reported to have said and this led to issues from the minute it was conceived right up to the second it was handed-over to the park's management. The lawsuit eventually alleged that the developer breached its mutually agreed contract terms, violated all collateral warranties and failed to properly get the ride into a working order for park guests. The list of faults compiled by the third-party consultants was extremely lengthy.

By early 1990 the scale of the problem was finally realized and park president Tom Williams announced to the press that the ride would now be closed to until at least 1992. "We are undergoing a comprehensive engineering effort that will translate into an opening that has yet to be determined," Williams officially said. It was at this time that the park had let slip via the lawsuit, that the ride had cost MCA $630 million to build and that whereas Kong and Earthquake could be repaired, the mechanical shark was beyond any such repair. Despite this, the company was not discouraged and once the third-party consultants had finished their investigation, the park started to investigate the possibility of refurbishing the ride in-house with their own engineers. It was rumored that throughout 1991 and early 1992, Universal tried to get the special effect (namely the explosive section of the ride) to work again but with no success. Rumors spread that the electronics used in the sharks deployment mechanisms were badly damaged due to insufficient waterproofing which led to the sharks ceasing-up 'mid-bite' with no means of releasing them. Universal quickly realized that the ride was not salvageable in its current state, so a new approach was required.

Since the closing of 'Jaws' the two companies continued to investigate and talk over the matter, the dialogue was reputed to be almost daily. Discussions continued to until April 4th 1991 when finally a deal was struck and Universal settled out-of-court with the ride's developer. Ron Sikes the park's vice president announced to the local media "In the settlement agreement, we have both agreed that we would have no further comment beyond the fact that the matter has been amicably resolved." Even the developer was reported to have said the matter was resolved amicably and that no further comment could be made, other than the fact that their services to redesign the ride would not be undertaken and that they hoped that they could one again work with the theme park in the future. The developer that had been started in 1984 by former Disney Imagineers and is still trading to this day (in fact the company actually worked on the original Monorail at Disneyland).

After the out-of-court settlement, the park got on board Totally Fun Company (who had worked on other opening day attractions such as E.T.), ITEC Entertainment (which would go on to make the park's 'Mummy' ride), Intamin and Oceaneering International in a collaboration of efforts to refurbish and enhance the ride. Top of the list of requirements were the re-engineering of the ride system and installing an entirely new track, with new special effects being devised to create an almost entirely new version of the ride. The re-design also included the replacement of two major ride scenes. Whilst the others worked on the ride systems, it was Oceaneering who had the task of providing life-like animatronic sharks for the re-engineered ride, which was their first ever theme park project. The ride was then officially re-opened by original cast members Roy Scheider (who had been at the park shooting Seaquest DSV), Lorraine Gary and the park's creative consultant and the movie's director, Steven Spielberg in the spring of 1993.

Winding the clock back to the spring of 1992 and the ride's refurbishment was well under way. Construction crews would access the ride from the parking lot behind, so as not to further impede on the guests' experiences. The famous sign appointed to the ride's entrance of 'Captain Jake's Amity Boat Tours' and all Jaws signage were removed. Construction walls went up around the lagoon which left a very large empty piece of real-estate adjacent to the south side of the ride: that of the queue building and the extended queue building. Taking up almost a fifth of the Amity area, the queue building and extended queue building (both linked at the entrance) could be temporary repurposed, which was an idea that was initially thrown around at the time. What else could they fill this space with? Could it be a temporary attraction? Perhaps a walk-through museum? The park's Art Director John Paul Geurts along with his colleague Project Coordinator and Manager Julie Zimmerman had just the answer…

Notes (Various articles and relocations used for this chapter):

Orlando Sentinel June 10, 1990
Orlando Sentinel Aug 23, 1990
Orlando Sentinel Aug 27, 1990
Orlando Sentinel Dec 13, 1990
Orlando Sentinel Aug 22, 1990
Orlando Sentinel Apr 10, 1991
Orlando Sentinel Aug 28, 1990
Orlando Sentinel Sept 14, 1986
Orlando Sentinel Oct 24, 1995

From ravenous rats to actual ravenous rats…

"Universal Studios Plans 'Fright Nights' For Halloween" ran the article in the local newspaper. "Capitalizing on a library of horror-movie classics, the park is planning three 'Fright Nights,' said Randy Garfield[1], executive vice president of marketing." Disney was the biggest player in town and Universal, who had at the time suffered from lower than expected attendance levels and general negative headlines, needed something to draw the crowds. It is said that at many times in the history of the resort even before it was built, it was in a constant power struggle with its mousey neighbors to the north. Disney pretty much owned the holiday season and family activities, particularly those focused on younger children. Universal needed to find its niche and it did that in these early days by focusing on Halloween and on the young adult and teenager demographic. Disney at the time was pulling no punches and around the time the event was known to be in the planning stages, Disney just happened to announce special activities to celebrate its 20th anniversary, with no underlying motive being seen just bad luck on the part of Universal as it really was the resort's 20th anniversary after originally opening the Magic Kingdom on October 1st, 1971. Garfield continued, "This isn't a response to Disney's 20th. It's an attempt to establish our franchise on Halloween and to take advantage of the legacy of monster movies we've had for 60 years. And it's strictly to take advantage of people's desire to party on Halloween." And the key word was "party", this would be a hard-ticketed, ticket holders only affair that would be held after park closes each day for three select nights. It would contain a cacophony of freaks, side-shows and monsters all made up to scare, delight and entertain guests in a laid back party (almost Mardi Gras like) fashion, where having a good time was as important as the scares.

The papers were awash with notices from Universal that "From 6 p.m. until midnight Oct. 25, 26 and 31, the park will open at a special price for ghouls and gals[2]." Garfield continued, "We've had a classic movie monster franchise for 60 years," referring to movies in the Universal library. Included in its archives are Frankenstein, Dracula and modern creatures, such as Chuckie, the doll with the attitude." Whereas Disney had years of animation legacy, Universal had years of horror legacy. Garfield and others hammered home to the media that this would include your classic favorites such as Dracula and The Mummy but also modern favorites such as Beetlejuice and Ghostbusters (though they were used under license as not strictly Universal properties but were present during the day hours). Other adverts in local shopping malls had pictures of Jeff Goldblum's portrayal of 'The Fly', Hitchcock's 'Psycho' and even a character wearing a hockey mask (ahem!); though some of these more modern franchises did not appear at the event.

Tickets to each of the Fright Nights event would cost $12.95 per person, plus tax and small service charge if purchased in advance, or $15.95 on the day of admission. On Oct. 25, 26 and 31, the Studios would close early at 5pm instead of the usual 7pm and the event would go on until midnight.

Before tickets could be sold the park had a lot of work to do in preparation for this fledgling event. Zimmerman who was mostly in charge of park entertainment and events called on Geurts to help build a concept that could be built in the fall or spring of every year that could attract guests to the new theme park during the slower times of year. Geurts who had worked on the Universal Orlando project from day one had actually worked on the design and build of many of the opening day attractions. "One of my favorite projects was the Hitchcock attraction and show. I worked with a team who were as dedicated as myself to making a true memorial to honor the work of Hitch." Geurts said. "We tried a number of concepts before the final attraction was designed. We had for many months wanted to build a bar on the first-floor, so guests could ascend the famous 'Vertigo' steps before stepping into a cocktail bar with Hitchcock themed drinks. Unfortunately the City required that any such bar would require restrooms to be located up there too and we simply couldn't do that due to space requirements." Shortly after the park opened Geurts tried to see if it was still possible but to little avail, "it was around that time that I was asked to sit down with Julie (Zimmerman) and explore the event that management wanted to stage." He continues, "Ideas were thrown around that we should do a Christmas event or a spring event, though it became noticeable to us both during these brain-storming sessions that we really couldn't compete with Disney, and at the time Disney seemed to own the spring and Christmas sections of the calendar. Fresh from my Hitchcock meeting, I made the idea of utilizing his brand in some way, this way quickly followed by Julie with a concept to expand that idea to a larger degree by utilizing other Universal brands of the same nature to create a Halloween themed event." The idea was set, it was pitched to senior management, who immediately asked the pair to go away and draw up a full concept.

It was around late 1990 that Geurts, who by this time was employed as an outside contractor, sat down with Julie to design what they could utilizing the best of the new park but also understanding that whatever they did would be on a very tight budget (as the park had only just opened). He said, "Julie acted as producer for the event and was key to finding the Universal owned concepts that we could play with and finding the talent to fill the streets. Whereas I was took on the other areas of the event, such as the design, the lightening, the music and the general park atmosphere. So we didn't have to compete with Disney we really wanted to aim at the local young people and adults to make an event that was adult orientated but played out more like a party, where everybody could attend and have a good time. This was going to be no kid-centric operation."

Planning went right into early 1991 when the project was finally greenlit by the management around the spring of 1991, ready for staging the event that fall. He continued, "As we worked on the details, the park's senior management referred the event to the central marketing department of the company – who absolutely loved the concept. They had a lot of fun utilizing the classic Universal monsters and our idea of placing a woman inside a glass casket filled with rats, idea that they used to great effect in an effort to drum up trade for our new event. Selling a new theme park for a second time took a lot of thought and by using the classic monsters (who hadn't featured in the original marketing) and the rat lady idea, was a great was to tap into the different demographic we were aiming for." Marketing also devised the name of 'Fright Nights' which seemed to sum up what the producers of the event were going for. Unfortunately after the first event, Universal received a firm letter from the copyright holders of that name, something that everyone had not been aware of. "Nobody thought it might be copyrighted, so when the project was greenlit for a second time, we changed the name ensuring to check all possible variations with the US Copyright people, before finally opting for 'Halloween Horror Nights' – which is a better name anyway".

The event's key performance goals were: to create a party environment, ensure the whole park is utilized so every guest knew wherever they were that they were in the party and to ensure every guest had a good time by staging a huge variety of entertainment. These were no easy tasks, as Geurts recalls, "Our budget was very limited but we wanted everyone who entered the park to know that this wasn't business as usual. We did this in a number of ways, which I guess most of which was myself just out there after park closing testing and experimenting with different light effects. We probably had more light effects utilizing technology that was built but no used often from within the façades to create the illusion of horror. Swopping out lenses with different colors to spots and putting in projectors really helped create the spooky environment. A lot of the projections were just drawings or patterns projected onto areas where their lights had been switched-off, this combined with a moving light enabled the backlot to look very different from the daytime with very minimal physical changes. This was long before the video projections they have now, we were just experimenting with simple patterns and effects but to great results." The lighting effects combined with the music and dry-ice machines to create environments unlike anything at any East coast park, he continued "we started using the term 'street-mos-phere' back them to define what we were doing. I don't know if we invented that word or not, but we definitely used that terminology back then."

The idea soon came about to build a haunted maze within the event, something that could be built relatively cheaply inside a redundant building that wouldn't affect the park's day-to-day operations. Management decided that the 'Jaws' queue building was to used, owed to the fact that the ride was now closed and would be so for quite some time. "We initially didn't want to utilize the Jaws queue for the house. It has a great atmosphere there which when combined with the lake can be utilized to great effect, however for building of sets we wanted to use one of the soundstages. We were told that they were being used for TV and Film production at the time, so we couldn't use any of them," said Geurts. "We set about using what we had and by the end of the construction I was really happy with what we had created. The queue building, despite its limitations, actually added to the claustrophobic vibe we were going for. We wanted guests to feel trapped inside this house, and that's why Universal have always called them 'mazes' for the simple factor that from day-one with our house design we wanted guests to not be so sure of where exits are – its more frightening that way. Unfortunately, over time due to the massive popularity of the event and certain building codes, we can't build them like that anymore."

"We worked around the clock to get everything in place before the event," said Geurts. "We had a team that were so dedicated to staging this event that we had created from nothing, so absolutely nothing was left to chance, we ensured we checked everything twice before opening," he said. Geurts and Zimmerman's efforts paid off when news came that the event was selling extremely well before opening, with visitor number expected into the thousands. "It was great news and a great time to be working in theme parks" Geurts said[3].

Notes:

[1] Susan G. Strother article, Orlando Sentinel, September 30, 1991.
[2] Orlando Sentinel article, November 4, 1991.
[3] Interview with John Paul Geurts.

Fright Nights

"Dying for a good Halloween party?"[1] the theme park publicized. Posters in stores, leaflets at every tourist spot, radio commercials, magazine placements and even a brief TV spot on the local Fox network highlighted the "huge" event that was coming this Fall at Universal Studios Orlando. Pepsi Cola who was the official supplier of beverages at the time paired up with the resort to market the event across the local TV networks. "If you want to come party down with your favorite monsters" savings of a 'devilish' $16 could be made if you buy special Halloween themed 2 liters of Pepsi[2] and present the coupon on the back. Locals were also encouraged by offers of buy-one-get-the-second-half-price. On opening night the car park was full (admittedly the car park back then was not as large as the multi-stories they have now), quickly queues formed around the block and onto the I4. The main draw of the evening would not be a lavishly detailed house or packed streets of scareactors but the chance to party (and they mean party!) with others in a creepy and cool Halloween environment.; a sort of lock-in afterhours party with those who were on the guest list only. "Come see the park after dark and experience it like never before" commented several of the Universal Management. This was surely to be a unique experience and totally unlike anything Disney were doing down the road.

The streets were packed[3], like never before or since, with performers of every type, including: A snake handler with a boa constrictor wrapped around his neck walked along the sidewalks, freaks and clowns stormed along the main gates, side shows from every carnival you've ever been to lined the streets, fire eaters performed near Hollywood Boulevard, a sword swallower astounded guests near Exposition Boulevard, men hammering nails into noses, and even street magicians performing card tricks and pulling coins out from people's ears were spotted deep in the park and these were just the random street performers!

Specially pre-selected schools of Central Florida[4] were asked for their students and their families to attend the event for free on different nights of the three nights offered, the catch? They had to come in costume. In all the press releases costumes were banned, because park management did not want members of the park confused with park performers but a special nightly costume contest was performed with winners selected by the guests cheering for the best costumed kid or who brought the most family and friends with them. Named 'The Monster Mardi Gras Costume Concert' (maybe that's where the idea for Mardi Gras spawned from?) it was held nightly at 7.30pm at the top of Hollywood Boulevard. Guests were asked to view a ménage of misfits and maniacs where 'intellectual 'properties (or IPs) were discouraged. Parents had to ensure their kid(s) who were taking part were in full makeup and at the park before the park had closed for the day (5pm), ready to be inducted and prepared for the Halloween party (as some at Universal were referring to it). The gates opened at 6pm but the exactly 400 costumed kids were kept backstage until show time at 7.30pm where they were held in a pen during the show. It was the Ghostbusters team and old Beetlejuice himself who congratulated the winner, James Glore, 11, of Southwest Middle School in Orange County on winning the contest. After the short show and awarding ceremony the kids were all sent back stage to de-frock their costumes and remove their makeup before being released back to their families for them to enjoy the rest of the park for the evening.[8]

A massive hit for the park and the one aspect which caused the most crowds was the event's only haunted house. Named 'The Dungeon of Terror' the haunt was located in the Jaws additional queue building (as prescribed earlier) and was unlike any temporary haunt that had been seen before. Taking 10 weeks to design and a further 6 weeks to build, as Universal wanted to bring everything it knew about movie-set building to a whole new level. Randy Garfield, executive vice president of marketing, promised before the event that this house would be "a murderous assortment of mazes, along with monsters and nightmarish images."[6] The facade was a stony entry port to a terrifying dungeon of mixed horrors. Fog machines bellowed out smog to knee level, strobes lights cut the scene and a real eerie anticipation filled the air, this was to be a very special experience like nothing you had seen before. Quickly queues formed with three-hour waits being the norm for each evening. After night one, it was seen that locals, who had been the night before, were rushing to this attraction on each of the two remaining nights before the queues built up.

Passing the stone façade the public travelled into a world of torture and misfortune. Poor unfortunate souls were left dangling above spiked pits or being stretched on various apparatuses, all done with the skill and good humor that only Universal Creative can produce. The layout was a series of prison cells in a maniacal dungeon where the freaks ruled and guests, just like you (well, cast members made to look like guests!), were being tortured for your viewing pleasure. In fact it was a serious of ingenious but elaborate props made to look like implements of torture when in fact they were completely harmless. The creative team had made sure the experience was exactly 12 minutes in duration from the moment you pass the façade to the second your feet walk you under the final exit sign. "A lot of times it takes much less because people are literally running to get away from these monsters," Tim Sepielli of Universal Creative said[9].

There was one problem though, no air-conditioning in the claustrophobic and confined house. The guests sweated and the performers' makeup melted, it was reported that as the night wore on, the makeup became more and more terrifying as the heat made the latex sag and the grease paint drip. The house was also incredibly short and many people tried to queue again to get another experience of the house. People were proclaiming to those in the queue, "you'll want to queue again when you finish, it's different every time!" And people did and the queue grew longer and people shuffled through like vastly slow moving conga lines. The house was also incredibly intense compared to what we now accept as the norm. One performer from the Nickelodeon Studios got so overenthusiastic that he brought buckets of slime from the attractions there and used them in his performance, unfortunately he managed to dump a vast quantity onto some un-expecting guests who were shuffling along in that particular scene. But there was one scene that would later go on to become a Halloween Horror Nights tradition. Towards the end of the house one cell had a particularly lackluster victim contained within, however the scare was not in front of you, it was below you. As quickly as the flick of a light the misdirected guests' attention was quickly turned from the room beyond to the floor below, where incased in a glass walkway was a lady being eaten alive by ravenous rats. The lady would scream loudly, scratch and bang the glass when illuminated by the light to make people jump. Scores of the rats would run and creep all over her. The glass walkway was specially built for this scare and would go on to be used many times in the events' of the future to become a tradition – 'The Rat Lady' was born. "When you walk down one corridor, you're walking on plexiglass," Sepielli said. "It lights up and there's a crypt under your feet with a girl banging and clawing at the plexiglass. I t's filled with live rats that crawl all over her body. Of course, the trick is that we smear peanut butter on her so the rats really nibble on her. That's a lot of fun!"[9]

Beetlejuice from the popular 1988 Michael Keaton movie made the rounds and actually starred in two of the night's shows. Perfectly choreographed to ensure no cross-over was seen for the make-up-ed actor who played as the park's official Beetlejuice. The movie which was a massive hit drawing in a reported $73million at the box-office starred Michael Keaton in the titular role as the mad yet comical ghost who tries to aid the recently deceased Alec Baldwin and Geena Davis in scaring away the incumbents of their former home. Beetlejuice who at the time was a part player in a day-time show with the Ghostbusters and occasional roaming character, would have two shows per nights with eight respective performances. He was a big draw for the event, so-much-so that the following year, the lackluster show 'An American Tail Theatre' was completely repurposed and refurbished into Beetlejuice's own 'Rock and Roll Graveyard Revue', which continued right in its original format right up until to 2002.

The first show of the night for 'Old Betelgeuse' was 'Beetlejuice's Graveyard Tours'. The setting was the Bates Motel set from the movie Psycho IV, which had been dressed to represent a ghostly motel from the movie's Netherworld, had regular performers "Joliet" Jake and Elwood Blues, aka The Blues Brothers'. As the show begins, the Brothers eager to get a room for the night see a sign off the old-highway for available rooms, they pull up in the Bluesmobile (1974 Dodge Monaco sedan in Police stripes), where Mr. Psycho himself, Norman Bates, greets them. Norman instructs them that they have to meet his host for the evening and with that Beetlejuice would appear from the grave, leaping from an actual grave. Together they performed a number of song and dance routines.

Next up for the "ghost with the most" was 'Beetlejuice LIVE (dead) in concert' which ran every night for two performances backed by the cast of the daytime park show, 'Ghostbusters Spooktacular'. Ghostbusters which had been a runaway hit in the 1980s with two fantastic movies and a cartoon TV series was the perfect outlet for the park. The nightly show was similar to a seasonal show held on the steps of the New York Public Library within the park called 'Streetbusters'. 'Streetbusters' would later be replaced in 2002 by 'Extreme Ghostbusters: The Great Fright Way' which itself would be replaced altogether in 2005. The 'Beetlejuice LIVE (dead) in concert' however would be a beefed up version of the former show extended with more tongue-in-cheek bad humor and less kid friendly gags. An unsightly cabaret performance from our Ghost Host would begin the show, he would open by singing (or screaming?) with 'My Favorite Things' from the movie 'The Sound of Music' with the lyrics changed in best Beetlejuice fashion to "frogs in your oatmeal, dung in your sneakers, blackheads and whiteheads, squirts and leaches with moustaches, roaches with wings - these are a few of my favorite things." Long gone were the Raindrops on roses and whiskers on kittens! After 'The Sound of Mucus' (sorry!), he then went on to perform 'I got (you) Mildew' where he was disrupted by our heroes, The Ghostbusters'. Arriving in their classic ECTO-1 vehicle, The Ectomobile, was a 1959 Cadillac Miller-Meteor limo-style (with ambulance conversion) used in the first 1984 film Ghostbusters. Arriving on the scene the team would stop Beetlejuice in his tracks, interrupt his rendition and then perform their songs. They would start with their own version of Gaye Marvin's – 'Aint No Mountain High Enough', along with a medley of C & C Music factory's 'Everybody Dance Now', Madonna's 'Vogue' and then 1990 chart topper MC Hammer's 'U Can't Touch This' aka 'Hammer time'. It was then during the final number that Beetlejuice would join in and depart with the gang in the Ecto-1 played out to their Ray Parker Jnr signature theme song. "Who ya gonna call?" they asked; "Beetlejuice" he shouted over the cheering crowd as the team majestically departed.

Just over the street from this show situated on the corner near Finnegan's Bar and Grill - was another show and much more grotesque, the 'Chainsaw Massacre' debuted, for what would over the coming years evolve into another Halloween Horror Nights tradition. The show which was based around a number of chainsaw wielding maniacs who had taken to the stage to sacrifice supposedly unfortunate guests (in fact they were perfectly situated members of the crew). As the adhoc victims were carefully selected and pulled unwillingly onto the stage, the chief of the chainsaw maniacs would begin their induction by describing the things that were about to happen to them. Then as quickly as it had begun various body parts of the "guests" were cut off live on stage and then tossed into the audience. Plastic body parts were thrown into the crowd along with sprays of fake blood (water) to ensure ultimate horror compliance for the gasping audience members. Such was the success of this humble show, that those wielding chainsaw maniacs would eventually evolve into the chainsaw Drill Team and the variations of that which would be seen in the years to come at the event.

Also in this area was Dr. Death's Show, The Human Pincushion, Magical Mania, Madam Kuszel – The Gypsy Fortune Teller, Cobra Woman and Dragon Breath. Whereas the other shows used fixed stages these performers and their assistants mingled in with the crowd and acted as great mini-attractions. There weren't any official scarezones at this first Halloween event but if there was anything that resembled a scarezone it had to be the New York area. It was like a travelling circus had taken over downtown New York and were putting on an impromptu show for any and every one present. From magicians doing close-up magic tricks to a man eating fire, these were the days when activities like these could be performed at close quarters and everyone stood back and gasped in sheer delight and amazement. The level of detail here was definitely different as performers here were mostly independent and provided their own makeup and props, some of which were truly terrifying!

Between the newly opened Back to the Future: The Ride and The Swamp

Thing Sets a newly installed stage was erected. The park map declared The Gravediggers would be performing and it would feature Laurel and Hardy. The Gravediggers were a rock-come-punk band of the 1980/90s who had reasonable success throughout the States, as they performed some of their songs and covers two Universal staff members dressed as Laurel and Hardy would entertain the crowds. As the band performed 'Monsters At Play' Laurel was spotted crying due to being scared by this perfectly suiting horror based band. Also in this area another stage was set for 'Universal Science Band' right behind the Animal Actors stage. A troupe of park employees with musical talents playing various instruments bellowed out 'The Monster Mash' and 'My Skin Crawls' to the gathering audience. Behind them inside the Animal Actor's stage was a magicians' act from the group The Pendragons, performing five times per night. The Pendragons, were a husband-and-wife team based in California that called their magical act the 'physical grand illusion'. Numerous set pieces and props were used including a scene where Jonathan caught a bullet in his teeth. They later collaborated again with Universal at Hollywood where their show, 'Cinemystique: Illusions of the Night' ran in the Castle Theatre in the Upper Lot for three months between June and September of 1994. It was later crowned the winner of the "Best Magic Show of the Year".

Over the lagoon at Amity, Prince Dragon performed between the now closed Jaws lake and Lombard's Seafood Grille, which was primarily a sword and stunt demonstration. Further down the street in the San Francisco area we had Iron Belly who performed right outside Lombard's. Iron Belly was primarily a tattooed man with assistant who ate fire and ice in front of a gathering crowd. It is quite foreboding that immediately behind where this small stage was temporary situated in the lagoon a timed fire canon would be installed for later Halloween Horror Nights events, almost like homage! (though probably and completely coincidental). Up the road from Iron Belly was Dr. Frankenstein's Theater featuring Mistress of the Night, Frankenstein and Dracula. The show was a horror-comedy style show taking place in the then American Tail Theatre, and featured characters such as Victor Frankenstein, Count Dracula and Frankenstein's Monster. It shows the power of this event that this opening day attraction was then completely re-themed to become Beetlejuice's Rock and Roll Graveyard Revue show, which borrowed the costumes, songs and story from this temporary Halloween show to be played out daily to day guests. The main difference being that the host for each performance would rotate. Most nights Frankenstein (well his monster) would be the host at the 8pm show and then Dracula would take over at the 10pm show. Also in this area, just over to the side of Richter's Burger place, was the Human Impaler who had five nightly shows to perform.

Over in the Hollywood area of the park, Starshower performed as the warm-up for Paul Revere & the Raiders. Starshower had performed locally for many years. Paul Revere & the Raiders had been formed way back in 1958 but had come to prominence in the 1960s with their first official release in 1961. Their classic tracks such as 'Kicks' which was ranked number 400 on Rolling Stone magazine's list of The 500 Greatest Songs of All Time was performed high on the temporary stage erected across from Mel's Drive-In, along with 'Hungry', 'Him Or Me - What's It Gonna Be?' and their Platinum selling number one hit 'Indian Reservation (The Lament of the Cherokee Reservation Indian)', which got park guests in the groove nightly at 9.45pm.

Along with all these great temporary shows and attractions some of the regular day attractions were open, these included[5]: The Funtastic World of Hanna-Barbera (Production Central), Murder, She Wrote Mystery Theatre (Production Central), Ghostbusters Spooktacular (New York), Kongfrontation (New York), Earthquake: The Big One (San Francisco), The Wild Wild Wild West Stunt Show (Amity), Back to the Future: The Ride (World Expo), E.T. Adventure (World Expo), The Gory Gruesome and Grotesque Horror Make-Up Show (Hollywood) and Alfred Hitchcock: The Art of Making Movies (Production Central) which even had an actor posing as Norman Bates at the exit just to give an extra scare or two. There was also for special guests of the event's main sponsor 'Pepsi', a special VIP party which was held on select nights by invitation only.

As the park closed a little after midnight on 31st October 1991, the clean-up began and the I4 was once again filled with worn out party goers, Park Management knew they had a hit on their hands and so did Disney. Reports quickly spread of the first ever mention of Universal within the Disney World departmental newsletter[7]. "Universal Studios Florida and Walt Disney World are tough competitors. So it was surprising to see Universal's Fright Nights event for Halloween praised in a Disney departmental newsletter", ran the article at the time, written by a Disney cast member who had attended one of the nights at the Fright Nights event. They described how successful the park was in turning itself into a Halloween attraction for weekend. The article read "While it is true that Universal Studios is the competition, they do have a great product (although E.T. leaves something to be desired) and can put on a great show." Suddenly, if only for a moment Disney was starting to notice what their smaller competitor could achieve.

Notes:

[1] Magazine advertisement, September 1991
[2] Pepsi Cola bottle label, obtained September 1991
[3] Interview with Mike Pressman.
[4] Interview with Mary Paula Jones.
[5] Park Map for the event, Universal Studios Fright Nights 1991
[6] Vicki Vaughan article, The Orlando Sentinel, October 14, 1991
[7] Orlando Sentinel article, November 4, 1991
[8] Orlando Sentinel article, November 7, 1991
[9] St. Petersburg Times, October 25, 1991
[10] Interview with John Paul Geurts

"Looks like Halloween Horror Nights is auditioning again…"

Icon Issues...

Ok now you've read the chapter about the actual Fright Nights event, I want you to pick up your device of preference (tablet, cellphone, laptop etc.) and type into a search engine the following phrase "Fright Nights 1991 Universal Logo" and then click on to search for just pictures. Hopefully you will see a logo of Fright Nights featuring the six icons for this event. The icon or icons of each Halloween Horror Nights would grow to become an important tradition and for this initial event the park opted for the ultimate horror icons, that of the Universal Monsters. So look carefully now at this logo, from left to right it features 'The Wolfman', 'The Bride of Frankenstein', Frankenstein's Monster', 'Dracula', 'The Creature From The Black Lagoon' and 'The Mummy'. However, one of them does not look as he should. The Wolfman looks perfectly like Lon Chaney Jnr's classic version, Boris Karloff's The Mummy and Frankenstein's Monster all look spot on, The Creaturea and the Bride, the latter made famous by Elsa Lanchester both respectively look exactly as they did in their classic movies, but Dracula does not look anywhere near what he should. Dracula was played most famously for Universal Studios by Hungarian born actor Bela Lugosi.

Lugosi who had been starring in silent movies since 1917 (that year alone he made 12 films!) starting in Hungary and then in Germany. Germany at the time was experiencing a boom in its film industry where masterpieces such as the first sci-fi Franz Liszt's 'Metropolis' was created and a young Alfred Hitchcock first cut his teeth learning the craft of early German expressionist styles; Soon after the debonair and enthusiastic actor hoped on a ferry and travelled to America where their film industry was starting to emerge. Working initially as a laborer the actor soon found his feet and appeared in a number of films in smaller roles, it wasn't until 1927 that he was signed to star in a Broadway production of Bram Stoker's Dracula adapted by Hamilton Deane and John L. Balderston. The production was very successful, it ran for exactly 261 performances before touring the States for just over two years, soon after Lugosi relocated to Hollywood to star in more character parts in early talkies.

In 1931 he was signed to portray his stage version of Dracula onto film. Universal produced the film that was directed by Tod Browning. The film was a colossal hit with audiences around the world and forever immortalized Lugosi as Dracula. A type-casting he would later learn to love and build a brand around. Lugosi went on to play the vampire on numerous occasions and was a crucial part of the franchise of monster movies produced by Universal during this time, playing not just the vampire himself but a collection of other creepy characters, most notably Ygor in 'Son of Frankenstein.'

It wasn't until after his death, that the image he had struggled to shift which later he capitalized into a personal franchise for himself where towards the end of his career in the 1950s he starred in scores of low-budget movies, started to cause problems for his descendants. He passed away peacefully on his couch in 1956[3], however by the 1960s the brand was in high demand and new monster movies were being made in vast quantities in both the States but also most notably in Britain (with Hammer films) and in Italy. Renewed interest in the classic Universal Monsters was starting to peak again.

It came at the height of this renewed popularity in 1971 when his descendants Hope Linninger Lugosi and Bela George Lugosi (his fifth wife and son) took Universal to court over their use of their late father's image which was wildly used with the other Classic Universal Monsters during this time. Such was the advent of television, syndication, mass production of merchandise and pop culture that the Universal Monsters were in demand all over the world, and Lugosi's heirs felt his constant use and popularity should not just benefit the Universal corporation. Initially discussions were held informally before court action was processed at California Supreme Court around 1974 and then reviewed in 1977. The case rumbled on until a decision was made formally in December 1979[1]. Headlines in the national newspapers quickly capitalized on the story, citing that "Dracula rises from the dead to haunt previous employers". The question the court considered was whether Bela Lugosi's film contracts with Universal included granting of merchandising rights for his portrayal of the character Dracula from his original 1931 movie, and whether these rights could be adopted by his descendants. The hotly debated case was initially ruled in favor of Universal as personal likenesses could not be transferred, however the case was appealed.

Justice Roth for the Court of Appeal, Second Appellate District, upheld that the right to exploit one's name and likeness is personal to the said artist. The Supreme Court of California awarded the heirs $72,000 and ordered Universal not to enter into any more licensing agreements with the actor's likeness for the purposes of marketing or merchandising, however the ruling stopped short of losing all rights and licenses to that of the original 1931 Universal movie. The decision was later appealed citing that Lugosi himself made little commercial gain for exploiting his image as the classical Dracula. The State Court of Appeal overturned the original trial court and then two years later (prior to 1979) the State Supreme Court decided the appeal court was actually right. This left the whole issue much more conflicting but left Universal in no doubt that they had lost their use of Bela Lugosi's likeness of their famous movie character.

California's descendibility statute, which was the right enacted in the final court case for their decision, which covers the rights of publicity and their entitlements (named Civil Code Section 990)[2], was later brought about at court again in 1988, where Lugosi's descendants now have the rights to license for any commercial use of his Lugosi's name and image from any of the movies he was portrayed in. Depending on the suit filed the right of publicity in some states remains for 50, 70, 75, up to a maximum of 100 years past the date of the death of the performer. Therefore by the 1991[4] Fright Nights event Universal would have had to pay for his image to be in the logo and that is why he unlike the others is not present. It is not known if it was a monetary issue for the fledgling event, as the budget was likely strict for an event where it was not known how successful it would be or whether the courts' decisions just made using the character as portrayed by Lugosi far more problematic.

This is a nice little unknown fact that is easily missed by the public and fans of the event but is equally important to know and forms part of the legacy of this great event.

Notes:

[1] Los Angeles Times, Dec 4th, 1979 by Philip Hager
[2] http://corporate.findlaw.com/litigation-disputes/practitioner-s-guide-to-california-right-of-publicity-law.html
[3] "The Road to Dracula", a supplement in the DVD "Dracula (1931)" [Universal Studios Classic Monster Collection, Universal DVD.
[4] Interview with Clive T. Bowley.
[5] Universal Studios Monsters: A Legacy of Horror Hardcover – 8 Sep 2009 by Michael Mallory.

Halloween Horror Nights: 2nd Annual

The event in 1991 called Fright Nights had been such a success for the new park that this year would be bigger and bolder with some five nights of Halloween entertainment. This year the event would have a larger budget (reportedly $1million[3]) and would aim to reach out to all fans of not just horror but anyone looking to have a truly unique experience and good time. The previous event had surpassed even the highest expectations for the park's management. "We [at Universal Studios] see Halloween growing into a 10-day observance" said proudly by Universal Studios Florida PR Manager Joseph Curley. The park now had the confidence to pull-off what could be a world staging event. Articles in the local newspapers ran rumors and speculation that Universal was starting to think bigger for the next event but also long-term, the Orlando Sentinel wrote: "All Hallow's Eve: Do people actually pack up and take Halloween vacations? And, if so, can Orlando become the destination of choice? Universal Studios Florida is betting on it". Such is the dedication of Universal that they knew from these very early days just what their small dedicated team of production technicians, artisans and craftsmen and women could seek to achieve.

Marketing was stepped-up a gear for 1992 and they needed to as the name was about to change. Fright Nights of 1991 was about to become the name that is used to this day. It is not known officially why the name changed, however there are two main theories. The first is that the name may have been changed due to the film rights to this name being used in 1985. Fright Night (not Nights) was a 1985 American horror-comedy-fantasy movie written and directed by Tom Holland (a former assistant and student of Alfred Hitchcock). It starred William Ragsdale, Roddy McDowall and Amanda Bearse. The film's plot follows young Charley who discovers that his next-door neighbor, Jerry Dandrige, is actually a vampire. When no one believes him, Charley decides to get Peter Vincent, a famous Vampire Hunter and local cable TV presenter, to stop Jerry from starting a local killing spree. The film also spawned various sequels, comics and a remake some years later. Did Universal feel their newly formed brand may get confused with this movie? Nobody is sure.

The other formative theory is more complex but boils down to trademark usages. At the time in 1980/90s America there seemed to be a number of events across the country using the same or similar name to Frights Nights. First up was the country-wide Six Flags theme park corporation which held select 'Six Flags Fright Fest' or 'Fright Fest', and had done so since the late 1980s, though smaller events had been held going back to the late 1970s with no official naming of the event. They also trademarked the use of the name Fright Nights on December 20, 1988 for their first official 1989 event at their Texas park, though seemingly changed their minds and actually stuck with 'Six Flags Fright Fest' instead. The Anheuser-Busch corporation who also operated a small number of theme parks, and were starting to think about getting into the Halloween business. They even trademarked the name Fright Nights in September 11, 1987 for use at their brewery in St. Louis, Missouri but nothing came of this and the Busch Gardens we know today only started offering their response to Halloween Horror Nights in a bigger way in 2000. There were also smaller events dotted across the country with fairs and travelling circuses that had used the name in the last 30 years. So was it due to some possible confusion with other operators that Universal changed the name? Though we are not certain on both theories, Universal was certain about this event and billed it the 'Second Annual Halloween Horror Nights'. We do know though that a decision must have been made on or before September 2, 1992 as that was the day Universal applied for a trademark to the use of the name 'Halloween Horror Nights' and it was officially trademarked on September 2, 1992. The name had been borrowed from the smaller event of 1986 held at the Hollywood Studios Park, along with the use of the pumpkin receiving a blow from above as a ripping chainsaw was cutting into it; both of which soon became synonymous with the event.

"[This year] it would be like Mardi Gras in New Orleans. People would say, 'It's Halloween, let's head for Orlando.'" Joseph Curley[10] was reported as saying (though his words were like a strange premonition for their own Mardi Gras event that would one day start at Universal in Orlando). The aim would be to bring everything that worked well in the first year back for the second year, add some new attractions, enhance some of their own attractions and really tailor the event to the people who were buying the tickets, and those buying them were adults and teenagers. Due to this shift in direction, the park actively made the classic Universal monsters take a side-step, no longer would they be the draw of the event, though they were featured on the streets and in some of the marketing. The classical monsters were definitely kept by the Pepsi Cola Company's marketing of the event as they preferred their more wholesome appearance whilst plastering their images over their bottles across the isles at the supermarkets and gas stations of Central Florida. In their replacement would be a more dedicated emphasis on popular culture that Universal would try to sew into every attraction on offer. Keeping festivities relevant, contemporary and wholly unlike anything their Mousey neighbor could possible put on. Joseph Curley said, "One way you can tell Halloween Horror Nights takes place at Universal and not Disney: There's a show featuring a Madonna impersonator, complete with the cones!" You couldn't get more contemporary than that.

As the previous year's event held over three nights sold out, this event was held over five nights on Oct. 23, 24, 29, 30 and 31, the park closed again daily at 5.30pm, reopening at 6pm for guests of the hard ticketed event. A separate admission for the event of $22.95 was charged with the park closing at 1 am. Day visitors to the park could "stay and scream all night" paying just $12.95 to stay that same evening.

But it wasn't just the pop culture that would be ramped up, Universal was also aiming to ramp up the scares too. "We get the gears going inside your head" by slowly building the suspense, said Tony Peugh, who helped design Universal's Halloween haunted studio sets. Starting with scary music and the sense of frightening people nearby, Universal's studio gradually works to a crescendo. The idea is to keep the customer off-balance." Returning to the Jaws queue building due mostly in-part to the attraction still being under construction but also due to the fact that the location and size of the building was perfect for the creation of a haunted maze, was the exceedingly popular original house 'Dungeon of Terror'. The original house had been dismantled carefully after park bosses immediately noted that the first event was such a success. This time the house would be re-used but it would not be exactly the same. Criticisms of the 1991 house was that it was too short, "we'd waited in the humidity with no air-conditioning for 3 hours and the house was less than 5 minutes to walk through!" one annoyed guest had noted. This time the house will be longer with more set pieces and a few alterations to the original layout. "At one point, those walking through are threatened by monsters on one side. On the other side is a mirror. The effect is to have customers bouncing back and forth between each side, recoiling from the monsters on one side, only to face them in the mirror on the other" said Tony Peugh about the new house. The result of the changes lead to the three hour waits of the previous year to be extended to an average of four.

The other house at this event was based on a recent Universal Studios released picture called 'The People Under the Stairs'. The movie had been released the previous year in November of 1991 and was an American horror film written and directed by Wes Craven and starring Brandon Adams, Everett McGill, Wendy Robie, A. J. Langer, Ving Rhames and Sean Whalen. Craven had famously been the creator of the ever popular 'A Nightmare on Elm Street' franchise featuring the hideous Freddy Krueger character. The use of 'The People Under the Stairs' however was a Universal picture and had been reasonably successful. Filming of the movie had taken place the year before at Universal Studios Hollywood in one of the soundstages and fortunately due to Universal's investment in extending their prop warehouse to be one of the largest in the world, all of the sets and props from the movie were put into storage. Universal Executives had hoped that a sequel would be in the pipeline, hence the use of the storage and once the hopes of this were dashed the Studios in Florida came calling. Around the summer of 1992 the sets and props were all boxed up in Hollywood and carefully shipped down to Florida where they were assembled again but into a house formation all inside Soundstage 23. Soundstage 23 had been used infrequently by all parties on the lot over the first few years, but had been used mostly in the early days by Nickelodeon Studios who often used the soundstage when their own soundstages were already engaged in filming. Nick's popular show 'GUTS' had used the soundstage as rehearsal space and were actively found other space to this to make way for the building of the house.

The construction was reported as being difficult from the outset within the massive 16,000-square-foot space. Piecing together sets that had been used from a movie and were wholly temporary for each shot had to be more robust to cope with the thousands of party goers that would no doubt cause damage to the sets if they had not been shored up thoroughly, which took time. So much time, that although the sets were already constructed when delivered the putting together, installing walkways and shoring them up actually took longer than the initial build of Dungeon of Terror the year previously.

"We also experimented a little in this house due to the fact we had more space because it had been located in one of the soundstages," said John Paul Geurts[14], producer of the event. He continued, "We had tried claustrophobic environments before to great effect, which were used throughout the house anyway, so we decided near the end that we would open up the house and put in a night's sky that would be beautifully dressed with stars and a moon etc., to make guests feel like they were outside but really inside. Unfortunately it came apparent very early on during 'night one' that this scene was causing a backlog. Instead of people remarking on the scene and then moving out of the house, people were actively taking minutes to pause which caused not only a back-up along the route so guests were getting stuck in some of the scary scenes but also the queue to move really slow. We then tried to pulse guests through rather than allow a continuous flow through the house, but that didn't work either. It was then we came up with the idea of 'scare-moving', whereby when guests would arrive at this final scene we would put scareactors lurking inside near where the guests entered, who would then jump-out at select times to literally scare the guests out the door. It became such an effective technique to keep the queue moving, that they still use that technique to this very day!"

Lifted directly from the motion picture the house featured themes such as cannibalism, incest, home invasion, sadism and poverty a mixed bunch of adult themes that proved the house to be a horrific as the movie it was based on. This was a modern event for a modern audience in a claustrophobic setting (like the movie) which snaked around the large soundstage to great effect. Simulated mutilations were played out in one room, human taxidermy in another and dangling body parts decorated the corridors with the gore setting set to maximum! One overly enthusiastic scaractor within the cryptic set actually took it upon himself to add more fake blood within his scene. With such realism he added to his performance the actual fake blood (red dyed corn syrup), which was reportedly sprayed over several guests while they enjoyed the house. Reportedly, one angry park guest with a now stained white T-shirt headed right for Guest Services to demand something was done. Universal reportedly responded by ensuring no future occurrences of staff members improvising with their own props was to ever happen again. But despite this minor setback, the house was a massive draw and lines quickly grew around the soundstage to get into be immersed straight into the hit movie. Before you could ride the movies, now you could physically be a part and interact within a movie!

'The People Under the Stairs' wasn't the only film franchise to be utilized at the event, for one of the first time and only times in the event's history different rides were repurposed into temporary Halloween themed attractions. Seeing the ride like never before was a true highlight and this process took the pressure off of the two official houses. 'Darkman' was immediately put into Kongrontation to become 'Tramway of Doom'. 'Darkman' was released in 1990, an American superhero action film directed and co-written by Sam Raimi (of Spider-Man and Evil Dead franchises). Raimi supposedly flew to Orlando to see his creation being applied at the event. The movie was originally based on a short story Raimi wrote that paid homage to Universal's classic early horror films of the 1930s. The film starred Liam Neeson as Peyton Westlake, a scientist who is attacked and left for dead by a mobster. Raimi was unable to secure the rights to either 'The Shadow' or 'Batman' franchises, so decided to create his own superhero and struck a deal with the motion pictures arm of Universal Studios to make his very first major motion picture.

The general theme of the ride was now changed, yes King Kong was on the loose and attacking your tram but you also had 'Darkman' lurking behind every corner. Inevitably the staff members dressed as the popular movie character would be lurking within the expansive queue, but also at the end of the attraction when to exit the attraction guests would then walk on the ground of the ride through the streets of New York that had been temporary repurposed as a short haunted house. Many guests remarked on the detail of the sets in New York, thinking that this level of detail had been added specifically for the event but it hadn't, the detail had always been there, such was the testament to the excellent quality to detail that Universal put into all their rides. Guests were also permitted to walk one final time on the ground of the attraction during Halloween Horror Nights XI, for show 'The Oozone Fright Club', where guests entered a staff members' only area of the queue line, and then had to exit to the ground where another haunted house had been constructed. It was also noted by many attendees at the event that some of the Darkmen(?) actually rode in the trams with guests, which totally unnerved some guests; One guest was reported as saying, "he looks like an evil cross between 'The Invisible Man' and 'The Mummy', totally freaky!" What a premonition that a *Mummy* might occupy the building…

And Kong wasn't the only attraction to have the creepiness beefed up for the event either. ET's popular ride had the queue temporary reimagined. The tranquil Southern California redwood forest of the snaking queue was pumped with bellows of dry ice and ghoulish scareactors awaited on every turn. Some guests were so terrified they ran through the queue to escape to the relative tameness of the popular family ride! The newly opened and extremely popular Back to the Future ride was also given a similar makeover. This time ghouls and fog machines made way for mad scientists and strobe lighting. A crazy disco theme played out and crazy longhaired mad scientists with blood splattered white coats lurked behind every corner of the expansive queue area. Some guests even reported being chased out to the gift shop such was the lengthy and twisting layout of the exit path from some of the attraction's higher load areas. And Universal wasn't finished there with their ride makeovers or 'horror-fying', Earthquake which had recently been tweaked due to on-going maintenance issues also got in on the act. At points mostly during the queue section of the ride and the pre-show various scareactors would be on the scene to scare up some frights and entertain guests before loading onto their ride vehicle.

Other rides and attractions that were open on these nights included: The Funtastic World of Hanna-Barbera, Hitchcock's 3-D Theater, The Horror Make-Up Show, (the recently installed) Beetlejuice's Graveyard Review and the popular day-time Ghostbusters' show. The Bates Motel[2] became an official photospot to take your picture with various Universal monsters and even characters from the popular syndicated show 'The Munsters'. The popular Pendragons[6] Magic Show from the previous year was back with fresh new tricks to amaze a waiting audience and the Carnival of Horror costume contest was also put on, with similar rules and restrictions as the previous year had implemented but it was only held on October 24 at 7pm.

Thunderdome debuted this year, based loosely from the motion picture 'Mad Max Beyond Thunderdome' (as it was not a Universal property), with the stage mounted half-way down the Hollywood Boulevard area of the park. The Queen of Darkness and her evil Thunderdome[4] henchmen, who seize guests from the crowd (well, cast members made to look like guests), to be tortured live (well maybe dead) on stage. Soon they would be locked in cages and lowered into a boiling vat of acid, reducing them to mere skeletons; which was neat addition that combined both horror and magic to great effect.

"Wanted - Person to share small, dark coffin with 100 live rats", ran on various ads in the local newspapers[8]. "Help-wanted ads ran over the weekend in eight Florida newspapers. The park has three Rat People but wants two more," said Universal spokeswoman Linda Buckley. The local ad would go on to make national headlines and for the first time in the event's history it would start to get national attention. "Those who get the job will wear Victorian garb and play possum in a coffin while dozens of rats crawl over them" she said. Several applications were received with a general mix of both genders applying for the part. The Rat Lady had been so popular as one of the main scares in the Dungeon house that bringing her (or him) back would be a must-do for Universal Creative. She continued, "These are the real McCoys - living, breathing critters with long tails and whiskers. And yes, sometimes they nip." It was a tough job and not for the faint hearted but the remuneration for the role was more vocational than financial. The pay you ask? "More than minimum wage, but not as much as (park president) Tom Williams," she said. However this time, she wouldn't be a fixed scare in that house, she would be mobile. Wheeled through the streets in a glass coffin (something that would later become her signature) the handler of the coffin would shout "come see a woman encased alive in a glass coffin filled with sewer dwelling rodents!"[9]

Like the previous year no official scarezones were setup[5], so instead assorted scareactors dressed as ghouls, vampires and monsters (including the Classic Universal Monsters) were deployed to roam the park[12]. 300 scareactors were employed that year to roam nightly in the park, something that was a real challenge for Universal's 40 employed makeup artists headed-up by Hollywood makeup artist extraordinaire Joe Blasco. He said,

"This is the biggest event of its kind ever. I was an apprentice to Ben Nye on the original 'Planet of the Apes', and we never did even close to this many apes at a time, maybe 80 at once at the most".

The scareactors each night seem to congregate mostly around the New York, San Francisco and Amity areas of the park. Amity was also home to a district loosely titled 'Midway of the Bizarre,', where scareactors named 'Blade Walker', 'Bone Bender' and The Hex Maniac' terrified guests as they left the signature house of the event from the Jaws queue building[13].

The event had many nationally famous acts attend for the festivities and done were larger (well physically at least) that the very popular Robosaurus who made his official debut at the event that year[11]. Robosaurus was a transforming dinosaur robot (like a transformer but not) created by engineer Doug Malewicki in 1989 but was later sold to new owner Monster Robots, Inc. Robosaurus is operated by a driver sitting in the head of the robot, and was built with the ability to transform from a 48-foot semi trailer into a mobile mechanical Tyrannosaurus Rex. It had hydraulically activated arms, large grasping claws, and jaws, and a flame thrower mounted in the head to give the effect of breathing fire out of its metal nostrils. It is still used today at motorsport and football events (particularly monster truck events) and even air shows to 'eat' and burn vehicles such as cars and small airplanes for various audiences. Mounted in the New York area of the park between the Ghostbuster's show and the New York Public Library steps the mechanical maniac acted as a giant weenie for entering park guests. Riding along the streets from the Boneyard area and then into position, the giant robot transformed into his trademark dinosaur appearance standing at a height of 40 feet when fully extended with a weight of 31 tons. Picking up car props that were provided guests stood in astonishment as the beast picked up and then proceeded to eat the vehicles. Then just as park guests were reconciling what they were watching the transforming mechanical reptilian spit vast lengths of fire from its nostrils and let fireworks off from its body. This surely was unlike anything that had been witnessed before.

Also making their debut this year were a small humble show duo of dudes who would go on to define the event but had started this year with very modest intentions; And that was Bill S. Preston, Esq. and Ted "Theodore" Logan, the wild stallions themselves, Bill and Ted in the ever popular 'Bill and Ted's Excellent Halloween Adventure'. Performing over four shows each night with two different casts alternating through the event. The first pairing was cast member Toby Miller who played the part of Bill who at the time was a ride attendant at Kongrontation, picked for the part for his uncanny resemblance to Alex Winter from the original movies and Ted was played by Back to the Future ride attendant Joel Buntin who also had a great ability to mimic Keanu Reeves. Buntin said, "I've seen the movie 26 times . . . definitely know it pretty well. We each have friends that look like the other characters, so we've been doing it with them for about . . . well, I've been doing it for about three years." "I've only been doing it for about a year and two months," Miller went on to say, "I saw *Excellent Adventure* and *Bogus Journey* like back to back in the same week, and I've never seen it before, ever. And I totally fell in love with the dudes!"

The other respective duo were John Gallagher who was working as a Studio Tour Guide at the time and Robert Ramos a cast member from The day-show of the Ghostbusters. Ramos was reported as saying at the time that he got into character by watching the original movie "about 550,000 times".

The main actors along with supporting cast had been carefully selected some months prior with full rehearsals occurring exactly one month to opening night. The show, which was held at Wild, Wild, Wild West Stunt Show building, would feature singing, dancing, comedy and event stunts. The show was set in an old western cowboy town, the lights dimmed and Queen's 'We Will Rock You' was blasted out of the speakers prompting the audience to sing along (a song that would return almost every year with the show).

The show began with a stand-off between the town's Sheriff and a plucky bank robber. Just as the guns are drawn Bill and Ted arrive on the set in their iconic phone booth, apparently lost from their mission to go trick or treating through time. The evil bank robber decides to corner the boys and steal their time-travelling booth to round up a new bank robbing gang from history. After he leaves in a cloud of smoke in the booth, Bill finds that he has a portable telephone for emergencies which he can use to remote control the booth and bring it back to the town. But after he dials the number, instead of their booth appearing a DeLorian appears in a blaze of Huey Lewis' rock ballad 'The Power of Love' driven by none other than Doc Brown (from Back to the Future)…

The Doc explains that they must bring back the devilish bank robber, but with the aid of famous musicians from past and present to help out. Just as the travelling booth re-appears with the robber it contains an evil assortment of villains to aid in the robber's attempt to rob the town's bank (no less than Freddy Krueger, the Terminator and Jason). Fighting breaks out between the two groups where various stunts are undertaken including falls from various buildings (this and others lifted right from the Western Show the temporary show had replaced), a fall down a supposed well, explosions and various props being smashed over each other's heads. The fighting climaxes as the town's Sheriff gun downs the bank robber. As the bank robber was no more and the villains had dispersed, Bill & Ted decide to hold a "most excellent" musical concert with their favorite performers, including: MC Hammer, The Blues Brothers, Madonna and an extremely portly Elvis! As they collectively sing and dance various contemporary musical numbers including guitar solos (ex-cel-lent) they end with a version of Elvis' 'Shout!' where the audience is encouraged to sing along. As the number finishes the house is literally brought down when the classic house façade in the middle comes tumbling down right to the actor playing Doc Brown's surprise. The audience immediately stood, they cheered and clapped and so a Halloween Horror Night's mainstay was born.[7]

The performances didn't go without issue though as various special effects did not work on select performances. Both duos were reported as being extremely professional and even adlibbing lines to make-up for the minor setbacks that were seen. The audience didn't care though, they loved the show! The park stationed merchandise carts at the exits selling T-Shirts with Bill and Ted sitting on their phone booths with the Universal classic monsters cramped inside, along with baseball caps featuring the classic Bill and Ted logo. The carts were reported as being sold out nearly every night such was the demand for this very early example of event merchandise. The 'Wyld Stallyns' had arrived and they were here to stay!

Other attractions at the event which were more party-like and musical was a mini-rock concert that was held at The Mel's Drive-In Theater area (with the lights first turned off at this event to read 'Mel's Die-In'). The radio presenter and personality Wolfman Jack DJ-ed this attraction and compered the show with three nightly performances. Performers included Roni G and Joe Savage 'The Madman of Rock n' Roll'. The latter, a leather wearing larger than life character bolted out covers but in his own particular style of Neil Diamond's 'America' and Queen's 'We Are The Champions'.

"You have to keep saying in your head, 'It's fake, it's fake,' but it's hard to believe it because it looks so real!" said park guest Michelle Martin. "Gross" others said. "Scary! Really scary!" said Nicole Porter, from Levittown, N.Y., who said she had seen the movie and was more frightened by the live production. Ronnie Bach, 49, of Palm Harbor said, "That was the scariest experience I've ever had in my life. Better than Disney."[1] Phrases like, "this is completely unique, like nothing we have seen before" and "last year was ground-breaking and this this year is even better" were all common responses from guests who had attended. Universal's expectations had been smashed, the bar had been lifted and now the quest was on to plan for the next year. Universal knew they were on a roll.

Notes:

[1] The Orlando Sentinel - Friday, October 23, 1992
[2] The Palm Beach Post - Sunday, October 18, 1992
[3] The Tampa Tribune - Friday, October 23, 1992
[4] Miami Herald, The (FL) - Sunday, October 18, 1992
[5] Miami Herald, The (FL) - Sunday, October 18, 1992
[6] 1992 Official Event Park Map
[7] Interview with the cast from the President of Bill and Ted's official fan club.
[8] Orlando Sentinel Oct 13, 1992
[9] Interview Michael Branch
[10] Orlando Sentinel Oct 30, 1992
[11] Orlando Sentinel Oct 30, 1992
[12] Orlando Sentinel Nov 1, 1992
[13] Orlando Sentinel Oct 8, 1992
[14] Interview with John Paul Geurts

Halloween Horror Nights: 3rd Annual

"The Shark Bites Back!"

Halloween Horror Nights in the late September press of 1993 was dubbed as "The 3rd Annual Universal Studios Florida Halloween Horror Nights"[10], though this year there would be some changes and none-more-so than the return of Jaws. Charting back to the summer of that year and rumors were spreading amongst the local residents and Universal fans that their beloved Halloween event would be toast. Thought was that now the shark is back, and it needs it's massive queue buildings for, well queuing, where could the dungeon house be sited? And would Universal even bother to take it down and then try to rebuild it again? Things were starting to look bleak for the event, in at least the fans' eyes, as many had perceived that the shark returning would make way for the event to go for that year; after all it had come and gone in Hollywood a couple of times. Fans were concerned.

"Biting Back"[11] the national headlines read in February 1993. Linda Buckley a park spokeswoman said, "Universal Studios Florida plans to reopen its Jaws ride in June [sic]. The water-based attraction will be the key offering in the park's 1993 season and will be the cornerstone of new advertising." The June deadline was missed due to further testing required as there had been some issues with the new pyrotechnics, the new ride was from concept to closure (in 2012) the largest ride of its kind to utilize the most amount of pyrotechnics (particularly gasoline for the finale) and things just couldn't get fixed right. Technicians and engineers worked around the clock throughout July and by August on select days only it was tested with park guests. By August 12th of that year Leslie Doolittle of the Orlando Sentinel had heard from hundreds of park guests that the new ride was amazing and unlike anything anyone had ever experienced before (in fact Universal were quoted as saying that just over 500,000 park guests had been selected on select days to ride the attraction in August to get all the bugs with the attraction sorted for the grand opening), she wrote "Judging by the screams, shrieks and cheers from tourists lucky enough to catch a test run of the new Jaws ride, Universal Studios Florida in Orlando is about to open an immensely popular attraction. [sic] People who venture out on an Amityville harbor cruise are terrorized, drenched, rocked by explosions and seared by heat. The ride is a life-and-death, hide-and-seek game with a massive killer shark." The park's marketing executive Randy Garfield was quoted as saying "You really think you are going to get your arm bitten off!"

The summer had been missed but Universal were not about to repeat the mistakes of the past and open a ride that was not perfect. The date was set for the official opening of 1st October 1993[9] ready for the celebrities of opening day to return and cut the ribbon once more. After all, Steve Spielberg allegedly got caught mid shark attack when the ride broke down on opening day, so Universal was not prepared for that to happen again when the main man himself was due to have the inaugural voyage. "Bringing Jaws on at this point really closes a chapter for us, and allows us to move forward," said Bob Ward, senior vice president for design and planning at MCA Recreation, Universal's parent company. "Obviously, we are all very excited that Jaws is becoming part of the family." The ride was then ceremoniously opened by original cast and crew members: Roy Scheider, Lorraine Gary and Steven Spielberg who all enjoyed the attraction completely problem free. In fact, the attraction ran all day without a single fault at all. But there was a problem for the fans, the ride had reopened just when Halloween was fast approaching but not only that, it was also now problem free and running daily from October, all hope was surely lost now, the event can't surely be coming back? But then there was a glimmer of hope on the horizon…

The hope came in an advertisement placed in the local press for "roach wranglers" and "rat ladies" to apply immediately at Universal Studios, "send us your resumes" the peculiar ad wrote[8]. The advertisement was placed the very day after the grand opening of the Jaws ride, finally central Floridian fans could air a sigh of relief so unless Universal had a massive vermin problem (hugely unlikely!) then Halloween Horror Nights would be back!

The roach and rat advertisement started again to make national headlines across the country and this really was the first time that Universal and fans alike started to see more attention from the event in other parts of the country than had been seen previously. By October 8th Bubba Smith had been hired as Universal's official roach wrangler, whereas four other women had been hired to the Rat Ladies for the event. Smith, who was a large man with a long natural scraggly beard debuted with his collection of real roaches in the People Under the Stairs house, which retuned that year. Universal used the appointments to further fan the attentions of the national presses, the Orlando Sentinel wrote: "Baker was one of 300 hearty souls who fired off resumes to Universal last week after the company advertised for "roach wranglers" and "rat ladies." Wranglers are a new addition to the grisly lineup of characters to be used in a haunted house Universal opens for Halloween. Two bug handlers were hired. The men will play deranged people caught inside the wall of a house. Their only friends are the roaches - so there's lots of nuzzling and cuddling going on.

Some of the bugs are the hissing Madagascar variety, while others are the smaller, and equally vile, American cockroach."[7]

It was then by October 15th that all fears could be laid to rest (then other fears renewed when the event starts!) when Universal officially announced that the popular Halloween event would be back for the third time to run for five nights on October 23, 24, 29, 30, & 31. In fact Universal had no such intention to not stage the event, they had little to anyone's knowledge (outside of park management's) been planning the 1993 event since as early as February 1993 and various members of the Park's Creative had gone on specific fact finding missions to Los Angeles and New Orleans to aid with idea development. The news quickly came when around March of that year permits were filed to show 'careful dismantlement and application of screeding' was being applied for in an area known only as Nazarman's. Nazarman's Pawn Shop and nearby facades in the New York area of the park was mostly used for storage. Nazarman's had been constructed as part of the robust facades that the original park designers wanted installed before the park opened to attract filmmakers to Orlando but also for guests to wander around and explore, like they couldn't at Universal's Hollywood backlot. Nazarman's Pawn Shop actually comes from an Allied Artists movie called 'The Pawnbroker' made in 1964 and starring Rod Steiger. The areas behind the shop and immediately around were worked on all summer to create a space that future Halloween attractions and houses could be temporarily installed. The construction created various back alleys that regular day guests could not venture onto and large spaces within the mighty steel frame ready for rooms to be set up, along with rigs and discreet towers to control the lights and atmosphere of any future attractions. This wasn't the first time that the park had undertaken real construction specifically for the event, but this level of construction here went on to show that Universal from 1993 had true long-term ambitions as to the quality and frequency of the beloved event.

"In terms of our haunted houses," said John Paul Guertz, the event's artistic director, "we've created some really dramatic situations that people can find themselves walking into and our haunted houses are definitely more upscale than your neighborhood haunted house. People come to see our haunted house attractions, but we try to make the most out of our streets with roaming characters," said Guertz. "People feel very comfortable out on the streets and then suddenly one of the characters leaps out and scares the heck out of them. There's something lurking for guests around every corner." And every corner was true! Where the 1993 summer season had seen a slowdown in park attendances, which was likely attributed to the promised Jaws ride that only opened shortly before the event was held, some park employees were repurposed to work the streets to become scareactors with more actors than had ever been at the event before plunged onto roads to chase and delight the guests in equal abundance. However, this year a more concerted effort would be made to better organize the streets with hordes of roaming scareactors characterized into loose fitting groups rather than appearing at random (though still no scarezones were officially set-up yet), these included: a sword swallower, a fire-eating contortionist, the Chain Saw Drill Team and the Dead High School Cheerleading Squad. This marked the first outing of a Halloween Horror Nights tradition, that of the Chainsaw Drill Team. The team consisted of five males dressed in faux-marine combat attires and were particularly robust on the streets of New York where frightened guests queuing to get-in could hear bizarre roars of chainsaws in the distance followed by blood curdling screams there after – a new tradition was born. "The idea of maniacs with chainsaws throughout the park had been there since day one", remarked John Paul Geurts, the event's co-producer. "Julie Zimmerman my co-producer can be directly accredited with creating the idea. She researched the concept of using chainsaws with no chains and then using them to scare guests with. It's such a neat idea that had really stood the test of time, as them guys and girls who are employed to be in the Drill Team really are as popular and iconic back then as they are to this day."[13]

There would be an increase this year in the number of houses; such was the popularity of the two previous houses where waits of over three hours were exceedingly common nearly every night. First up was a return of a house that had been present for the first time last year, 'The People Under the Stairs' which would be located in the expansive 16,000-square foot Soundstage 23. The house was intended to be dismantled after the event in late 1992 and put out back into storage or sent back to Hollywood (as the house was a mixture of additions and real sets used from the movie). Operations department intended to wait until Studio Operations called for the house to go to make-way for a new studio production before it would be dismantled, however no such call was given. It was around this time that Universal much like its neighbor Disney, was starting to see that Orlando was not going to become the next Hollywood. Production demand decreased and the productions that did need space such as 'SeaQuest DSV', Hulk Hogan's 'Thunder in Paradise' and various Nickelodeon shows could easily be made in the other expansive soundstages that surrounded Soundstage 23; therefore in the Spring of 1993 the decision was made to leave the house where it was, to fix it up and repair it from the previous year's use and then re-open it for 1993 with pretty much the exact same layout and numbers of scares. Though minor alterations had been made,

the house was incredibly scary. "Each room is familiar yet spooky - a bare light bulb illuminates the ghostly attic, creatures lurk underneath the stairs and roaches scurry through the kitchen.
We like to tap into subtle, familiar fears," said Jerry Abercrombie, Universal's props manager. "The attics, the basements, the closets . . . the things you know you shouldn't be afraid of, but you are." As previously mentioned, the Roach Man was located somewhere in the house, which brought a different almost creepier dynamic that had not previously been seen for this house.

As in the previous house where actual sets from the hit movie were used, the next house was the actual sets from a TV movie, that of Psycho IV – The Beginning. The direct-to-TV movie had been the final official sequel to the hit original 1960 movie of the same name and the last to star leading man Anthony Perkins. The horror-drama movie that was both the third sequel and a prequel to the original movie, as it includes both events after Psycho III while focusing on flashbacks of events that took place prior to the original film. It was first broadcast on the Showtime cable network on November 10, 1990.

"I couldn't wait to build a 'Psycho' house", said John Paul Geurts. Geurts who had worked previously on the original Hitchcock attraction was a great fan of Hitchcock and wanted to bring all the best set pieces from the famous movies into one house. "For my time working on 'Halloween Horror Nights' it was possibly the hardest house to physically create. We knew we were going to use the sets from 'Psycho IV' but the problem lay that the motel especially had been built solely for the purposes of filmmaking, they just assumed that it would be torn down after production wrapped and then trashed. We went in to see where we could run lighting equipment, where we could make enough space to put 'boo-doors' in etc. but we just couldn't do it, there was no space and no actual floors built. I was quite upset about this, as I had really wanted to use the original sets from this movie," he said. The movie which had been the first movie to be shot entirely at Universal Orlando (filmed onset during the initial weeks of park operation), had built sets using forced perspective that were entirely for the temporary use of film production, with no regard whatsoever for future uses. "Unperturbed we went back to the drawing board, and one evening I was out the back just surveying the area and I thought to myself, 'you know, between the motel and the Hard Rock Building, there's plenty of space', so the idea hit me of building an extension to the back to accommodate a maze," he said.

It had been noted that during filming the production crew had asked that the nearby Hard Rock Café to extinguish all lights and turn their music off due to the proximity of the restaurant, though just enough space could be provided to fit an extension to the motel[14]. Geurts continued, "So what we did was we propped up the front façade which was fully retained, we removed the side walls and replaced them with large wrap-around walls (all in the similar materials), we then built-out the back area and demarked it on the ground and poured a concrete slab. The roof we raise up slightly and put in additional supports (as we had removed the rear walling) and then to infill the rear area we approached a company that built a kind of tent over the back of it that would be obscured by the front façade." Installing a tent for the purposes of building a house for the event was the first time the technology had been used, prior to the 'Sprung Tents' being installed years later, though as Geurts remarked[13], "our tent was far more simple in design than the technology they now have in the Sprung tents." He continued, "We were actually given free rein to do what we wanted with the Bates set as it had been earmarked from early 1993 to be demolished in or around 1995 to make way for an extension to the 'Fievel's Playland' [which would be 'A Day in the Park with Barney' that opened in 1995]. So they let us do what we wanted as long as it was within budget."

The house and motel for the shoot had been the first official production at the Universal Resort. Where the house and motel had been moved in Hollywood and was now a part of their popular tram tour, the decision was made to move the production to the newly opened park and construct a complete new outdoor set for the filming, with the set construction to occur shortly after the main construction of the attractions had completed. Therefore site contractors were utilized for this run-on work. Bill Nassal of The Nassal Co. (which is still trading to this day) was an external contractor who built many of the early attractions at the park, including: the interior and external train for the Back to the Future ride, the interior for the Earthquake attraction, the swamp for the set of The Swamp Thing television show, the sets for American Tail and American Tail II, attractions based on the movie; and the Lagoon Boathouse and restaurant, which was then a part of the set for the lagoon stunt show. In fact the company would continue to grow when in 2006 it was handed the contract to work again with Universal to help bring to reality the Wizarding World of Harry Potter at Islands of Adventure and then again at Diagon Alley at the Studios.

Bill and his excellent company of engineers and technicians soon got to work to create the house and motel for the production. Most of the construction and then the subsequent filming was all undertaken with guests watching with it becoming its own unique attraction where not since

1910s in at Universal's Hollywood Studios could you come to a working studio and see actual movies being shot in-front of you. Bill said at the time, "For instance, Nassal has cabinetmakers who can undertake complex jobs, such as the intricate woodwork of the Psycho House, and artists capable of painting just about anything." And intricate it was. Using plans from the original construction, that were amended to build all four flanks where in 1959 only two sides were built as filming didn't require the camera to see the other sides, so they weren't built. In Orlando, like all the sets that had been built for actual and potential filming they had to be strong and withstand tropical conditions. Whereas concrete padded reinforced steel structures had been built in Orlando for the soundstages and outdoor sets, in Hollywood everything had been built and framed in timber, including the outdoor sets. The original Bates house in Hollywood had been a composition of other sets knitted together to save money, as Hitchcock had famously wanted to make this classic movie for a very tight budget. The Psycho house was built from a number of Universal's stock units to save money. In fact, Hitchcock staked his reputation on the fact that the movie could be made for less than $1million, in the end its final budget was close to $800,000. The front elevation of the house and the distinctive tower facade was removed from a house on what is now Wisteria Lane (then Colonial Street) and had been used in the 1950 Jimmy Stewart classic movie 'Harvey'. Therefore Nassal and his team had very high expectations to not only build an exacting replica of the 1960 movie but to also make sure it passed various building codes for outside buildings in terms of bracing for severe weather conditions. It was therefore around the first week that construction of the sets were completed and the delayed production began shooting. The production of Psycho IV being delayed in order for the opening of the studios to occur, as park bosses were keen for park guests to get a taste for seeing actual motion picture (well made for TV) productions being shot at the studios.

Skipping forward to 1993 and Studios Creative had thought that unlike the 1991 event where the sets were used as a show for Beetlejuice and co, and then underutilized for just a photo-spot in the previous year – what if the sets built for the movie could be used to put the park guests through the actual movie. Quietly over the summer of that year the house and motel were converted into an ambitious house for the event. Guests would enter in in via their nightmare via the main Bates Family Mansion's looming porch and into the main house that had been dressed to look like a combination of the actual house from the movie and a weird composite of old-timey movies from Norman Bates' mind, from there guests would venture down the famous path and into the actual motel. Norman and his mother were the main antagonists and they were everywhere! In the house's living room a cozy fire is roaring and a large oil painting of a scenic view is hung above the fireplace but wait, just as you are lured into a false sense of comfort the painting would be flipped and Norman in full mother's garb would start plunging his kitchen knife right in front of your face from above; it was said to be one of the most popular scares from the house. Later a recreation of the famous kitchen scene from Psycho 2 would see Norman appear from inside kitchen cupboards, there were Normans everywhere in this attraction! A corridor from one room in the motel to the next would be a closet filled with old lady clothes when suddenly a scaractor dressed in a Mrs. Bates special would pop out and scare guests from behind the clothes rail. But it wasn't all just from the mind of Norman, there was one scene in the motel that was lifted straight from the original movie, and it was one of the most famous too, that of the shower scene. Bernard Herrman's eerie score would play as guests passed a bathtub with shower screen pulled around. Inside a puppet controlled mannequin would be showering (including shower cap), whilst a Norman Bates look-a-like would creep up and plunge his knife repeatedly into the back of the dummy just as the musical crescendo would occur[12]. This scene located near the end of the attraction would send guests running into the streets!

Next up was The Slaughterhouse located in the Nazarman's area as detailed earlier, and it was hands down the goriest the park's creative had made thus far in the event's small history. Guests would enter in near Sting Alley and into a packing and processing facility for meat but this wasn't any old meat, this was human meat. Corpses were hanging from the ceilings like cattle in a butchery store, hairy brutes with blood splattered aprons would jump in front of you carrying large cleavers and proceed to start hacking to bits poor victims who had not been so lucky. The general idea was what if a load of insane mutant cannibals were left to run the local meat factory and with the ability to retro-fit and build a purpose made haunt facility for this house, the Creatives at Universal took to military precision in designing the house. "Designing a haunted house turns into math, eventually," said John Paul Geurtz, the event's artistic director. "You have to calculate each step people will take and engineer their every move. There's nothing random about this." It also marked the first house to have its tongue firmly pressed into the side of its mouth, where humor and light relief (if only for a second) were as important as the scares. "We do have bodies that hang or dunk or drape or spew, we also use a lot of humor and a lot of subtle scares" Geurtz said. Creative Director Julie Zimmerman said, "People love to be scared as much as they love to laugh. We all need to get that out, to scream and yell and do all the things we can't normally do."[6]

A bumper crop of attractions were open this year including: Kongfrontation, Ghostbusters, Funtastic World of Hanna-Barbera, Hitchcock's 3-D Theater, The Gory, Gruesome, Grotesque Horror Make-Up Show, ET, Earthquake, Back to the Future: The Ride, Beetlejuice's Graveyard Review and the newly opened Jaws. It was the latter of these offerings that was ironically the most impressive. As described earlier, fans of the event had thought that the return of the shark would mean the end of their beloved event, what actually happen was the creation of a new Halloween Horror Nights tradition and one that sadly now can never be repeated (least in Orlando) and is, Jaws at night. Jaws at night took the attraction to a whole new level of terrifying. The Park's Creative department had not made any alterations to the ride, it just came into its own once the sun was down. The dark and sometimes foggy atmosphere made the experience more terrifying as the shark seemed to be coming out of the water at random locations, such was the dark foreboding ambiance that lead to regular park guests becoming temporary disorientated.

Other than the three house and roaming scaractor hoards there were also a number of smaller shows, these included: Hex Maniacs[3] (a magic act that featured a "live" cremation), the Human Blockhead (a gross-out sword swallowing and pinned head maniac), Robosaurus returned performing much the same act as last year, Crossbows of Death (as it says), Burn and Bury (an improvisation comedy act offering quick and easy burials) and Rock Inferno (a horrific rock concert) with Herb Williams and Gibraltar headlining[4]. Herb and his band were a popular performer and rock band that performed extensively in the south of the country during the 80s and 90s. A mixture of classic rock, old school funk, Motown covers, smooth ballads, jive, swing songs and even dance classics. Herb played a plethora of hits that were popular with all age ranges in attendance. His silky smooth vocals combined with his natural showmanship were a welcome lively addition to Hollywood Boulevard. Playing four times per night, the final show of the night featured more slow dances and ballads. Other act performing on the same stage included: Country and Christian band 'Diamond Rio', who had then recently won the Country Music Association vocal group of the year award and who are still performing to this day, and R&B trio 'Jade'[2] who had released various singles to mixed success in the early 90s. The event was keen to retain the party atmosphere, which it did in spades during the performances.

Also appearing four times per night was the returning and increasingly popular Bill & Ted in Bill & Ted's Excellent Halloween Adventure II. The show was as popular as the previous and only minor tweaks had been given to the script that everyone at Universal's Creative team had decided that the original show was such a hit then perhaps the original script should be used. The guests didn't mind as every single performance played out to packed crowds.

The new national media darling of the tabloids was back too, the ever-popular Rat Lady. "Our Rat Ladies have really taken a liking to their job," said John Paul Guertz. "Rat Madames" Stacey L. Virta and Catherine Greenlief, he adds, "have even put together a Rat Lady Manual" to help others play the role. Some of the four-page manual's tips include: Before the show: "You are encouraged to get to know the rats on a daily basis - (by) arriving early before the show, or stopping by during the week. The only way you can get to know your rats better is to show you care." (For the record, 500 applicants applied for this job.) In the coffin: "Aussie Scrunch hair spray works best. . .this brand keeps the rats coming back." Also, "it's a good idea to keep rat food or treats handy during performances in case the rats get the munchies." Suddenly the popularity of the role and press attention had led to the role becoming more like a vocation than a temporary regional haunt.[5]

The event was a hit and Universal had achieved the impossible, they'd raised the bar yet again to create an 'institution'. Nights had sold out of pre-sales tickets and people were starting to come from afar. The Orlando Sentinel wrote: "Three years ago Universal Studios experimented with a new idea, Halloween Horror Nights. It has quickly become an institution, particularly with teenagers who love to tour the specially themed haunted houses and can also ride on Earthquake, Jaws or the other attractions too. Be forewarned, however. Buy tickets in advance at Ticketmaster outlets because they sell out quickly". And sell out they did. Nearly every night queues at the ticket windows would form and stay long well into the event. The ticket prices were $24.95 (plus tax) in advance for Florida residents, $35 (plus tax) for the general public, $28 (plus tax) and surprising even kids(!!) had their own ticket for ages 3-9(!!!) which cost slightly less at $29.95 (plus tax)[1].

Notes:

[1] Orlando Sentinel Oct 22, 1993
[2] Orlando Sentinel Oct 22, 1993
[3] Official park map from 1993
[4] Interview with Michael Leonard
[5] St. Petersburg Times, October 23, 1993

[6] Orlando Sentinel Oct 15, 1993
[7] Orlando Sentinel Oct 8, 1993
[8] Orlando Sentinel Oct 8, 1993
[9] Orlando Sentinel Oct 2, 1993
[10] Park advertisement, circa 1993
[11] Orlando Sentinel Feb 22, 1993
[12] Interview with Dawn Peterson
[13] Interview with John Paul Geurts
[14] thepsychomovies.com

1st Ghost: "*I'm going to be icon this year...*"
2nd Ghost: "*Don't lie to me as I can see right through you!*"

Halloween Horror Nights: 4th Annual

"The Scareactor is born!"

The event this year in 1994 marked the first occasion of the infamous 'Ghoul School'[1]. Universal wanted to take everything it had learned from the last three years of being in the fright business and now take the scares to the next level. Starting in late August of that year everyone who had previously worked the event as a scaractor was invited back to attend the classes before the new willing participants were inducted. The 'Ghoul School' opened to much media attention at the time and made headlines in some of the local newspapers. The classes consisted of how to apply one's makeup correctly so as to create your character but to not use too much of the products; costuming and how proper attire should be worn for maximum effect and techniques of terror and etiquette; the latter being everyone's favorite part of the day. Rob Anderson was the main coach of the training and had the task of making the zombie's zombified and the mutant's maniacal.

A show of how the auditions and training were being undertaken was held at the Monster Make-up Show Theatre on October 6th that year. A fake zombie training class was quickly performed to the press to highlight the exacting art of walking, groaning, moving and even speaking like an actual zombie. Jim and Debbie Klingensmith[2] were in attendance that day. This was the third year the Kissimmee based married couple had worked at the event as scareactors. "It's become a tradition," said Jim, to which his wife replied, "Each year gets better." By day the Klingensmiths working together selling time shares, but by night the corporate suits were off and the make-up was donned. Debbie went on to recount a fateful night last year (1993) when working inside one of the houses she scared a couple so bad she had beer accidentally poured right over her! "It's a fright reaction; it's never bothered me. I'd do it for free!"

Also in attendance were Andy Campanaro[3] and Mick Pless, a retired journalist and postal worker, respectively, who were being trained for this year to become the gruesome 'Roach Men' of the event. And these weren't just normal cockroaches, again like last year the use of 2 to 3 inch big Madagascar roaches with their hard shells and ability to hiss like rattle snakes were to be used. "They're like turtles with little personalities," added Campanaro. Universal Studios public relations representative Amy

Moynihan said that hundreds of applications are recieved all year long now by their HR department to work with the roaches and the rats. She explained that although they look disgusting, the rats and cockroaches alike were actually bred by specialist companies for the event to ensure they are completely germ and disease free. She also went on to explain that during the event the animals are cared for onsite but after the event they are re-homed. "The rats (of Rat Lady fame) go for pets (when Horror Nights is over). They're adopted by employees and their friends," she said.

During the Ghoul School successful candidates were asked to pledge their allegiance to the event and promise to give the best scares they can. After which with a cheer and smile every successful participant had graduated and were given their notices as to where they were to be working on the event. Some 400 actors were inducted on this course, such was the increased demand that year for scareactors.

Halloween Horror Nights 2 & 3 had started with just 5 nights. For this event this was increased to 8 nights: October 14, 15, 21, 22, 28, 29, 30, 31 (1994). This meant that the three weekends leading up to Halloween would all be 'owned' by Universal with Disney at this time only offering to decorate the water tower at Disney-MGM Studios with fangs and a small cape and then hosting a smaller Halloween party at Pleasure Island named 'Halloweird Bash'[4]. The event would run only on October 31st and would see the plucky party island filled with lots of dry-ice and chances to do the 'Monster Mash'. Universal on the other hand, was offering more haunted houses than ever before, more musical acts than ever before and the set-up of the very first scarezone.

The first ever scarezone was situated between the Hollywood area and where the Hitchcock 3D (Shrek) are situated, this large piece of real estate was then mined for scares by three roaming groups. The ever-popular 'Chain Saw Drill Team' were back, complete with their chainless saws (shh!) plaid shirts and greased up muscles. They shared the streets with the 'Lizzie Borden's Band and Axe Corps,' who sang and danced with large axes in tow. Finished off with the 'Monks in the Hood', a weird bunch of mad friars who had painted white and black faces who hide behind corners and jump out on unsuspecting members of the public. Along Hollywood Blvd. were a collection of sets and large fixed props to complement the actors, the placing of such items had never been done before. Cages, podiums, pedestals and prisons were all installed for the duration, leather clad muscle men and sexy animal furred bikini clad go-go dancers with fangs danced up. The sexiness of the event had definitely been increased.

Lizzie who was acting Queen of the first scarezone was modelled after the famous case of a woman who was tried and then acquitted for the 1892 axe murders of her father and mother in Fall River, Massachusetts. As the actress strode the streets with a powdery white face glaring at the masses of public she held up high her axe, for which her assembled cast of weird period dressed singers would chant "Lizzie Borden took an axe, gave her mother forty whacks, then she hid behind the door, and gave her father forty more." Then just as the final word of the chant was over, Lizzie would point out into the crowds to show the chanters to go out and round-up a willing victim. The showmanship of this first scarezone was a fantastic foundation and although not perfect, mostly due to the large area it was held in, it would serve the event well and ensure that scarezones would quickly become a tradition for the event in the years to come.

Though four houses were advertised there were technically five, though some argument to this has been given over the years. Officially there were four and first up this year was a return for 'Psycho' Norman Bates. The house which debuted the year before inside the house and motel from the movie 'Psycho IV' was a huge hit with the public, the house was re-dressed and where many of the popular scenes were retained, some new ones had been added. A graveyard scene was added just outside the motel, this had been used during the original Fright Nights for the show with the Blues Brothers and Beetlejuice. Having the gravestones and graves already dug were a no-brainer for repurposing into a scene for the house. They also added a horrific attic scene after using production stills of the attic from 'Psycho 2', this mostly contained stuffed animals with dust and the ever present Norman with mother's garb was there too. Returning was the kitchen set with pop-out Normans in nearly every kitchen unit, the creepy closet walkthrough scene and the infamous bathroom scene.

The Psycho house was not the only house to return this year. 'The Dungeon of Terror' which wasn't present at the previous year (thanks to Jaws reopening) was for HHN4, having moved from one queue building to another. The Earthquake attraction's extended queue building would be the home of the new house, which marked the first time the queue building had been used for a house; it would go on to be a popular venue for staging houses. The house was very similar to the one that had been seen before where 'faux-guests' and other victims had been imprisoned and tortured in the inaugural maze. It featured the Rat Lady again incased in her trademark glass coffin, along with a new character, the Snake Master. A man covered by two boas greeted guests halfway round the house. And although reviews were positive the house lacked the hot, claustrophobic atmosphere of the previous incarnations.

Although if you wanted heat in your houses, you needed look no further than the house that was built over in Nazarman's. The brand new original idea house was Hell's kitchen. Nazarman's had been used in the previous year as a slaughterhouse type maze and although some of the props were left to be repurposed the rest of the house was entirely different. Hell's Kitchen, was an industrial kitchen, complete with chefs with blood stained aprons and huge cleavers, pots and pans rattled on the stoves, blood parts scattered everywhere and blood n' sweat dripped from the ceilings etc. This house purposefully fully had the air-conditioning switched off to create a steamy (thanks to the Floridian humidity) and hot atmosphere. Makeup melted on the performers and extended breaks were given to the scareactors with the most energetic roles. Head Cook of the house was a 6ft tall hunchback covered in blood and swinging knives at guests, he was played by John McVay[5] "It's right up my alley," said McVay, a resident of Winter Park who by day is an employed carpenter and painter. The Roach Man was located back into this house in one of the smaller kitchen scenes trapped inside a big glass case. Hissing roaches crawled over him, up his beard and into mouth whilst crawling over rotten food and pots filled with slime; it was quite shocking. "I'm here to create hell and have fun!" remarked McVay of his time in the house.

The Boneyard, an area since disappeared at Universal, was an area of concrete located between where Twister stands today and the Music Plaza Stage. The area was an outdoor attraction which opened with the park in 1990. The attraction featured a variety of larger props and sets from past Universal Pictures films and TV shows including Jurassic Park and its sequels, Waterworld, Back to the Future, Jaws IV and Ben Hur. Guests could get the chance to walk around the large props and see how they were built, no real tour of sorts just an outdoor scattering of props for guests to look at. A replica of the swimming 'Bruce' (Shark) prop from the movie Jaws IV pulled in most of the crowds, along with sets from Jurassic Park and its sequels.

The house that was located here was a combination of sets built with timber frames and then covered by a fabric roof, it appeared as though it was a giant tent but strictly speaking the buildings weren't a tent, they were just sets that needed protecting from the Floridian weather. Also to add to the confusion was technically two mazes inside as different entrances were used, however the park map billed the location as one single house. The first theme was an old abandoned insane asylum had recently been excavated, it had been abandoned many years prior but had now been reopened. Bloated corpses half dissected, melting zombies and maniacs controlling large machinery such as giant grinder greeted guests throughout its winding corridors of doom (such was the space the house filled). Props from the actual Boneyard were temporarily moved and not repurposed for the house. The other theme was science-fiction with mad scientists and evil clowns tying down helpless victims to large tables to experiment on. Large lamps and hideous ghouls disorientated guests which made for good scares in this labyrinth of a house.

Bill and Ted made a welcome return this year with a show that, although had many themes from the past shows, it was entirely different. The show dubbed 'Bill and Ted Meet Timecop' was held at the regular Wild West Show building and was tied into a recent Universal picture, 'Timecop'[8]. The film starred Jean-Claude Van Damme as a police officer in 1994 and a U.S. Federal agent in 2004, when time travel was possible. It also stars Ron Silver as a rogue politician and Mia Sara as the agent's wife. The story follows a special agent's life through time as he fights time-travel crime and investigates a politician's unusually successful career. As the movie had been released in September that year to mixed audience responses the idea was sprung to tie the movie into the popular Bill and Ted show in an effort to give the movie one final push at the box-office. He's a time traveler and they are time travelers it seemed the perfect fit. As soon as the show started the title characters danced and sang covers of AC/DC, Nirvana, Queen and Offspring. Followed by Bill and Ted travelling through time to make very comical pop culture references, these included: Nancy Kerrigan and Tonya Harding fighting, cracks at O.J. Simpson and then Arnie's Terminator coming to save the day. And although the Timecop tie in was a little dubious, the show was again a massive hit drawing crowds at the increased five performances per evening.

Robosaurus was also back this year. This would park the last time the metal giant would be at the event before returning for a one-off in 2006. The show was incredibly similar to previous years and had been located again in the New York area of the park. Changes this year included some stunt performers working alongside the giant to add to the action. Three shows were on Fridays with four on the busier Saturday nights. Though this was the first year not to have a magic act of some kind take part there were other shows and attractions this year. These included 'The Price is Fright' gameshow with Beetlejuice and a Vegas style act called 'The Devil and His Showgirls. The former being a spoof gameshow where guests of the park could compete for ghoulish prizes with 'Wheel of Misfortune' and 'Win, Lose or Draw Blood' with a red glittery clad Beetlejuice on hosting duties. The other show being a sadist musical revue which featured a fair number of scantily clad Vegas-like showgirls, such was the sexy theme that the event had this year.

These two shows were both pretty forgettable; however one couple would never forget the 'The Price is Fright' show. Starting in 1994 from the solid foundation of the previous year lead the central Florida event joining the culture of the local communities like it had never before. Soon a special type of fandom was starting to emerge that enjoyed not only the great scares that could be had but also the amazing craftsmanship that the park created. People were celebrating events onsite and couples were starting to use the event as date night; the event was becoming something very special. So special in fact that this year marked the first time that the event actual real weddings. Two Orlando based couples held small ceremonies and said their vows during the event. The first wedding held was for Heidi Danzig and Hank Miller[7], who tied on the first Friday of the event, right on the 'Price is Fright' stage which was located inside the Animal Actors stage. The second wedding was for Cynthia Lopez and Peter Nazario at the other Beetlejuice show the permanent day show of 'Beetlejuice's Graveyard Revue' stage. Lopez and Nazario got married onsite on the final Sunday of the event with witnesses to the ceremony of no less than Herman, Lily and Grandpa Munster.

A special Rock n' Roll Inferno stage was erected for the event that included a good number of musical acts this year. These included: 'Flash Flood' a local band that performed covers of various rock groups, 'Sass Jordan' a female singer from Canada who had at the time had a number of hits, and 'Jerry Lee Lewis' the rock legend who needs no introduction. Obtaining Lewis for just one night was a great means for advertising the park and was a huge deal at the time. But he wasn't the only big-named celebrity to be at the event that year. Some of the cast of hit TV show 90201, namely heartthrob Jamie Walters and Stacey Piersa performed songs at the Beetlejuice stage. It was reported that evening that others from the hit TV show were also present. And finally Fox TV and ABC respectively taped special programs onsite during the event on the Saturday, Fox's was for 'Fox's Halloween Bash' a live party report from the destination resort. Fox having flown a number of stars from various hit TV shows to star in the live broadcasted program. The show ran on more than 100 Fox stations across the country, and helped generate plenty of out-of-state interest in the resort. ABC's was more subdued and featured other haunt attractions from Central Florida in 'ABC in Concert', though both were taped at the same time on the same night. "It's a huge deal - it's very big for us. Halloween is becoming a mega-holiday," said Fred Lounsberry, Universal's marketing spokesman. Soon after the broadcast people were reportedly clambering for tickets. "We've been slowly building the event to make Universal the place to go for Halloween." "We get media calls from all over asking what's new in Florida for Halloween," said Gary Stogner[6], a tourism spokeman. It was quickly realized that Halloween was becoming big business for the park.

Notes:

[1] The Tampa Tribune, October 14, 1994
[2] The Orlando Sentinel, October 14, 1994
[3] The Orlando Sentinel, October 14, 1994
[4] The Orlando Sentinel, October 31, 1994
[5] The Orlando Sentinel, October 14, 1994
[6] The Orlando Sentinel, October 31, 1994
[7] The Orlando Sentinel, October 29, 1994
[8] Fort Pierce Tribune (FL), October 14, 1994

Halloween Horror Nights V

The Curse of the Crypt Keeper

The competition that had defined both Universal and Disney in the 1980s would return for Halloween Horror Nights V. Every year the event at Universal, who at the time was still a relative newcomer to the market and had only just fixed their centerpiece ride (Jaws), was growing and growing. Disney at the time had owned the Christmas holidays but it wasn't enough. Executives at Disney had become increasingly interested in trying to grab a piece of their own share of the Halloween festivities. Last year they had dipped their toe only gently into the water with the redressing of the Earful Tower and an adult only Halloween party at their party island, Pleasure Island, but it wasn't enough. Quickly a decision was made by park executives that although what Universal was doing was very successful, it just wasn't Disney. Disney needed a way to bring adults and children alike to their parks but without scaring the life out of them. So Mickey's Not-So-Scary Halloween Party was born.

The event for Disney would be a special one-night hard ticketed event held after hours in the Magic Kingdom and would specifically be aimed at families and young children. "If it's successful, we'll do it again," said Disney spokesman Greg Albrecht. Attractions at the first Not-So-Scary party would include: Cinderella Castle being shrouded in fog and eerie lights, Frontierland will become an old-fashioned ghost town, where guests will hear a stage coach approach passed unseen. Weird aliens will roam Tomorrowland, Adventureland will become a dark torch-lit jungle and the Headless Horseman will haunt guests around Liberty Square. Complaints had been received by Disney that guests staying during the Halloween season had nowhere to take their kids during the festivities if they wanted to trick or treat; they either had to venture off property or stay in their resort. So for $18.50 ($16.95 if bought in advance), guests could trick-or-treat from 7 p.m. to midnight along Main Street with Mickey and his pals, whom were all decked out in their own Halloween costumes in this specially designed hard ticket event. "You can go several places around town and get scared to death," spokeswoman Sarona Soughers said at the time. "This is a place to go to have fun without too many nightmares."[1] Disney keen to keep the scares to a minimum, also chose not to decorate Fantasyland at all, so kids who didn't want the scares but wanted the candy could trick-or-treat without fright.

Universal's mantra for every event was about building on the previous year and making it bigger and better. So this year they decided that someone needed to headline the event, bring it altogether and present the houses as though they are a collection of gruesome haunts that have been specially selected and approved for your enjoyment. Many ideas were put forward including Beetlejuice (whose star was starting to fade a little), Norman Bates (though he lacked the showmanship needed) and even characters from Jaws were considered. The debate rumbled on until a decision was made to go outside of Universal's own characters and licensed agreements to see who else could host the event. Quickly a decision was made to approach the licensing company that owned the right to the Crypt Keeper. The Crypt Keeper and his TV show 'Tales from the Crypt' had been running successfully since 1989 shown on HBO and had in 1995 been made into a movie named 'Demon Knight' which had been released by Universal to much success. A deal was soon granted and the Crypt Keeper was officially licensed to host the event that year, making him the first official icon of the event.

The Crypt Keeper had been born out of the boom of superhero, sci-fi and horror comics of the 1950s, a boom which was triggered when the older more family orientated comics were starting to seem old fashioned. Originally made by EC Comics as an anthology comic containing moral stories that were presented in a gruesome way, a medium which really spoke to children and young adults of the time, the stories were very poetic justice or eye-for-an-eye in their telling of stories. Gone were the bible stories and innocent family cartoons and in were the likes of Spider-Man and The Incredible Hulk. Some of the illustrations were incredibly detailed in a horrific manner and it was thought that many of the artists had been returning veterans who had served in World War Two, whom were drawing off their own experience of witnessing firsthand the atrocities that had been seen in Europe and Asia.

The comics came under serious attack in the mid-1950s from parents, church members, teachers and other commentators who believed the books were contributing to the then sense of perceived illiteracy and juvenile delinquency of the 1950s. In June 1954, a highly publicized Congressional subcommittee held hearings on the effects of comic books upon children which left the industry reeling. The subcommittee put a highly restrictive Comics Code onto many companies that were in the same market, this lead EC Comics publisher Bill Gaines to cancel his wildly popular Tales from the Crypt and its two companion horror titles, as they just could not tailor the comics to meet the code the subcommittee wanted. Skipping forward to the 1970s in Britain they were experiencing a huge boom in horror related media, particularly in film, with the likes of Amicus and Hammer who had been turning out their own British versions of Dracula and Frankenstein since the 1950s. It was the former, Amicus who acquired the rights from EC Comics to make their own movie version of the comic book and then a sequel 'The Vault of Horror', though in both the Crypt Keeper as we know him today was sadly missing.

In the 1980s EC Comics and other providers of 'classic horror' went through a revival with a high demand for reprints of the 1950s comics being demanded (the subcommittee's code now being dropped in modern America). This led to the production of a TV series that ran from 1989 to until 1996 on the HBO network , a network that could get away with more horrific or explicit shows that mainstream TV. The series actually moved production to the UK towards the final episodes to get the benefit of the then Government's tax breaks that were being offered to production companies at the time. The show would start and end just like the original comic books with the mysterious Crypt Keeper himself hauled up in his own haunted mansion ready to tell a tale of foreboding or sorrow that inevitability would include a twist along the end or some kind of horrific set-piece; introduced by a Beetlejuice-esque haunting yet catching theme tune that funnily had both been written by composer Danny Elfman. Call the show a respective modern times version of the 1960s Alfred Hitchcock Presents or The Twilight Zone TV show. The show was a hit and lead to three movies being produced, a kid's Saturday morning series, radio plays and even a computer game. One thing was for sure, the charismatic Crypt Keeper was a huge deal in the 1990s, so Universal obtaining the rights for the character to host their event was a massive victory for the park.

The event which was unofficially titled 'The Curse of the Crypt Keeper' and would run on an extended 12 nights for this year[2], and park creatives were quick to point out that preparations for the event had taken the longest to date, "Imagine buying 4,000 pounds of dismembered body parts props. Or making blood, brain fluid and primordial ooze by boiling a brew of 600 gallons of methocyl cellulose -- a water-based gel.[3] Boil it and stir it for three days in 64-quart cauldrons." One of the creative team was quoted as saying, "More than 500 scareactors will star in Curse (of the Crypt Keeper), using 1,200 prosthetic pieces - protruding foreheads, extended chins, gaping wounds, disfiguring scars, gangrene-infected limbs." Production had been ramped up for the event, with more production crew, more screactors, more houses and more nights to entertain. The production crew had started way back in the Spring when they began a more extended tour of horror inspiration by travelling to the Cajun country, Hollywood's famous Haunted Soundstage (which was located at Hollywood's Universal Studios on soundstage 28 on the backlot, though now sadly demolished in 2015, it had previous held the original theatre set from the 1924 version of The Phantom of the Opera), abandoned New York subways, New Orleans historic cemeteries and other nearby real haunts. Armed with video and still cameras, the creative team sought to explore these settings and record scenes such as decay on tombstones, moonlit shadows, the howl of wind through trees and other iconic scary moments, all of which could be recycled for the event. "We specialize in complete sensory overload," said Universal creative member Jerry Abercrombie. "It's not enough to recreate the visuals - our guests must hear, smell and feel the experience in order to have a good scare." He went on, "We continually evaluate our product based on guest satisfaction, and in this case, the louder the scream, the better."

The first house, a nod to the house that had been before, was the Crypt Keeper's Dungeon of Terror, named after the event's icon and though it shared the name partly from the original Dungeon house, the actual house for this event had no other similarities to its predecessor. This house was a "heart-pounding, palm-sweating journey into an evil crypt of unthinkable horror," according to Universal Creative at the time. Built in the Earthquake extended queue area the house would heavily feature the house from the TV series along with the theme song bellowing out into the crowds to act as a draw for the house. Unsuspecting guests would pass through the mansion's dingy root cellars and a cemetery of the undead, a library full of ghost stories, a parlor, a trophy room (with human heads as trophies), and eventually meet Universal's legendary Rat Lady[4]. Dressed in Victorian fashion, the Lady lies in a glass coffin, with rats crawling over, under and around her. More than 125 rats, hand-raised at Universal, are used in the attraction. Before moving into the last room, the coffin room from the TV Show where your host is waiting for you. A life-sized puppet of the Crypt Keeper sitting upright in his coffin would greet guests for one final scare, "goodbye foolish mortals" the gravely high pitched voice of original Crypt Keeper actor John Kassir would yell out as guests passed.

Next up built into the Nazarman's area of New York was Terror Underground, Transit to Torment, a house that had been devised during the creative team's recent trip to New York. Guests would enter the house by walking through decaying turnstiles into the New York subway underground, soon they would be up against slime covered walls, through tight tiled maze like corridors and eventually enter into catacombs where the sense of all direction was soon lost. The house was exceedingly dark which played on many of the guests own phobias. The path would then twist, turn, and even double back on itself slightly before guests were brought face-to-face with the mole people, a crazy mutant race of creatures who inhabit this maze of tunnels.

"According to city historians, it's a whole other city down there - the `mole people' elect their own mayor, have their own doctors - they've completely abandoned modern life to live within this vast labyrinth of darkness," said Julie Zimmerman of Universal Creative. "Because it's a real life legend, the mole people are just as frightening - perhaps more so - than traditional ghosts and goblins"[5] she said.

The next house that was built was arguably another dual house. This was located on Soundstage 23 and was just as detailed as the other two houses. Where the Crypt Keeper's house had drawn heavily on the TV show and the Nazarman's house had been based on urban legends from underground New York, this house would bring back the classic monsters from Universal's history but bring them back in a wholly new and terrifying way. As part of Universal's creative team's extensive research, members of the department visited Universal Studios Hollywood. It was there they were given full access to the huge prop storage department located on the backlot, a resource that had been storing and protecting props from Universal's productions to as far back as the 1920s. The creative team reportedly spent weeks trawling through the collection until they found such relics from Universal classics including The Hunchback of Notre Dame, Frankenstein and Dr. Jekyll and Mr. Hyde. The team sent back to Orlando two tractor-trailers full of props and set-pieces from the Hollywood Studios for use in this house[6]. Sure Universal had used previous sets and props from their modern movies but never had they actually used props from classic horror movies, this was a revelation! And though most of the general public would go on to miss or not even recognize the classic props that were used in this house, it is nice to think that this house was probably the most authentic house that had ever been made for the event surrounding the classic monsters.

Universal's House of Horrors offered two different paths with two different queues. The house was so big and separate in its scares that it was the first official dual house, though a dual house had unofficially been offered the year before[8]. The Classic monsters from the gold era of Universal were offered on one side of the house with newer monsters on the other side of the house (Chucky had featured predominately on this side of the house). Though they weren't officially at the event the other house did contain non-Universal-like monsters which could have been reminiscent of other popular monsters of the time, though no licenses had been officially applied for by Universal. The house would prove so popular that it would be used again.

Hollywood Blvd would again become Horrorwood Blvd and be home to
one of the two scarezones this year, and would include the ever popular
Chainsaw Drill Team, along with various mutants and freaks, along with
distracting guys and girls in not much clothing. The other scarezone this
year would be located over in Amity named, Midway of the Bizarre. A
Mardi Gras gone wrong could be a perfect description of the event. Evil
clowns chased guests whilst a carnival voodoo lord of the cemetery would
seek to raise the dead and any evil spirits in the neighborhood. Like a
Mexican day of the dead festival, the scarezone featured bright colours and
skeletons in equal measure along with jesters dancing to freakish music and
cannibals a plenty. The scarezone was a sensory overload of smells, sounds,
colours, dry-ice and scares. Recognizing for the first time that not
everybody comes to the event to be scared witless, this scarezone was the
first in the event's history to offer a 'chicken path' for anyone not quite
brave enough to venture in, a discreet path to the south of the Jaws
attraction was offered. To compliment this 'chicken path' Universal also
created unofficial 'safe areas', in Central Park and Avenue of the Stars
where ghouls were not allowed to roam. They also marked on the park
maps skull-and-crossbones symbols so guests could recognize the scary
areas of the park. This was likely due to Universal wanting to attract more
people to the park (a response from Not-So-Scary starting that year?),
people who perhaps didn't want to be scared and wanted to enjoy the party
atmosphere without the fear of spilling their drinks or dropping their
popcorn!

Again like previous years, various shows were offered to keep the party
atmosphere alive. First up was Rock of Ages, a rock 'n' roll street party that
featured various musical acts such as 'Raven & the Nevermores' as well as a
DJ for the event who played pop songs from the 1960s to 1980s, Michael
Jackson's Thriller song was noted to have been played numerous times each
night. Beetlejuice also returned that year to host his four nightly interactive
game-show spoof 'The Price Is Fright' back in the Animal Actors Stage.
Bill and Ted were also back this year but minus the Time Cop from the
previous year. Other attractions for this year included: Kongfrontation,
Funtastic World of Hanna-Barbera, Hitchcock's 3-D Theater, ET, Jaws,
Earthquake, Back to the Future: The Ride and Beetlejuice's Rock n' Roll
Graveyard Review. The latter, the ghost with the most was also presiding
over Beetlejuice's Plague Ground, located outside the Animal Actors stage
the area became host to a number of carnival games. Such games had not
been installed permanently at the park yet and were a welcome sideshow to
the park's festivities.

The final show offered featured the park's icon for the evening, The Crypt Keeper. A lagoon show entitled 'The Crypt Keeper's Revenge: Knights of Hell' with the Crypt Keeper this time played by an actual person and not a puppet like in his house of that year. The show which was held three times per night and was the last show of the evening before closing saw boats with demonic symbols duel with other boats, undertake stunts and jump through fire[7]. Many guests commented that it was similar to the then Miami Vice stunt show that was offered during the day but being at night it took on a whole different vibe with additional pyrotechnics, lasers, fireworks and fire.

Notes:

[1] Orlando Sentinel, Oct 24, 1995
[2] Park commercial and map, Oct 1995
[3] Fort Pierce Tribune (FL), Oct 13, 1995
[4] Fort Pierce Tribune (FL), Oct 13, 1995
[5] Fort Pierce Tribune (FL), Oct 13, 1995
[6] Orlando Sentinel, Oct 13, 1995
[7] Orlando Sentinel, Oct 16, 1995
[8] Interview with Mike Pressman

"Well looks like we won't be playing baseball after the event now the bats have flown away…"

Halloween Horror Nights VI

Journey Into Fear

Halloween Horror Nights VI: 'Journey into Fear' was held on October 11, 12, 17-19, 23-28, 30, 31, and November 1, & 2 (1996) for an unprecedented 15 nights with the event starting earlier than before and now ending in November. The event was going from strength to strength. Not much was said all year for the event until around the beginning of September when Universal ramped-up the marketing, choosing this year to make Frankenstein's monster the unofficial center of the marketing campaign. The monster was paraded on various TV spots including many on Fox which were seen around the country. During this time Fox also partnered with the event and Doritos to sponsor many TV shows to gain more advertising for the event. Popular teen orientated programs such as 'Goosebumps'[1] which aired at the time ran competitions with Frankenstein's Monster to attract people to call in to local radio stations (such as Kiss FM) to enter for a chance to win all expenses paid vacations to Universal just for Halloween Horror Nights. Buzz was growing around the country and the event was starting to be the place to go if you wanted a true unique Halloween experience. "Nobody does Halloween like we do," said Universal spokesman Fred Lounsberry. "October, traditionally a slack period for Florida theme parks, shows up on Universal charts as an attendance spike as a direct result of Halloween Horror Nights" he said.[5]

The dates for the event were leaked[3] to the media around the 8th September when auditions for the event were taking place. For the first time in the event's history there were to be less parts for potential scareactors, with only 400 official parts to be casted; they did however, have a good reason for this...

For the first time in the event's history Universal wanted to provide a parade. It had been this very year that earlier in the season in March that Universal had the first in another long-running annual event, with their version of Mardi Gras; a similar party-like event which prominently featured a parade as the highlight of each night. The event's icon from last year was back, The Crypt Keeper and he would be appointed the grand marshal of the parade activities. The Chainsaw Drill team along with a firing of fireworks and fixed roof-level flamethrowers would sound their saws as the fireworks and flames would fire high into the sky to signal the start of the parade. The first float from the backstage area was the Crypt Keeper's own with the maniacal zombie himself perched high above on a regal looking throne. Next up was a float that showed a human sacrifice followed by a float dedicated to snakes with a large serpent head mounted at the front. Along with the unofficial icon and drill team there were skeletons dancing in the street with elongated arms, werewolves, horned demons, voodoo dancers, ladies with fake snake appendages, funky vampires playing pianos, exactly 75 trained stilt walkers and a stilt walker with made-up to look like the Devil himself from the movie 'Legend'. 'Legend' was a 1985 British-American fantasy-horror adventure film directed by Ridley Scott and starring Tom Cruise, Mia Sara and Tim Curry; with Curry playing the devilish role as Beelzebub himself. At the very end of the parade we had an undertaker throwing ashes at the crowds (instead of beads), though dressed similar to a character that would be born soon at the event, the character provided popular and provided a good deal of banter to parks guests. As the floats passed along the streets, ghouls and goblins of every type would throw beads into the assembled crowds, in true Mardi Gras style. There were five floats in total, all had been re-themed from the Mardi Gras event that had started earlier in the year at the park. The parade route started at the top of Hollywood Blvd by Mel's Diner, it would run down Hollywood to Production Central where it would turn to go into the park and along the main path, through New York and exit behind Kongrontation.

Universal had in the previous year formed a travel company to deal directly with customers wanting to book Universal packages to the resort. With low expectations the fledgling subsidiary had done very well, so well in fact that the Halloween event this year was the first time that direct packages had been offered. The travel company had sort in the previous year to add cruises and beach trips to its current offered travel packages, and expanded the offering by adding packages including ground transportation especially for Halloween Horror Nights and Mardi Gras, respectively. Since September that year the company had offered both one and two night packages for the Halloween event, which included theme park tickets, Halloween tickets and accommodation. This would later go on to be called 'Stay and Scream' but the name had yet to be realized. It had been seen in the past year that attendance was growing significantly for guests coming from out of State. It had particularly been noticed that nearly a 20% of the guests attendance was coming from Georgia. So along with the usual adult and child prices (yes child tickets were still sold in 1996!), the discount for Florida residents was extended for this year to include Georgia[2] residents too.

The Crypt Keeper wasn't only restrained to being on the parade this year, he again like last year had his own house back in the Earthquake queue. The house was called 'The Crypt Keeper's Studio Tour of Terror'[5] and was not a copy of the previous year as it was an entirely new attraction. Instead of the tour of his old decrepit manor house this time guests would tour a haunted studio backlot, complete with a Norman Bates shower scene with mother, an electrifying room showing a studio worker getting shocked and various other dusty and cob-webbed props and sets.

The next house located in the Nazarman's area was 'Toy Hell: Nightmare in the Scream Factory'[4]. Toy Hell was a combination of toy factory and back alleys immediately around the factory where the insane toy makers had decided to use actual human body parts to make the toys seem more life-like, think 'Pinocchio' gone wrong or the movie 'Child's Play' (though Chuckie was not present in the house). The Franken-toys had all come to life and eventually killed the toy makers and were now setting their sights on plucky park guests. The house was filled with great scares, one notable example was a huge pile of discarded stuffed-toy-animals in a heap on the floor, but actually inside the pile was a scaractor ready to pounce on unsuspecting guests. Combined with the good scares were costumes unlike anything that had been seen before, with fur like covers "sewn" onto flesh and human arms "stitched" onto teddy bears it was an exceedingly creepy house.

As in the previous year there was a final house located in Soundstage 23 that was again a dual house with separate entrances and queues titled 'Universal's New House of Horrors'. One half of the house featuring the classic Universal monsters was entirely similar to the house that had been seen the previous year, however the other side was altogether different. The other section was 'Reel Life Horrors' and featured a bizarre wax museum where a rogue lightning bolt had brought the horrors of the museum to life. If you thought the classic Frankenstein's monster and Dracula were scary then you would be terrified on this side as you would soon be up against 'real monsters' with the likes of Jack the Ripper and the axe owning Lizzie Borden. Rumor had been that the previous year's monsters had been swopped out to make way for real frightening monsters, so in their place true-life villains were presented, much to guest delight.

Due to the parade's route the number of scarezones was reduced to just one, with Midway of the Bizarre in Amity being offered again. The scarezone was again offered and although larger it was entirely the same as had been held the previous year. The Chainsaw Drill team was also not restricted to being just in the parade and were aloud (after parade duties) to roam the park at will. Along with the solitary scarezone the park brought back the magical offering and provided a magic show with a twist. 'Tricks, Treats and Trances' would debut in the Animal Actor's stage providing four shows per night. The show was hosted by Cindy Layn who combined traditional magic with hypnotism to great comedic effect. The rock n' roll party that had been seen at previous years was also back, titled 'Welcome to my Nightmare' it was located outside of Mel's Diner and played to three shows per night. Various lookalikes were used to depict rock bands from the time including: Kiss, Alice Cooper and Black Sabbath.

The Bill and Ted show was again back this year and as popular as ever. The whole script was based around the hugely popular franchise at the time of 'The X-Files'. The same TV series' main villain The Smoking Man was the head villain for the show and kicked off proceedings by kidnapping our plucky hosts leaving the Agents Mulder and Scully to track them down, along the way they meet fellow Agent Ethan Hunt there (from the successful 'Mission Impossible' movies) using every Tom Cruise gag in the book including a scene from 'Risky Business' where the actor dances on stage in just in underpants and sunglasses just like Cruise had done in the movie. Gags abound for all agents of the large screen when James Bond was introduced to help out, along with The Terminator, who had just seen his show open that year at the park (Terminator's show had opened on April 27, 1996). All topped off with a Will Smith lookalike rapping as his character from Independence Day but in the style of his earlier character 'The Fresh Prince'; at the very end our heroes were reunited with the X-Files crew for a singalong with Kiss (the band) lookalikes singing various hits including their 1975 hit 'Rock and Roll All Nite' whilst the others all danced about. As Bill and Ted shows go, this would be a very memorable show.[6]

Notes:

[1] Local Fox Commercial, Oct 1996
[2] Orlando Sentinel Oct 11, 1996
[3] Orlando Sentinel Sep 8, 1996
[4] Orlando Sentinel Oct 25, 1996
[5] The Tampa Tribune Oct 14, 1996
[6] Interview with Mike Pressman

Halloween Horror Nights VII

Frightmares (*You'll never sleep again!*)

The marketing for Halloween Horror Night's seventh event entitled 'Frightmares' started in earnest around mid-September. This year a little fanged goblin (unofficially named Igor or "eye-gore" – get it?) floating above a terrified looking eyeball would go on to become the event's logo and be used in all marketing. Universal employed a local animation studio to create the creature just when CGI technology[4] inter-spliced with actual film footage would be in its early days of use. It may have been genius or pure chance that the little creature would bring much publicity to the event, but not for the ghastly reasons intended but for copyright problems[1]. A European heavy-metal band named 'Krokus', who had received some success in the States, had released a single called 'Stayed Awake All Night' in 1989 and the artwork for the cover had featured an almost identical little goblin attached to a brow lifting an eye lid on an unsuspecting person, which was extremely similar to the one Universal was using for all the marketing at the event; apart from the color of the eye ball, the actual image was near on exactly the same! The image around early October was rolled-out to billboards, TV commercials, magazine advertisements and supermarket points-of-sale, the image was everywhere. And although Krokus had at the time disbanded (they have since reformed the band), the image was still unmistakable to the original album sleeve from 1989. And as quickly as the image had been rolled out rock n' roll aficionados were quick to spot the similarities. Colin McCormick, editor of an online magazine about tourism to Orlando was one of the first to spot the similarities when browsing that month for CDs at a local music store. "The similarity is phenomenal," said McCormick, who noticed the album art in the store whilst looking across the street at a poster of the very image attached to the Halloween Horror Nights. McCormick, like many others voiced their concerns to the local Orlando Sentinel who were quick to point the matter out to Universal. The paper thinking that Universal had made a grave error of judgement was quick to extinguish all concerns when Universal's Vice-President Jim Canfield issued a note to the local media saying that Universal loved the artwork so much they actually bought the rights to use the image specifically for their event this year.

'Frightmares' as the event's tagline would read would be expanded out again to another milestone, that of 18 nights and would again contain a parade, one scarezone and 3 houses with one being the dual house that had been seen in the past. The other key feature of the event this year would be the expansion and anticipation of the houses' facades. Though the facades had been prominent at the event from the very start, it was this year that thorough design and consideration was given to these house entrances. Creative believed that as the houses were attracting such long queues, the need to build anticipation through the house entrance would be essential to the overall enjoyment of each house.

The first house up would be exceedingly detailed, located in the extdened Earthquake queue area, 'Tombs of Terror' would take guests on an extraordinary tour of New Orleans and The Bayou, which had been specifically designed to fit the parade and scarezone of that year where the horrorific Mardi Gras theme had spread and rooted across the park. The house featured: pirates, ghosts, zombie soldiers and vampires, set in the area's many mansions focusing mostly on a decrepit funeral home at first. After clearing the buildings, guests would be lead into creepy deserted cemeteries before being taken into the misty swamps where the swamp monsters and ferial vampires lurked. The famous streets of New Orleans and the Lafayette Cemetery had both been heavily surveyed by Universal's creative to ensure all the details of the area could be included to make the experience as authentic as possible. The Rat Lady was also present in the house during one of the graveyard scenes, encased in a tomb surrounded by her rats (which were really starting to become celebrities in their own right by this time!).

Next up was a return[3] to 'Universal's Museum of Horror' which had moved up the road to Soundstage 22 still retaining its dual house status. house of horrors: slight name change, more museum like, dual house. One side had the classic monsters pretty much the same as in previous years and the other side had modern day horror films, loosely based on recent horror movies such as Scream and Candy man. The soundstage had two large facades built that year to mirror what was being done elsewhere to build the suspense in the queue. A gothic interior with stone vaulted ceilings and columns welcomed guests into what was billed as "the world's only museum where the guards have to warn the exhibits not to touch the visitors!"

Last up for the houses was a return back to the popular Nazarman's area with 'Hotel Hell'[2]. The house had a large fake hotel façade built in Sting Alley which had been made to look like a hotel that had gone out of business and had been boarded up, once inside guests would venture into the hotel's check-in lobby, rooms (which was not all too dissimilar to a certain ride in a certain theme park which may or may not include a hotel), then on guests would explore the kitchen, then the dining room and some of the guest rooms. Ghosts of the dead hotel guests, staff including the bell boy and a sadistic chef were all present ready to jump out at unsuspecting guests. This also marked the first time that the Rat Lady would be located in more than one house as here she was incased in a sewage pipe with glass around, located in the laundry scene.

Midway of the Bizarre was back and still located in the Amity area, no really changes were seen here other than the addition of carnival games, which had not yet been added to the Amity area. Likewise the parade, Festival of the Dead was a near mirror of the previous year, following the same route and having nearly all the same floats. One large addition was instead of the Devil from 'Legend' being on stilts, he had his own float towards the front of the parade. A magic show was also back this year, entitled 'Abra Cadaver' it was again held in the Animal Actors' stage for five performances a night. The show included the usual mix of thrills and guest participation where a plucky member of the audience was hauled out and cut in half. The show had been presented with different magicians and did not feature any hypnotism like the previous year.

The Bill and Ted show[5] was back again for an impressive sixth outing and was as popular as ever. The overall theme was based around original Star Trek versus the Next Generation Star Trek crew (as both franchises had been making movies and TV shows recently). Both captains Kirk and Picard would do battle over who was the best with the audience cheering to decide. Various banter like gags are batted to and fro amongst the two characters about wig wearing and being 'a true number two' instead of a number one (Picard's famous nickname for his second in command Riker) as they explore Gotham City. They are soon joined by the performance's villains who were the Borg Queen from the recent Next Generation movie 'First Contact' and a Klingon to represent both franchises respective villains-au-jour. Ripley from Aliens soon shows up, along with a lookalike Will Smith from the recent Men in Black movie, along with the Terminator (again), and Batman and Robin from their recent Batman movie 'Batman & Robin, soon the villains from that movie both Poison Ivy and Mr Freeze show up. The Terminator and Mr Freeze on the big screen had both been played by Arnold Schwarzenegger, so two lookalikes of Schwarzenegger both square up with some funny back and forth gags about the two roles by the same actor. The cast of Seinfeld arrive to much comedic affect in a stolen DeLorean time machine followed by Darth Vader. The song 'Grease Lightning' is performed from the movie 'Grease' with Kramer on lead vocals. At the end of the song Bill's cell phone rings and it is the classic Ghostface voice from the 'Scream' movies who soon appears on stage, he is then quickly defrocked to reveal his true identity that of Austin Powers. The assembled cast dance to his signature theme before the Men in Black interrupt and start performing their signature theme. Finally Elaine from Seinfeld interrupts and performs the Spice Girl's number one hit 'Wannabe' (which was still riding in the charts at the time!). She is joined during the performance by the Borg Queen, Batgirl and Poison Ivy characters. As the song continues it blends into 'Smells Like Teen Spirit' by Nirvana where the whole cast reunites on stage to sing and dance with Bill and Ted taking center stage. At the very end of the song it is the lookalike of Kramer from Seinfeld who gets the signature chance to bring down the house as in previous years.

The final remarkable aspect of the event this year was the first occasion that Universal had expanded its travel company's operations abroad to offer packages for tourists from the UK. In the previous year packages for transport, hotel and tickets had been offered domestically to US guests, which continued to be rolled-out this year to great effect. It was this year however that the roll-out included UK guests. The reasoning behind the decision was that in the previous few years the company had witnessed a growing number of guests travelling especially for the event from the UK. To capitalize on this growing movement of fans from abroad, Universal were quick to offer complete packages just like they had done to domestic guests for the past couple of years.

Notes:

[1] Orlando Sentinel Oct 23, 1997
[2] Tampa Tribune Oct 11, 1997
[3] Park map from 1997
[4] Park TV commercial from 1997
[5] Interview with Mike Pressman

House Designer: *"Nope I can't tell which witch is which either…"*

Halloween Horror Nights VIII

Primal Scream (The last scream you'll ever hear)

Originally starting as a humble three night event back in 1991, the event this year grew to another milestone to span 19 nights for this year, it would increase the house content to feature five haunted houses, three shows, one scarezone and a nightly parade. There was a great emphasis this year that the event had become a juggernaut that with every year that passed it would pass new boundaries and become even more successful than the previous. To match this demand Universal had to keep pace and ensure they were providing an upscale event that always built on the previous years. The event had grown so rapid by this point that attendance was increased by almost double every year, year-on-year. It was projected in 1998 that by 1999 it would finally become the most attended Halloween event in the entire world. Michael Gilligan, Universal's senior vice president of marketing said at the time, "Our goal is that by this year or next year, no one will be able to come near this (in terms of attendance figures)." The gauntlet was laid down by Universal, as the owner of this title of 'most visited Halloween event' was over on the West coast in Southern California with 'Knott's Berry Farm'. Knott's had been in the themed Halloween entertainment business far longer than Universal, starting their event back in 1972. Knott's were keen to retain their title, so after Universal's impressive announcement they went ahead and bumped their event out to 16 nights, a decision they made due to the fact that 'most of the nights had already sold out'. Knott's spokeswoman Dana Hammontree[1] said at the time, "We are still the king of Halloween". Universal weren't daunted by the challenge. They countered Knott's offerings by providing stage shows featuring internationally acclaimed acts, using the best acting talent in the business and by providing some of the largest most ambitious houses it could image; Universal did not disappoint...

The first house, which although billed separately, was a dual house with a shared theme and it was unlike anything the park's creative team had built before. S.S. Frightanic would be built into the whole Earthquake queue housing, a life-size ship of epic proportions the house would borrow heavily from the smash-hit movie 'Titanic' which had been released the previous year and had smashed all then box-office records. The house would offer two unique and detailed entrances with separate queues that would provide guests with two very different experiences; these were Carnage Crew and Fear in First Class. The ship had taken all summer to construct and when fully realized it was an impressive 520ft long. Nobody could surely take credit within the Halloween industry for creating such a large detailed set as this before.

As the event had now by this year become a year round venture to plan and construct, the Creatives at Universal were keen to draw on all experiences of the 'fright-science' to create the world class haunts that were constructed. It was having this time and space to create that led to this very ship being constructed. The backstory of the damned vessel was the Frightanic ship (a luxury liner) had just docked in San Francisco after a mysterious voyage to Hawaii where the ship was sucked into a black hole and into another dimension. When it returned to dock the crew had gone insane and the ship is in an awful state of dilapidation where ghosts and ghouls of every caliber lurk behind every corner. Jason Surrell, a manager of show concepts and scripts said, "It's like the Titanic gone bad, if that could have gotten any worse." The idea for such a house had been kicked around for a while but park's creative struggled to bring the concept together, it wasn't until this year when the trophy of 'most visited haunt event in the world' was within reach that the button to proceed with the elaborate plans was pushed. "We've had the idea to do a death ship or ghost ship for three years without success," says T.J. Mannarino[2], Universal's scenic designer. Now was the time to proceed!

Inside the ship guests will find: lights flicker and water sprays from over the deck, along with sounds of creaking metal as though the ship is starting to sink. Narrow corridors with exceedingly low ceilings direct guests into various scenes including, the office of the ship's dentist where a zombie is sprawled in the operating chair, his teeth drilled so painfully that the smell of burned teeth is pumped into the air. Rotting corpses of former crew members lay in swing bunks along the ship's crew quarters. In the old-fashioned smoking room, the chandelier and furniture are installed with mechanical arms discreetly hidden to give the effect that the ship is moving with the tide, with the aim of evoking real feelings of seasickness. On the bow of the ship a pair of rotting skeletons made to represent the characters of the movie was seen with sprayed out arms, all done firmly tongue-in-cheek, as you pause to chuckle that's when the scareactors get you. In total across the two areas of the house there were a cast of 80 scareactors (a new record), all in costumes and makeup playing the crew and dead passengers of this damned voyage. A luxury carpet moves underfoot to add to the disorientation. The level of the floor changes height to add to the claustrophobic nature of the house combined with multiple paths ahead. The acts of disorientation reach a crescendo when as you try to gain your bearings a scaractor will jump from behind that fake mirror or wall to get the best scare. "All it takes is one second of not paying attention and we get you," boasted Universal's J Michael Roddy, the show director[4].

Each room was designed to have at least one moving part to create the illusion that you had left Florida and were now on the open seas with the crew from hell. In the glitzy ballroom of the ship the team even installed fans and mechanical arms to propel human looking mannequins in a waltz around the dance floor while real dancers would twirl with the dummies before breaking the dance pattern and giving the best scare to unsuspecting and disorientated guests. "There are 'boo corridors' of quick jabs that prepare you for the big one up ahead," Surrell said[3]. In fact due to the level of staffing within the house, you could be no more than a couple steps at a time from being got at for a perfect scare. "People have got a three-second attention span in a room while they try to see what's safe," Mannarino said. "So if we can distract them for a second or give them a sense that an area is safe, then we can scare them. The thrills are choreographed and timed to catch the crowds of 10 to 15 guests just as they are halfway through a room. We scare from the side or behind so that they will run forward rather than backward and keep the line moving," Mannarino said. There truly had never been such a large detailed house built for what was just a temporary haunted attraction; Universal had upped their game in big style.

The next house offered this year was Hell's High… School's out forever! Located in the purposely crafted Nazarman's area the house was a combination of low-budget slasher movie (ala 'Scream' or 'I Know What You Did Last Summer' which were all popular at the time) and a teen comedy, it was the latter that was just starting to come back as being a very popular cult comedy genre. The combination of the two made for scares and laughs in equal portions. The storyline was that a slasher movie was to be shot in a real high school but the unsuspecting film crew had inadvertently used real murderers. Add evil substitute teachers, zombified nerds and cruel gym coaches and you have a recipe for a great house. Guests would enter into classrooms, a puke filled cafeteria, science labs, the nurses office (complete with a needle swinging deranged nurse), the gymnasium with countless body bags handing up from the ceiling and moving along with cries and screams of the nerds placed within and even a disgusting kitchen. The tradition of having a least one house that contained an element of comedy in equal measures to the horror was greatly seen from this year onwards.

The event also had a return of the 'Universal's Museum of Horrors' house that had been seen in previous years and again it was a dual house; this marked the first time that Universal had held two dual houses in one year.

Split in two with two queues, two entrances and two huge facades, the houses were very popular with the park's guests. Billed as 'Chamber of Horrors' with the original monsters from Universal's back catalogue come out to scare and then 'Unnatural History' where modern horrors lurk. To change up the classic monsters section of the house, the park's creative focused on creating elaborate sets and facades to ramp up the feeling of being in the actual movie. The Universal movie 'Casper' (the friendly ghost) had wrapped filming a few years prior and when scouting for props on the west coast the park's creative spotted the pipe-organ from the film, shipped it to Orlando to repurpose it as The Phantom of the Opera's organ for a loud spectacular scene half way through the house. Classic scenes that were reimaged that year include: 'Frankenstein', 'Psycho' and 'The Shining'.

Midway of the Bizarre was back, slightly bigger than previously. The ghoulish Mardi-Gras gone wrong scarezone was held back in Amity much to the event's fans approval. Along with the scarezone the parade was back. This year a couple of floats were tweaked but largely it was the same as previous years. Grand marshals for the parade were Chucky and Tiffany from the 'Child's Play' franchise. The Universal movie 'Bride of Chucky' happened opened to much success a mere week before the event started. The black comedy horror film was the fourth installment in the 'Child's Play' film series. The film was written by Don Mancini and directed by Ronny Yu. It starred Jennifer Tilly (who plays and voices the titular character Tiffany) and Brad Dourif (who voices Chucky). Heading the parade in their matrimonial parade float the characters also starred in the first ever webcast for the event which had been streamed live on the main Universal Escape (the then name for the Orlando resort) website. The webcast featured a ghoulish looking minister forming the marital bond between the two characters with Beetlejuice and others as witnesses – guess who caught the bouquet!

Along with these attractions the park also built the largest set for any show they had put on before for the event for 'Inferno'. A spectacular gymnast meets circus performing acts, similar in content to a Cirque du Soleil performance the show combined acrobatics and daredevil like acts against a huge spectacular backdrop, held in the Animal Actors' stage the show performed three shows per night. Next up was the rock festival that was again held outside of Mel's Drive In. Big named actual bands were mixed with local sound-a-like bands to give a great atmosphere to the proceedings. 'Horrorpalooza' was the name of the event and such real acts as local Florida band done good, Lynyrd Skynyrd[5] bolting out 'Sweet Home Alabama' and Free Bird' to cheering crowds with Peter Frampton, Tommy Shaw and sound-a-like band Kiss Army all performed during the event.

Bill & Ted were back again for a very similar show to what had been seen from the previous year. TJ Hooker, Lethal Weapon, Goodfellas, Zorro and the characters from Titanic all starred in another comedy romp with the time travelling dudes. Like the previous year songs from the movie 'Grease' were added for the climax where the house literally comes down. This also marked the first time that James Michael Roddy (then Universal Creative) took the reins for the writing duties of the show, and it was an "excellent" addition that year.

Another first this year was the using of an outside contractor to help build the sets that were required, mostly due to the success of the event and the ever increasing expansion of requirements. Fake Productions, a local specialist in this field first helped out in 1998, they would go on to be appointed again for future years to help with set construction[8].

Other notable firsts for the event this year include the opening of Universal Studios' Classic Monsters Café[6], which was heavily included in the marketing. On some of the nights the queues were reportedly out the door! The use of interest marketing was really pushed this year to maximize the event's world-wide credentials; after all if you wanted to seek to be the biggest in the world you had to reach out in every way you could. The other big change for this year was the use of scents. Remember the burning teeth smell I mentioned earlier? Getting the right smell[7], how it was to be distributed and to what levels took a huge amount of planning. In preparation for the event Universal bought gallons of custom scents with titles such as 'Eau de Dead', 'open coffin', 'rotting corpse no.5' and 'Burning Flesh (general)' from a New York perfumer to add a sensory dynamic to the houses and one scarezone.

Notes:

[1] Orlando Sentinel Sept 29, 1998
[2] Tampa Tribune Oct 2, 1998
[3] Tampa Tribune Oct 2, 1998
[4] Orlando Sentinel Oct 2, 1998
[5] Park map from 1998
[6] Park map and poster from 1998
[7] Tampa Tribune Oct 24, 1998
[8] Linkedin, various profiles

Halloween Horror Nights IX

Last Gasp *(Sayonara!)*

Halloween Horror Nights IX: Last Gasp would debut at the park in 1999 and this would be what some people call 'the last of the formative years' of the acclaimed Halloween event. The events from next year onwards would still utilize everything that had worked before but with new twists, which I shall speak more of in the next chapter. It was August 8th of that year when auditions for the various park roles were being undertaken with the usual required mix of actors, actresses, performers, dancers, stilt-walkers and people who are "very comfortable with rats". It also marked the first occasion that people who auditioned were given jobs based purely on their looks, and no not how you think. Show Director J Michael Roddy explained at the time, "There were auditions and some characters were added to the show based on their talent, at that audition. A prime example was the American Pie characters. I had toyed with the idea but couldn't figure how to include them. Two of the performers auditioning - June Lindle and Dave Tomasi came in and I knew I had a Jim and Michelle that would start the pre-show and be a thread throughout. Another example was Meghan Maroney as Heather Donahue from the Blair Witch Project." In fact that day alone 500 people showed up to audition for the 25 parts for the show[1].

The announcement of the park's event actually happened exceedingly early by the earlier years' standard when a press-release was issued[3] on July 26th. The release mentioned that the event would run for 19 nights (the same as the previous year), a house based around a new concept of using 3D technology would be added and that the popular dude duo Bill and Ted would return, but that was all. Anticipation was building as to what a 3D house could be and how it could be implemented? The wait was over and the opening night came, fans flocked to the Nazarman's area to see for themselves. On that very night the queue for the house quickly exceeded 3 hours. "The 3-dimensional haunted maze was my favorite," said one guest. "After an hour-and-a-half wait, I was given my 3-D glasses and then realized it was worth the wait," another said[4]. Neon strobe lights and luminous paint would combine together with the guest's free 3D issued glasses to deceive their very eyes into believing they are seeing things in front of their face, which weren't in fact there until an actual scareactor jumps out. The house was receiving high praise from all guests.

The house was called 'Universal's Creature Features in 3D', and used many of the classic horror creatures but presented using this interesting technology. The house like many this year included very detailed and elaborate facades again. This house had a whole New York theater frontage that had been boarded up to make guests look as though they were entering a dilapidated old cinema. It also blended well with the Nazarman's New York setting. Frankenstein's monster, Dracula, the Wolfman were all present for the technology's initial outing. A forest scene was seen the Wolfman on scare duties with little nods towards the recent hit 'Blair Witch Project'. There were monsters coming from below, from the side and even from above on cords; any which way was utilized to confuse and disorientate using the glasses. It was something that had never been seen before.

Though the Mummy ride at Universal would not be open for a few years yet, this year did feature a Mummy house that too was wildly popular. The park had also reimaged their popular Stage 54 exhibit with props, sets and costumes from the summer blockbuster. On top of that the event's logo for that year featured a ghoulish looking mummy as the centerpiece for the marketing. Universal had gone Mummy mad! Some speculation based on the reaction from guests at this event and the box-office success of the modern franchise was having led directly to the Mummy becoming a permanent fixture at the theme park. The house, entitled only 'The Mummy' was based on the popular movie that had been released in May of that year to much critical and financial success. The film totally refreshed the old Karloff version of the movie into a new edgier dynamic adventure movie that played well to all audiences. Located in the Earthquake queue building the house tied directly into the movie where actual scenes were recreated putting guests right into the heart of the action. A scene showing a 'live' mummification was added, along with sounds and projections of beetles crawling everywhere, secret passages, ancient crypts, scenes of torture and lines of those dog-faced zombie soldiers queuing up to scare guests. The house was a massive hit for the park.

Norman Bates was back again this year and it was understandable why he was so furious, as Universal had at the time just demolished his old house, the Bates Manor, which had been used as the location for the fourth installment to the popular franchise. Not having his own actual home to be located in, Bates was moved to Soundstage 23 where the past Psycho house themes could be built on and expanded due to the larger size of Soundstage 23. 'Psycho: Through the Mind of Norman Bates' would start off in familiar settings but would quickly take guests try into the twisted mind of the man himself. A shower scene in a replica of one of the infamous motel bedrooms would soon see 'mother' jumping out around every corner with a further descent into his madness. Rooms full of wet blood drenched shower curtains were hung around where guests had no option but to pull their way through until a dark path leads into a room full of huge 6ft tall knives with mirrored faces added to the disorientation, before dumping guests onto a spinning runway (which would later be used very often in houses at the event). The house was loosely associated with the remake of the original Psycho which had been released by Universal Pictures in 1998.

Next up was a house called 'Insanity' and it was, completely. The house is important as many fans of the event will testify that this is the first house to start using the Shadybrook association with the event, however there was no direct tie at this time, that would come later. This house though was intense, event staff were directed by Creative to slow the queue down to stop congo lines, so scene by scene could be presented more intensely. The fear of not seeing ahead or seeing where the exits are were prominent in this house. In the first room the lights would go out and it would be pitch black, then suddenly you'd hear doors open, creatures scratching at the walls and dogs growling, though the room was completely dark with no light. Some believe this house to be the first early test of an 'extreme house' where the scares were notched up a level to great effect. After the initial dark room scare the house would proceed to lead guests into an insane asylum, with padded cells, strait jackets, before leading guests face-to-face with an evil clown come jester, who would dance about and distract guests before other inmates would jump from around the corner for the ultimate scare. After his area guests would walk corridors filled with body bags hung up from the ceiling that twitched and moved to show victims contained within while a heavily tattooed inmate with a knife and another with an axe would prowl as guests looked for the exits. The house was intense!

The final house offered this year was also located in the Earthquake and was entitled 'Doomsday'. Guests were led on a journey through the underground of New York City as the clock strikes midnight on the New Year's Eve 1999. The house played on an unfounded myth that the world would end in 2000. Those that will remember the time will say how some people believed this was a genuine threat to humanity at the time. Some people called it the 'Millennium Bug' or 'Y2K', which defined that as computers could not comprehend the 21st century within their databases they would stop working and would therefore cause the world to end. Some states and countries around the world actually issued advice to citizens as to what to do if Armageddon was about to happen. Looking back in retrospect it was a crazy time but this house was created to play on people's fears and present a scenario of 'what if'. Initially guests were taken down into the New York subway where trains had derailed (similar to the attraction that the house was based near to), hooded freaks from subterranean worlds were present to oversee the end of humanity. A more religious overtone of the Book of Revelations was presented where witches were being burnt and demons were present, as guests explored deeper into the house and closer to hell. Towards the end the hooded freaks were revealed to be demons and heating was cranked up much to guest annoyance (as the Earthquake queue is technically outside).

The parade was back again this year and followed the same route as previous years. New additions this year included: a float filled with spiders of all sizes, a rat float, a Mummy float featuring characters from the movie, and the snakes float which had been vacant for a year was back. Also back was the accompanying Midway of the Bizarre scarezone located again in Amity. Due to the parade every year the park could not facilitate further scarezones, except for a few roaming gangs such as the Chainsaw Drill Team or the Rat Lady. The merchandise for this year was also increased substantially. Universal noticing that past event merchandise was selling very well on online auction sites during the event, decided to sell more merchandise at the event to attract more dollars their way. It also marked the first time that the 'I Survived' t-shirt made an appearance, a tradition that follows to this day. 'Trick or Treat – Deadman's Party' was present this year, a rock show featuring heavily made-up sound-a-likes singing monster rock and pop songs from the 80s and 90s. 'Deadly D'illusions' located at the Animal Actors' Stage was billed as "You won't believe your eyes as you witness this spellbinding display of unbelievable effects, magic and shocking illusions." A magic show at heart the show also featured death defying acts like fire eating and sword swallowing[5].

As announced back in July, the popular dudes were back again this year (though they would be back every year). Famous and popular movies of the time were given the Bill & Ted treatment, including: 'Austin Powers 1 & 2', 'Mystery Men' and of course the very popular 'American Pie', plus appearances by Jerry Springer and Marilyn Manson lookalikes. J Michael Roddy show director had taken the reigns that year as script writer and producer for the show, an appointment that would see the show obtain the highest guest satisfaction level that had ever been seen for the show.

Three other notable events happened this year. The first was that Universal had purchased a warehouse down near the Orlando International Airport, due to reaching capacity storing everything onsite. The warehouse could be used to build props and sets all year round and would provide important storage for their collections of ever growing props. The warehouse would go on to be featured in the marketing for a later event (Halloween Horror Nights XX), though to date no guests or fans have ever visited the now infamous warehouse. The next event that is significant to timeline of the event happened on the West coast of Florida in Tampa at competing park, Busch Gardens. 'Spooky Safari'[2] would debut this year at the park and would feature, for just two nights, Dr. Livingsdoom's Haunted Jungle Trail (their first ever house), a large pumpkin patch for families to explore, various children's activities and the ability to ride all your favorite rides during the night. The special after-hours hard ticketed event would be Busch Gardens first ever foray into the Halloween business, such were these first two nights being a success, the name would soon be changed and Universal would start to see some real local competition.

The final event, and possibly one of the most important in Halloween Horror Night's history, was taking place very quietly right at the park exit. Every night guests were asked about their experiences by Universal employees hoping to secure feedback from their visit to the event that year. After all the questions on houses and shows were answered the poll-takers would ask one final question, "what is your biggest phobia or what are you most scared of?" The answer to which would prove to be the catalyst in the creation of an icon that would go on to define the event.

Notes:

[1] Bill & Ted Fan Club
[2] Tampa Tribune Oct 29, 1999
[3] Orlando Sentinel Jul 26, 1999
[4] Orlando Sentinel Oct 29, 1999
[5] Park map and advertising from 1999

Halloween Horror Nights X

Not afraid of the dark? You don't know Jack...

"A star is born!"

The next decade in Halloween Horror Night's history would focus more on originally crafted content and less on obtaining external intellectual properties (IPs) for the event's many houses and attractions. This initial step change many have speculated could have been brought about due to pressures of the new park, which had only just opened (Islands of Adventure), where time and or money were more constrained to help open this new park. Or possibly as Universal Escape was no more and now Universal Resort was here to stay could this have led to a change in direction? Or possibly as a new generation of creatives had slowly taken the reigns at the in-house creative team[11] and perhaps wanted to take the event in a new and exciting direction; perhaps we'll never know. What we do know is that the event this year was going to be unlike anything we had previously seen.

Quietly, in late August of that year, near the area where people pose for photos with the newly erected Universal globe a small sign was deployed, it read: "HOT SET! Beware of demented clown! He's been known to scare the socks off people! Universal Studios is conducting a test to determine the scare factor of a key Halloween Horror Nights character. Please avoid this area if you are not interested in entertainment of this nature." And so Jack the Clown was first introduced to the general public at large. Jack, who had been born out of the surveys from the previous year, was to be the event's first icon that had been wholly developed in-house. Created by then Universal Creative J Michael Roddy, he said at the time of these tests said, "[He's the] Scariest clown every seen! What we've seen today shows we're right on the mark, and this Halloween [Horror Nights] will be the most extreme and the most scary we have had up to this point."[10] The tests were carried out on a dry sunny afternoon with no sets or props just Jack in all his awfulness and park guests were terrified. Universal knew from these early tests that they had created something very special.

Jack Schmidt would have an elaborate back story to create his character that would be a kin to any horror icon of the last 100 years. He would be bolder and more dynamic than any character that the park had used before. No longer would lengthy IP negotiations be needed where detailed analysis of what characters can and can't say or can and cannot do. The park had free reign to deploy their new creation in any horrific manner they wanted. The first step was creating that very back story, and although it was added to and changed a little over time, the rough original outline was this:

"Jack Schmidt was a circus performer. He loved to entertain children with his practical pranks and prat-falls during his stint with Dr. Oddfellow's Carnival of Thrills. But underneath the greasepaint and clown nose, he held a hideously dark and sinister secret. Jack was a twisted murderer. He was wanted for the abduction and disappearance of several small children throughout the Southern states. Police officials soon caught on that the missing children followed a pattern that led them closer and closer to the travelling freakshow.

On Halloween 1920 the police were closing in on the Clown killer. Fearing capture, Jack revealed his sinister secret to Dr. Oddfellow in the hopes of possible concealment. The Good Doctor was himself wanted by the police for the accidental death of several patrons in a freak circus accident years earlier under a different name. The Doctor was not sympathetic to Jack's cause; in contrast he quickly admonished him for potentially bringing the police down upon the entire band of miscreants. He asked Jack to show him what he had done with the bodies of the children. Jack revealed the bodies of thirteen children hidden in the confines of three small trunks that were kept in his travelling coach.

Fearing the worst, Dr. Oddfellow had Jack murdered and his body hidden within the travelling carnivals House of Horrors as an exhibit, along with the bodies of the children. Years later the Carnival was sold by Dr. Oddfellow, and the various dark rides and exhibits were split and sent to various owners around the states, including the House of Horrors and its grisly secret.

Sixty years later, in the Fall of 1980, a television crew from the BBC was documenting the great Dark Rides of America. They journeyed throughout the eastern seaboard looking for forgotten carnival rides and attractions. They stumbled upon the House of Horrors as it sat abandoned in a Louisiana Junkyard. The crew asked permission to film the interior. Twenty dollars later, the film crew pried open the doors of the forgotten relic and stepped inside. The smell of decay was overpowering as the bright camera light illuminated the darkened corridors. Moving past the faded walls and hanging fabric, the smell began to increase. The cameraman wretched as he panned his camera towards a series of trunks. Behind the trunks was a large wooden box stenciled like a children's toy. One letter filled each side of the box: J-A-C-K.

The Cameraman steadied his camera as the Host of the show investigated the box. He found a large crank on the side of the box. He turned the crank with some resistance, but after a few twists, it freely moved in a clockwise rotation. A clanky musical melody played out as the Host smiled into the camera.
"It still works!" said the Host. Suddenly the Music stopped. The Host's smile turned to an embarrassed clench of teeth. He rotated the crank once more with no result. Suddenly the Light from the camera died. He turned to see the Cameraman move away. He heard the sound of something wet. He grabbed his flashlight and clicked it on. The Cameraman was standing a few feet further away. "Sorry - My light died." he grinned. Then, without warning the crank rotated a few spins. The top of the box flew open and a form sprung out. Affixed to a giant spring was the decomposing body of Jack Schmidt.

After a thorough police investigation, the bodies of the thirteen children as well as the body of Jack were shipped to the local Louisiana Coroner's office for further examination. The bodies of the children arrived later in the evening. At approximately Midnight on October 31st, the van carrying the body and box of Jack disappeared into the Louisiana swamp. A freak accident. Later that week the bodies of the BBC cameraman and Host were found the result of a grisly and unsolved murder.

Throughout the following years there have been urban legend retellings of this tale, with a corresponding story about the decomposing body of Jack killing again. The legend states that Jack is searching for Dr. Oddfellow, in a thirst for vengeance. The legend also states that Jack will reward anyone who releases him from his toy tomb by turning the crank with a very special reward. (This also tied into the emergence of the media gift which debuted this year. A small detailed prop would be sent to select members of the press with the aim of inviting them to the press preview but to also shock them enough into writing about the gift. Impressive media gifts from over the years include: Bloody Mary's jewelry box with sound from 2009, 2010's popcorn box with 'real' werewolf hair and SAW recorder to this year's Jack-in-a-box prop).

The local press ran the story: "October 2000 - Universal Studios is bringing some of the original pieces of Dr. Oddfellow's carnival of thrills to highlight the popular Halloween Horror Nights event. The Publicity and Marketing Department have also decided to play on the urban legend of Jack.

Designers of the event have been able to acquire what has been sold as the original box in which Jack was trapped. No word yet on the actual validity of the find.[8]"

With the backstory in place, the creative team decided to focus on the look of the monster. A mixture of real-life clowning killer John Wayne Gacy, a hint of the chaotic clown from Stephen King's 'IT' ably played by Tim Curry, a splash of the Joker from the Tim Burton version of the original 'Batman', a dash of original Universal horror movie 'The Man Who Laughs' (1928 film) and a spate of any urban legend from the many regional carnivals that had toured, were all possible ingredients in the 'DNA' that created the character. "As we start to get older, we realize that smile is nothing but paint. And there could be something dark and sinister behind it[9]," said J Michael Roddy. And that was the point, Jack would be an amalgamation of all the urban legends that have been told, all the movies that used a terrifying clown and all the times you as a child saw a clown and wondered who was under the grease-paint; Universal played to all these sensibilities to great effect. Using Roddy's own face as a starting point, the look of the monster would use facial attributes of Roddy to exaggerated proportions, combined with the aged makeup, elaborate hair styling and sharp claw like nails installed the character was made to scare anyone, including the non-clown fearing masses.

Next on the building of the monster would be to select an actor who could play the character in a terrifying form, who could really get under people's skin and add all the little nuisances that were required to make a truly great monster icon. Park creative looked no further than Central Orlando theme park veteran James Keaton. Keaton had played Beetlejuice for the park's daytime show, commercials and other park events; in fact up until 2015 he had played the part of Beetlejuice for just over 18 years. Keaton would be perfect for the role, as he could nail the part of Beetlejuice every single day without fail, so to bring the true character of maniacal clown to life would be an easy task for such a gifted acting talent.

The initial tests were all positive. Universal knew they had created something special. The next step would be to unleash the character on the public at wide. Universal took the bold step to market the character via every media outlet they possibly could, such was the confidence of department. Jack would be everywhere, starting in September as just a jack-in-the-box on highway billboards that would open slowly through re-postering every couple weeks to reveal the character. The tag line of: "Not Afraid of the Dark? You don't know Jack!" a play on words with great post-modern emphasis to attach to the new era of Halloween Horror Nights was heavily used along with appearances of the clown. Along with radio ads, a new commercial where unsuspecting teens get murdered at a Halloween Horror Nights looking event, through to a heavily publicized outing at a Fangoria convention that was in Orlando at the time to actual interviews in the local press. Suddenly the lines between fact and fiction were starting to blur, a policy that would add weight to the character and increase the scares from members of the public who thought, maybe, just maybe this guy is real… In an early October interview with members of the press, the character said, "[To scare guests] Completely, to the very core of their bones. In every manner. Everything is planned for Halloween. No matter what you come to see, I will be there to scare you. If you go to see Terminator 2, I'll be there. I will be everywhere. So complete is the frightful experience this year that not only will people be completely frightened in the houses, they'll be completely frightened in between and even during the parade - with my bloody playthings." And he wasn't wrong. Not only would Jack be everywhere in every media outlet before and during the event but he would also be everywhere inside the park too, from rides to shows to just lurking in the streets, such was the confidence of the park's creatives that they had created a solid event icon, he was deployed everywhere with everybody coming into direct contact with him at some point; a strategy that would really pay off.

October 6th soon came around with park guests clambering inside the newly built parking structure, creating queues from the park gates that extended almost as far as City Walk7. 19 nights of horror were planned with 5 houses and not just one scarezone anymore but an increased 4 zones, 2 shows, 2 rides that had become specially 'haunted' for the event and they even had the parade back. The event was bigger and better than ever before. With guests desperate to get into the event to see the horrors that awaited and they weren't going to be disappointed.

The first house that was offered was 'Anxiety in 3D', a house that used the very popular 3D technology from the previous year. Built inside Soundstage 22 the house would again deploy the disorientating technology to fox and confuse guests with a video game setting; marking this the first video game house seen at the event. The house had been 'designed' by Jack to play on all the main phobias that people held but in a video game environment. Fears such as confined spaces, spiders, rats and heights were played to guests to make then terrified and disorientated in equal measures.

Sharing the same Soundstage as 'Anxiety' was 'Total Chaos'. It also shared the first mammoth sized entrance canopy of temporary scaffolding and staging to highlight their entrances and queue areas, built in the Boneyard area of the park. The house would feature an alien on the run inside an Area 54 type setting with freakish mutant aliens from outer space running amuck inside a secret government facility. It was also one of the first houses to install a slide as part of the house's path, the following treatment had been written for the construction of this area: "Room 106 – The Attack Tunnel[4]: "As we are propelled downward, we come to an abrupt stop and find ourselves in a four foot wide room filled with small glowing orbs (ball pit), painted with wildfire paint application, stretching out before us. A blast of air causes our guests to quickly get to their feet, as they stand, a triggered nine-light blasts our retina with a powerful burst of light. Our eyes begin to fix, and we can make out the forms of decapitated heads that seem to float in space around us. We force ourselves forward through the thigh deep round and gooey objects. From behind and above us, a large hideous disfigured creature rushes forward and attacks, his attack cues a monstrous scream. We move quickly forward up and out to escape its tentacled clutches and find some solace in rejoining our group." Universal built a pair of slides for guests to travel down that emptied onto a ball pit with scareactors lurking in the pit to frighten guests forward. In many ways, this was a genius addition to the normal mazes built which under current accessibility laws could never return.

Though being everywhere for the event, Jack did not have his own house this year, though this is a common misconception from fans. The house was actually the creation of Dr. Rich Oddfellow (Jack's nemesis) and was entitled: 'The Fearhouse' located again in the Nazarman's area the house would have a beautiful highly detailed façade of a clown's face installed to whip up terror and anxiety in the awaiting queue line. Similar to Krusty's face on 'The Simpsons' ride that would come much later in the Universal timeline, guests would enter on Sting Alley and walk up a red carpet installed like an elongated giant tongue that would wrap its way down the alley to the queue, like a showbiz carpet meeting a wet tongue the mood for the house was set before guests took one step inside. Once inside guests would be attacked by clowns from above and below, big clowns, small clowns, old clowns, toy clowns, clowns everywhere, including the master of ceremonies himself at the very end. If you had coulrophobia (a fear of clowns) you shouldn't be at the event, let alone be inside this house!

Over the road was the house 'Dark Torment', entering inside the popular Earthquake ride guests would be dumbfounded to find the pre-show was now a queue area for the same ride which ultimately would lead to the house. Entering onto the usual subway tram guests would be attacked by the usual fire effects, road collapse, tram collision and rush of water. After the effects had ceased the ride vehicle would remain stationary before Jack would pop up to the tram and proclaim to the guests that "Congratulations, you didn't survive, you're now all dead! Welcome to hell my pretties!" Disappearing as quickly as he arrived, the tram doors would open and guests would debark the ride on the set and into a side room where before a short queue guests would enter into a Dante's Inferno like house. The first room would be a graveyard, entering via "your grave" guests would appear to walk underground further to the second room where hooded creatures await, the following original treatment was written by Universal, "We move forward into a chamber of seven tall and ominous robed figures, they stand four feet above us along a circular platform which we must follow. The faces of the figures are masks representing the seven deadly sins. Across the faces, scrawled in blood the words: lust, greed, sloth, anger, pride, gluttony and envy. One of the masked sins, with the mask that reads 'envy' suddenly springs forth sweeping at us with a sharp ceremonial dagger."[6] Guests would move along from this entry port to various rooms depicting each of the seven deadly sins and the punishments laid out for each sinner per room with infill rooms in between; the house including pre-house ride was quite lengthy.

Another Universal Creative treatment was written for the Hades room, it read: "We exit the darkness and enter our next chamber through eight foot wrought iron gates are slamming and askew, forcing us to wind through them. Beyond the steely entrance lies a chamber of ghastly and grotesque fear, a precursor to the horrific experience that awaits. A wall of tortured bodies surround us to our left and right. Strobes gives the walls the illusion of movement. Concealed amongst the bodies are two tortured souls. As our new arrivals make their way through the carnage, the souls break free from the wall. Their eyes are bone white and their mouths sewn shut to hold their tongues in their hands, thrusting them toward you." The treatment went onto say, "4 scareactors required"[5].

The Earthquake queue area also housed another maze, that of 'Universal's Classic Monster Mania'. The classic monsters were back but this time for a new generation. Gone were the classical looking monster and instead were exaggerated monsters of pure evil. Frankenstein's monster looked like he had been assembled from former dead pro-wrestlers, Dracula had reportedly been twisted into a half-man-half-bat creature with razor like teeth and the Wolfman had become more wolf than man. These mutated misfits were totally unlike any incarnation of the classic monsters that had been seen before.

The next house was an unofficial house but was similar to that of the Earthquake ride's house in that guests would queue in the same manner for the Kongfrontation ride but instead of entering onto the ride, guests would be let loose to explore the highly detailed sets of New York. Billed as 'Nightmare Creatures 2' the house would return to original Halloween Horror Nights territory. Unlike a house where a strict path was used, this house/ride was more like an indoor scarezone where guests could explore at their own peril. The ride along with Kong were all switched off and the detailed sets were anyone's to explore. One of two 'haunted attractions' the sets held scareactors around every corner. Tall stiltwalking scareactors were complemented by shorter scareactors along with copious fog machines to give a mysterious foggy New York setting. Though the advertising didn't do the ride/house justice, the attraction would go on to be a fan favorite that can never be reproduced due to the fact that Kong (in this incarnation) is no more at Orlando.

The other haunted attraction this year was the Jaws ride. 'Bloody Waters' was the ride's new name for the event. Jaws was a particular fan favorite for many years during the event, as the park map would advertise "see the shark in the dark". Now, the ride would have a whole new repurpose and theme. All of the then current Jaws effects would be included, the change would be an addition to the boathouse scene where a haunted looking fisherman complete with steel shark hook would swing at unsuspecting guests followed by Jack jumping from behind a barrel and just when you thought you had seen enough the ominous shark would make his giant splashing entrance. Like the Kong attraction, the ride was a huge hit for park guests.

Four official scarezones would be seen this year unlike the previous few years where one large scarezone was always used. The scarezones this time would be sparsely decorated with little sets and props to make way for the twice nightly parade. In fact, the scarezones would simply disappear for the parade duration and reform after completion each time. 'The Gauntlet' located in the Bone Yard area scaring guests directly into the queues of the two soundstage houses was complemented by the Chainsaw Drive Team (who all seemed to have KISS like black and white face paint this year) that patrolled between here and the park's entrance every night along with Jack who had an official photo opportunity with photo booth from the commercial[12] installed to the side near the Twister store. The area also housed another official photo opportunity of the Classic Universal Monsters just outside of the Monster Café with Frankenstein's Monster, the Wolfman and a gothic looking Dracula completed the line-up.

'Midway of Dr Morose' was held in the Amity area where again a band of freaks and clowns descended on the area to create a mini carnival of terror. 'Apocalypse Island' was held in the Central Park area by the lagoon side, it featured lots of zombies and mutants running around and eating human flesh, with customary appearances by the icon at random times through the night. The final scarezone was 'Clown Attack' located in Hollywood[2]. The scarezone would again feature clowns of all sizes and ages that would terrify and delight guests in equal measures, the beginning of photo spot scarezones really began with this scarezone as the clowns were only too happy to pose for a quick picture in return for a good scare. The parade was also back this year and it featured much the same as the previous years with the only extra addition of (yes you guessed it) a Jack themed float, otherwise it was the same albeit they ran it the opposite way it had been run before, starting in New York and ending in Hollywood. But if you wanted even more Jack, he had his own show called 'Jacked Up' located in the Animal Actor's Stage, which was a mixture of magic tricks gone wrong, edge-of-your-seat acrobatics and performers dancing to deranged musical numbers. A DJ played howling tunes at the top of Hollywood and Bill and Ted had their usual popular show at the Wild West Stage. Pop-culture items that were lampooned this year included: the then content sharing website 'Napster', 'Mission Impossible', the new 'Charlie's Angels', Simpsons characters 'Mr. Burns' and his loyal sidekick 'Mr. Smithers' along with Britney Spears and Lil Kim impersonators. Finished off by a song-a-like Eminem singing 'Slim Shady', and then finally the whole cast assembled to dance and sing 'Bye Bye Bye' by N'Sync ready for the house to once again come down[3]. If partying with the time-travelling duo wasn't enough, guests of the park could gain free entry into City Walk's many clubs each night after the event, this was the first year that allowed this additional benefit.

When Jack was interviewed by the press he was reported as saying: "I'm hoping, personally, that they will be very afraid. I'm hoping that people will see me and say, "Ooohhhh, ooohhhhh, he's scary." And then boys will bring their girlfriends here to show how manly they are to not be afraid of such a big, spooky clown. Oh, look at the big spooky clown. Then more will show up, and then they will be afraid… That's the type of impact I'm hoping for. I'm hoping that people will see that clowns aren't so bad after all, and more people will show up here."[1] He continued, "Oh, I'm not done. I will be here. Universal thinks that Halloween will be done at the end of the month, but I have another plan. I'm going to stay…"

And stay he did…

Notes:

1 Orlando Sentinel, Oct 6, 2000
2 Park map 2000
3 Bill and Ted Fan Club
4 Generic event website with archives
5 Generic event website with archives
6 Generic event website with archives
7 Interview with Jo Powell
8 Original UO backstory for Jack from HHNVault then HHNCrypt
9 Orlando Sentinel, Oct 8, 2000
10 Video by UO showing the introduction of Jack
11 Linkedin profiles (various)
12 Official commercial for the event, 2000

The rat lady and friends on break…

Halloween Horror Nights XI

I.C.U. / Jack's Back

Speculation for the event was growing as far back as August for this year's event in 2001. Billboards featuring a bizarre logo with the letters ICU were appearing along the Interstate 4 road, and slowly over the next few weeks ahead of the event the boards would be updated to show a creepy pair of eyes glaring at you from the huge billboards. They didn't go unnoticed by local members of the community, some of whom made complaints to Universal and the local media[11]. One resident wrote to the Sentinel and complained, "In driving about town of late, I have been startled to discover the specter of sinister eyes peering down at me from the Universal Studio's current Halloween billboard advertisement. It's true that many older kids - high school and college - find it appealing and enticing. For them, after all, it's fun to be scared. As a grandmother and a former preschool teacher, I wonder if we might not have forgotten some of the little children who in their innocence do not have the ability to distinguish reality from make-believe. What responsibility do we have as a community in this regard?"

Universal knew that they needed to top their original character icon from last year (Jack) with someone who would be as equally mad and dreadful or if not more so. Universal again turned to surveys that had been undertaken by park guests to see what else made them anxious and frightened. At the time of the event there was much discussion about the ever increasing power of computers within our daily lives, 'Moore's Law' that computer power doubles every 2 years was of much concern for some people, and this was directly tied into the fact that discussion was moving onto how much power the Governments of the day should have when viewing our own personal computer usage. This combined with the then current spate of television networks putting out hidden camera shows and fly-on-the-wall documentaries; 'Big Brother' for example had just aired on CBS at the end of the previous year to much avail. So when Universal got around to asking the participants of the surveys what scared you the most, they said "clowns". Which Universal had done the previous year with Jack. They then looked at the second most popular fear of the surveys, and that was 'the fear of being watched'. Therefore Universal knew that the next horror icon for their event would have to have sinister eyes or at least a mysterious stare for the icon to be successful.

The original planning was for the event icon to be called 'Edgar Sawyer' and there would be a twist that he was in fact Jack all along. 'Edgar', because it sounded gothic like Edgar Allen Poe and 'Sawyer' because it sounded like 'saw-you', as the new icon would have a readily available chainsaw as his main tool of dispatch. However this brought problems, problems which only rose to the surface some months into the planning of character. Vivendi and Canal+ had merged back in 2000 and with that merger meant that the owner of Universal, then the Canadian company Seagram would be brought by the merged companies. The ultimate shareholder of the new company was a Mr. Edgar Bronfman, and due to this ownership the creatives at Universal decided to drop the name in respect of their boss. The other problem was the surname. The surname of 'Sawyer' was actually the surname of Leatherface and Co from the original 'Texas Chainsaw Massacre' movies. And as Eddie had been designed for the purposes of scaring people with his stare but ultimately via his large chainsaw, Universal did not want any possible lawsuits filed, so they had to drop their surname and effectively re-design their character's backstory and name.

The new idea was for him to be Jack's own younger brother named Eddie. Therefore they could share a surname and no one called Eddie or Edward was thankfully on any of the parent companies of the then media conglomerate! The appearance of the character would largely remain. Eddie would be a composite of all the best 'starey' horror icons from movie history. He would have the leather face muzzle of Hannibal Lecter, the glassy expressionless stare of Michael Myers with the shear violent rage complete with chainsaw of Leatherface. And to add a visual connection to his brother, some of the white and green face paint from Jack would be applied to his brow. Like Jack in the previous year, Universal were sure that this year they could increase the gore, increase the horror and bring the event to a new insane level of terror to scare guests like never before. There was however a tragic event about to unfold that not only changed the event completely but also changed the Western World.

Without going into detail of what happened on September 11th, because we all know what happened that day and we all know of the tragic loss of life that was suffered across the States. The auditions for this year were actually September 11th and 12th, so they were postponed in respect of what had unfolded over those days. As the auditions had been cancelled, speculation quickly grew that the event would be canceled altogether. "Despite last week's terrorism…" said Jim Canfield, a Universal spokesman, "…there aren't discussions at the attraction about canceling Horror Nights altogether, or at least postponing its start." Peter Stapp, a former operations[12] executive at Universal and now a theme park consultant said at the time, "I'm sure they will examine the appropriateness of the plans and make any adjustments that are needed." News finally came just over a week after the tragic events of 9/11 that the show would go on and thus ended the speculation that the event like many others at the time would be cancelled (events at Disney, Pleasure Island and various local conventions were all cancelled during this week). Cranfield spelled out the event that would be coming, "19 spine-tingling nights during this spookiest of seasons when the park is overrun with ghouls, goblins, monsters and mayhem. Horror Nights is guaranteed to disorient and startle even the most fearless of thrill- seekers with gleeful gruesomeness." No mention of the blood and gore that had been planned was made. Obviously, in an effort to respect what had happened and to not allow the whole event to get cancelled (though it had been postponed somewhat), Universal decided to tone down the gore, blood and horror of the event. Names of attractions were changed, blood day (the annual day the park's creatives go around and splash the 'red corn syrup' over each house was cancelled), bloody props were swopped out, anything that resembled confetti or dust were removed and any horror that showed too much peril was cancelled; this included the 'Opening Scareamonies'[13].

The 'Opening Scareamonies' a tradition of having one singular pre-opening show on the first night, a tradition that had loosely started in the previous decade, and which was used as a media type press preview event in the previous year, was due to be held this year where Eddie the new event icon would largely dissemble Jack live on stage. The original treatment[10] is presented here "On Hollywood Boulevard: Guests entering the gates of Universal will be corralled onto Hollywood Boulevard. Here we are treated to an opening ceremony in the grandest tradition. A Flatbed truck extends across the street. A makeshift hangman's noose hangs above. On the truck we also find a large box. It is a recreation of a children's toy block with the letters J-A-C-K all around. Fog pours from the box as we hear a rock version of "Pop Goes the Weasel". A low growl turns into a laugh as the maniacal clown Jack springs from the box. He bounds around the truck laughing at the audience. "Miss Me?" snorts Jack. The clown killer launches into the attractions and shows. He is immediately cut off by the sound of a rock guitar. We hear the Duane Eddy rock classic "Rebel Rouser" as EDGAR (Eddie – as mentioned earlier) our new master of scareamonies enters, Chainsaw in hand. "Who are you?" yells Jack. "Me?" glares Edgar. "I'm your replacement!" "You don't know the Saw! String him up Boys!" Two other Chainsaw Maniacs enter and grab the clown. They place the makeshift noose around his neck and lift. We hear the snap of bone as Jack's body goes lifeless. Then it springs back to life. "You'll need more than that to get rid of me, freak!" snarls the Clown. They lower the clown and place his head down on his box.   Edgar revs up his trusty chainsaw and tears through the clown's neck. Blood sprays as Jack is beheaded right in front of us. His head drops down. The new reigning champion lifts the clown's severed head high for all the audience to see. The mouth still moves as we hear Jack scream out his objection. "I'll be back!" yells Jack's severed head. "Time to go back in the box!" smiles Edgar. The evil chainsaw-wielding madman drops the head into the box. Then proceeds to chainsaw it. Suddenly the Chainsaw Drill Team appears from behind our audience and attacks. They chase our guests into the park as the New Icon screams – "Open for Business!" A pyro hit signals the opening of our event."

Due to the perceived violence and gore of the Opening Scareamonies, it would be cancelled for this year. In fact, as Eddie was already frightening people on the I4 the creepy monstrous and violent connoting character would at the very last minute be cancelled. The billboards were taken down and the commercial was redubbed. Months of planning on the part of both the resort's theme park creatives and marketing had to be either removed or re-designed. Some of the advertising couldn't be recalled, such a deals with Taco Bell, Walgreens and various local papers. Some fans of the event remember spotting both advertisements in the local papers for the event where one in the center had a photo of Eddie and another on the back had a drawing of Jack. Suddenly the pulled marketing of "I see you!" (I-C-U) was to be hurriedly replaced with "Jack's Back" and "There's no more clowning around." Eddie was rapidly scrubbed from history and the popular clown from last year was brought back to be the event's new icon.

Other changes include: 'Bloodbath Underground' would became 'Ooze Zone', where the blood splatter streets of New York inside the Kong attraction would now be covered in slime rather than blood along with the planned foam. Foam parties were going through a fad at the time. 'Deadly D'illusions' became 'Dangerous D'illusions', and the show remained largely the same. A slight tweak in the name of 'The Festival of the Dead Parade' saw the popular parade become 'Nightmares on Parade'. 'Terror Land' would become 'Scary Tales' (a name that would ultimately stick for this house's future use. And 'Slasher Alley' became 'Nightmare Alley'.

'Scary Tales' would be a successful house for this year and would ultimately ensure it be brought back in various guises over the forthcoming years. Soundstage 22 would be used for the house as large elaborate sets were required to present everyone's favorite fairy tales. The concept was that all the fairy-tale characters and stories we all knew as children have been locked away in an abandoned carnival for 30 years. They've morphed and mutated during their imprisonment and now they want revenge. Large cute sets would be juxtaposed by hideous large monsters hidden inside each room. The Snow White scene for example featured a large terrifying wolf complete with sharp teeth and claws. The Wizard of Oz scene would feature a room full of blood hungry vampire like Scarecrows. The Mad Hatter's Tea Party scene would feature a large long table complete with bodies hanging from the ceiling and a mad demented zombie looking Mad Hatter would scare guests forward into the next room which was Alice's Toy Room complete with made Frankenstein looking dolls. Another popular scene was towards the end of the house where guests were led into a darkened room where squishing and squelching noises could be heard complemented by a foul smell, before the lights were lifted and much to the guests' surprise they were walking on top of rotten pieces of guts, though they were actually walking on a glass floor. "We have these smells in these houses that are just vile," J Michael Roddy[9] of Universal Creative said at the time. "There's a company that provides them, a catalog you can order from. Soil and Rotting Flesh are especially popular this year." The house was wildly popular and would form long queues each night.

A house that was setup to be the former Icon's house had to be toned down. That house was 'Run' and it was built inside the Earthquake queue. Original ideas from the park's creative minds were to build on the previous year and have this the most extreme house that had ever been built before. Adrian LePeltier[7] was tasked with the design of the house. He along with other's from the resort's Art and Design department had holed themselves up in one of the Portofino Bay's suites for several weeks while the team brainstormed possible ideas for the event at large and the house. "Some ideas got thrown out because of safety or other issues," LePeltier said. "For example, we wanted to blindfold guests and have them feel their way along a gunky rope through a dark room to escape". He continued, "In the end, you're forced to acknowledge that some of these things can't or shouldn't be done. After all, it would take some people an eternity to find their way along a rope in the dark and we need to move our guests through quickly to keep the lines short." Eventually the design of the house would evolve to become narrow, twisty and dark (but not pitch-black). He continued, "Guests are thrown into a diabolical game show where freaks and maniacs menace with chainsaws. To escape, guests must literally run through a series of dark, winding corridors of padded walls and chain-link fencing, with hardly a chance to catch their breath, let alone scream." The house was planned to be as intense as possible to afford the largest terror of any house ever created. And to crown the house with the most scares, the park's new icon would be chieftain of the chainsaws.

The original treatment promised the most terror of all houses, ever[8]: "Universal Studios Halloween Horror Nights presents the most extreme Haunted maze in its ten-year history. As our Guest Contestant, you will be thrown into an environment that has no rhyme or reason, only the most diabolical combination of unsettling imagery and dark, winding corridors. Your challenge is simple: Get out as quickly as you can. Through chain-link barricades and padded walls, you must make choices to survive. Think you know the way out? Good Luck. Remember to keep moving. Don't stop, not even to Scream!" The treatment would go onto describe a gameshow host that would open proceedings from the façade, this would be followed by light tricks and sirens sounding, so as to allow the chainsaw maniacs free to come select their guests. Caverns and junkyards were seen as guests made their way through a twisted maze of confusion and terror, and it was the latter that was toned down. Gorey scenes were removed, the number of maniacs with saws was reduced and Eddie was pulled altogether. The event's icon who was replaced would not even be present in his own house.

Next-door to this house was 'The Mummy Returns: The Curse Continues' and would be directly tied into the then Mummy movie of the same name which had been released in May of that year. The park promised, "Venture through a maze of tomblike corridors and dark caverns in the Temple of the Scorpion King, where danger lurks around every corner." The house was not as detailed as the former house to bear this name but it had many good scares. It came at a time when The Mummy franchise was at its most popular, with actual sets from the movies being showcased in the Stage 54 area of the park, along with wax models of the original Mummy and co who were on display in the foyer of the Monster Makeup Show. Made by Madame Tussaud's the figures[6] were on a tour of America before they were permanently installed in the creator's New York branch. The figures were a part of the 70th Anniversary celebrations of the classic monsters as Universal were keen to highlight both the modern and classical Universal monster franchises. Guests could enter into the theater after inspecting the wax-works to see a continuous running of the film 'Boogeymen' which played clips of older horror movies, such as those featuring the characters depicted in wax in the foyer.

'Superstitions' a house that featured many of our popular held superstitions was built in the Nazarman's area of the park. The park map billed the house as "Explore a hidden warehouse filled with ancient relics and urban legends that will have you believing in the supernatural." The house had been toned down a little from the original treatment but it still featured black cats and witches a plenty.

The last house would be 'Pitch Black' and would share the Soundstage with 'Scary Tales' as many houses had in previous years. The house was lined up to give guests a thrilling experience. Guests would be plunged into a world of darkness that to some was extremely disorientating, though strobe lights had been added. The park map billed it as "A mysterious zone of darkness has appeared causing weird disturbances. It's up to you to investigate... if you dare." As with many of the houses, the scares were reigned in and the scareactors were asked to tone it down. What would have been a mysterious dark adventure into the unknown became a rather temporary light laden affair that unfortunately was not as good as it had been designed to be.

One of the most exciting shows of the event had been 'Dangerous D'illusions' with Franz Harary. Franz was a magician of international acclaim who had been made famous by television shows such as NBC's 'The World's Greatest Magic', which Harary made a NASA Space Shuttle vanish live on television. He had also worked with the likes of Michael Jackson and Alice Cooper[4] on their many respective tours. The show featured a mixture of mind bending illusions and feats of amazement. It was held four times per night in the Animal Actor's Stage.

Scarezones this year were all non-removable and located in areas that did not affect the parade, these were: 'Midway of the Bizarre' which had been reduced in scope and size unlike previous years, this had been held once again in Amity. 'The Unknown' in Central Park which was a gothic setting with ghoulish gargoyle like creatures hiding around every corner and 'Nightmare Alley' located between where the Hitchcock show had been down to where Transformers is now.

Both the parade (with slight name change) and Bill and Ted were both back in their respective attractions. The parade featured a return Mummy float, along with guests who had purchased 'Stay and Scream' tickets the chance to ride one of the floats and distributing the colored beads to the on-lookers. Bill and Ted's show that year featured: a lookalike of Christopher Walken dancing to the famous Fatboy Slim music video, American Pie, Sex in the City and a rendition of the 'The Lady Marmalade' music video featuring sound-alikes of Pink, Mya, Christina Aguilera, and Lil' Kim. This was all topped-off with an impromptu game of 'The Weakest Link'[5], which had been shown on TV around the same time as the event.

In efforts to boost attendance to the event, the park bosses decided to use their links in Hollywood and attract celebrities to attend the event as members of the public (rather than performing or signing autographs). Universal would go on to do this most years in an effort to attract headlines in the local press and attract more guests. This year it was confirmed that Howie Dorough[1] from the Backstreet Boys, and then couple Britney Spears[2] and Justin Timberlake of 'N Sync were all spotted at the event. And attract guests they did, but they needed to. This was the first year that metal detectors had been introduced, done so in response to the terrible events of that year. Though they were not popular and did create longer queues for entry, they would soon become a mainstay of the event as attendance grew. This year the attendance did fall, some people have estimated it still maintained between 10,000 to 20,000[3] guests, though over all it was down a hard 10%[14]. Park bosses were grateful for foreign tourists, particular British guests, who often pre-book their vacations months (even years) in advance, these went a long way to make up for the reduction in domestic visitors (mostly out-of-state visitors) which had significantly reduced due to 9/11. The local community did respond by coming back more often for the event and the fans by means of the internet did help publicize the event in an effort to try to attract more people to give it a try. And although the event was by no means a failure that year, Universal did do their best to try to pull the event back from being cancelled and provide the world-class event that guests had become accustomed to.

Notes:

[1] Orlando Sentinel Oct 31, 2001
[2] Orlando Sentinel Oct 23, 2001
[3] Orlando Sentinel Oct 22, 2001
[4] Official park map for 2001
[5] Bill and Ted Fan Club
[6] Orlando Sentinel Oct 19, 2001
[7] Orlando Sentinel Oct 4, 2001
[8] HHNMemories.com, originally Universal Orlando
[9] Tampa Tribune Oct 15, 2001
[10] HHNMemories.com, originally Universal Orlando
[11] Orlando Sentinel Oct 3, 2001
[12] Orlando Sentinel Oct 18, 2001
[13] Interview with Jo Powell
[14] Orlando Sentinel Apr 26, 2002

Halloween Horror Nights XII

Islands of Fear (Your time has come)

"A new home"

As early as late April in 2002 Universal was building anticipation of their forthcoming Halloween event. The event in the previous year had not been as successful due to the events of 9/11, this combined with issues of marketing the event ensured that attendance was, for the first time in the event's history, down. But it wasn't just the event that was suffering; park-wide attendance was still down about 10% for the main Studio Park and 8% down for the still relatively new park, Islands of Adventure. The new park had failed to meet attendance expectations since it had been opened in 1999[11].

Universal knowing that they had a mountain to climb had to think bigger than ever before. A process that started by feeding information to the press as early as April that year. A small article in the local Sentinel[10] provided the information required: "Universal Studios' top-drawing annual Halloween Horror Nights might get a new home this fall: Islands of Adventure. The proposed move being researched by Universal Orlando executives would be part of a major expansion and upgrading of the scare-fest." Susan Lomax, a Universal spokeswoman, confirmed the information from the paper, "We are looking at a variety of ways to dial up the fear factor. It's our signature event - the biggest thing we do all year." Other commentators were less than impressed with the news, Peter Stapp, a former Universal executive and an attractions consultant in Orlando, said, "You know the old saying, `If it ain't broke, don't fix it.'[9] I wouldn't tinker with something so successful." A local resident expressed similar concerns, "I don't see how the other park could be managed, it's huge!" But not everyone shared these sentiments, "Islands is a teen-oriented attraction, and the nature of Halloween Horror Nights really speaks to that demographic," said Dennis Speigel, president of International Theme Park Services, a tourism-attraction consulting company. "I think this could push Islands up a tick on the attendance barometer by bringing in new users who have never seen the park before." And that was exactly what Universal was hoping for…

The decision had been made in May of that year by park executives before it was officially announced to the media in June, "This is a scare-maker's dream come true," said Bob Gault, president of Universal Orlando. The event would be bigger than ever before and be staged in the newer theme park of Islands of Adventure, where the latest rides and attractions would be complemented by houses, scarezones and shows. Gault[8] teased, "…its narrow, winding walkways and many nooks and crannies, will be one giant haunted house. That tropical forest in the Jurassic Park area is really going to be frightening at night when we add weird music. Islands offers more places for monsters to jump out at people and plenty of theme-park story lines. In the Marvel Super Hero Island, evil super-villains will reign supreme." Starting the speculation as far back as April and then confirming proceedings as early as June was exceedingly early for the park and showed the resort's determination to turn around the event's fortunes from the previous year.

Around September billboards started appearing locally for the event, this was combined with posters and even a banner tied to the Pharos Lighthouse at Islands of Adventure. A sinister looking gaunt man wearing a top hat and clutching a weird pair of metal scissors was adorned to all the advertising. The park's creatives had taken great care and consideration in choosing who should headline the event for park icon. Some believed that Jack should return again, other believed strongly that a new character could be created, others wanted to see Eddie return and be the actual icon rather than last year when he had to be dumped right before opening. The debate waged on before selection of a wholly new character was agreed; new location, new character, it just made sense. Initially the idea of creating an icon for the event of an evil-child was proposed. She would be called Cindy (SINdy) and the park would be her playhouse, where everything she has created and would be brought forth for us to enjoy. She would then be tied to each house, each scarezone, each show, each area to create an overall themed story arch, something that was important to the creative team at Universal at the time. The event would be her thoughts, her will and her ideas from her evil little mind. Each Island would showcase the disturbed and frightening depths of her mind as we the park guests explore them.

The character was chosen and an elaborate back story was produced, the park's creative design manager, TJ Mannarino said at the time "We find that the story is as important to guests as the scare."[7] Everything was set for the character to be the event's new icon and this was set right up until September that year when concerns were raised right at the top of the organization. A number of child abductions had occurred that summer on both the East and West coasts, though not linked in anyway, they did put this topic on the news agenda for many months. Fearing a media backlash for being unsympathetic Universal quickly decided to revise their icon choice. Though only the minimum amount of park literature and marketing had been done with Cindy, it was relatively easy to swop her out for a new icon. The hard work would be deciding on a new event icon and then design this icon in time for the press deadlines.

Undaunted and fearing a repeat of last year, the park's creatives worked into the night crafting the new icon. Looking at Cindy's backstory they chose her parents as a starting point. Originally Cindy's obsession with the dead would come from her upbringing being in and around a mortician's office which had been owned by her father. The father's character morphed away from him being her father (though temporarily) and that the character would be an evil, demented mortician come funeral director who would be using unsuspecting locals as vessels from which he could explore whether bodies have souls, obviously by mutilating them horribly. The inspiration had come from many year's prior where for some of the year's that the event held the parade a character dressed like an undertaker would scatter ashes at the rear of the parade informing guests of their impending doom. The character had been played by park regular and local Orlando acting supremo Bryce Ward. Bryce's deep mid-Atlantic accent combined with his long drawn face (when make-up applied obviously) would be perfect for the role. Building on Bryce's former performance in the parade and the backstory that had been created, the park creatives used various sources as inspiration, including 'Something Wicked This Way Comes' movie which featured a gaunt top-hat wearing Jonathan Pryce, along with the foreboding Jud Crandall character ably played by Fred Gwynne in the Stephen King 'Pet Cemetery' movie and the Reverend Henry Kane character, the main antagonist of the 'Poltergeist' film series. Making a nod to the latter inspiration the character's name was changed from Dr Paul Bearer to Dr. Albert Caine (note the spelling), but who would also known as The Caretaker. Luring victims to his Victorian Manor, the Caretaker would seek to operate on them and find their soul. Finally the park had their icon.

The character was approved by everyone at Universal and marketing started the task of adding the character to all marketing. From billboards to posters, the character would be seen across the land. Back in the Art and Design department rushed from completing the development of the new icon, they quickly set about adapting the event's plans to make way for the new icon. Two houses which had been planned were due to be re-imagined, luckily these were the two that had not started construction at the time, they were a tropical voodoo doll house and a cannibal meat factory house. The latter was due to be built in Soundstage 20, a soundstage that had not been used at the event before due to filming requirements, particularly seasonably for gameshows and wrestling programs. The soundstage was so large that in coming years it would be used again but to house two houses in the one soundstage. Luckily, due to a slowdown in production and filming requirements at the time, the soundstage would be the perfect venue for a haunted house, not least because of its size but also because of its proximity to the neighboring park; being the physical closest or closest with ease of access and egress to Islands of Adventure. Having scrapped the idea of a cannibal house, the park creatives started the process of developing a house to fit the backstory of the Caretaker. Utilizing the space available in the Soundstage, the park's creative minds could build one of the largest houses they had ever designed and fill it with all kinds of unimaginable horror.

The house would become 'Scream House', and would take guests on a tour of the Caretaker's actual home. A full house façade would be constructed to give guests the illusion that they were entering into an actual building (within a building), this had never be done before. After designing and building the house, the team scoured all the thrift and antique shops locally to fill the house with peeling wallpaper, an organ, caskets, stuffed animals, vases, pianos, velvet curtains, fire places, glasses, and antique furniture; all dusted and distressed to give the appearance of age. "To have this level of detail is critical for us," said TJ[6] Mannarino at the time. "Our goal is to take you out of reality and put you in this imaginary world and give you that second of disbelief, `Am I really in a funeral parlor?' Then you see something move in the corner and you think, for that second, maybe it really could be some strange, disfigured monster." The scents of rotting flowers and dirt were added to ramp home the scares. Finally a cast was needed to staff this significantly detailed house, 26 scareactors would be deployed at any one time (allowing for breaks), which had been a record at the time to fill this huge house. The cast would be a combination of unfortunate house guests who were dying from wounds half-way through their operations to zombified former patients now inhabitants of the haunted house. Topped-off with several Caretakers complete with rusting metal shears.

The Caretaker also needed a show. It was too late to put him into a main show or create a special sit-down show for the event. The idea from previous years of having an 'Opening Scaremonies' was brought back. The idea would be perfect for the character, whereby he could introduce the event, what the guests would expect to find beyond the gates and to build anticipation. Brought to the event via a horse-drawn-carriage, the aloof character would appear on a small stage in front of the park gates. Selected guests (really actors) would be plucked from the gathered crowds before being tortured by snakes and scorpions inside a raised coffin before being gutted live. One victim's heart would be pulled out, still beating; the Caretaker would announce the opening of the event and for guests to go forth.

Inside the park, guests would enter into the first scare zone 'Port of Evil'. This followed, scarezone featured tortured souls in various levels of distress. Guest flow could be better controlled here than in the Studio park with most guests opting to go left entering into 'Island Under Siege'. Anticipation for this island was extremely high. Universal promised, "The super heroes have all been defeated. Now you're trapped on a decaying, lawless island under siege by the minions of the most vicious super villain of all, Carnage." Carnage was a popular character at the time from the Spider-Man universe. The island was like nothing that had been seen before or since with Thor's hammer laid on a crater in the ground, Spider-Man's webbing was seen applied to various walls, parts of Iron Man's armor had been stolen and strewn around, along with Captain America's blood splattered shield nailed to the Dr. Doom ride walling. There was smoke, overturned cars, burnt out vehicles, police running around with blood splattered uniforms and general destruction all about. Various villains from the Marvel universe prowled the streets with water pistols along with Carnage who was positioned atop a tower of scaffolding flicking his long tentacle like fingers down to the shocked passing crowds. The whole island looked like we had all just missed one huge battle to the death for which the heroes had lost spectacularly.

Carnage wasn't just situated on the streets; he also had his own house. Located behind 'Dr. Doom's Fearfall' in building B285A that would later be named the Carnage Warehouse (the building had been erected specifically for the event, then used for storage ever since), the house would be entitled 'Maximum Carnage' with Universal's park maps promising: "Venture into the labyrinth-like secret hideout of the malevolent Carnage, an insane criminal with incredible alien powers, who's bent on mindless destruction." The house would contain toxic waste splattered walls, chemical dripping, barbed wires hanging from the ceilings, laser beams and strobe lighting to disorientate guests, complete with villains and henchmen chasing everyone; the house was skillfully managed to give great scares. Skull masked leather clad chainsaw henchmen, complete with gas mask wearing scientists would chase guests into the classic turning tunnel (which Universal had used regularly), past waterfalls of toxic waste and through loads of scaffolding. Music would blast out of the speakers playing fast drum and bass, while guests have seconds before the nuclear reactor would explode, with alarms going-off and hot aired pumped in for maximum effect. The house would end with our host Carnage on top of a podium waving his tentacle like fingers down to unsuspecting guests.

The next island on would be Toon Lagoon renamed 'Treaks and Foons' and would be a welcome respite from the intense devastation of the preceding island. Originally designed as a scarezone for Cindy to deploy her twisted imaged characters on guests, the area included scores of charming cartoon-like characters that worked the area in pairs. Combined with the largest foam machine that had ever been deployed by the park it made for a very weird experience. The pairs of grinning ghouls would dance with guests while their other half would lurk behind corners or within the foam, before jumping out on the guests lured into a false sense of security.

The 'Scary Tales 2' house was also based here, built into the Popeye and Bluto's Bilge-Rat Barges' queue housing. The house had built on the reputation of the previous year and would mostly be about childhood fears. Little Red Riding Hood and Alice were back, along with the vampire like Wizard of Oz Scarecrows. The house also used the first attempt by the park's creatives to install black and white camouflage tactics into some of the rooms, complete with strobes and light effects scareactors would be dressed in black and white costumes before being posed directly in front of black and white walls to give the effect that the walls were literally moving and reaching out to the guests. A huge façade was constructed with a big blue goblin face on it, lots of nursery rhymes and child-like-chants was played throughout the house. One room had the infamous rhyme of 'Mary had a Little Lamb' which had been taken to the next level where she had slaughtered the poor animal plus other lambs and strewn them everywhere! Plus it wasn't the wolf that had killed grandma in the classic tale, it was grandma who had killed the wolf. Hiding behind her bed the grandma would push the decapitated blood dripping head in your face before scared guests would rush into the next room and be confronted by the Three Little Pigs all complete with roaring chainsaws. The house had everything!

Next up would be the Jurassic Park Island that was as wildly anticipated as the Marvel Island transformation. Props and set pieces formerly stored off-site and in the Boneyard were repurposed to become 'JP Extinction'. The concept was the island's scientists had started to experiment with the dino DNA by creating human-dinosaur hybrids. The hybrids along with the actual dinosaurs have smashed their way out and roam free within the island. Actual props from the Jurassic Park sequel 'The Lost World' were used in both the streets and the island's house. Raptor costumes were adapted to fit scareactors who hid in the bushes and jumped out on passing guests, along with a large life-sized Triceratops (though some speculate that this prop was from the original Jurassic Park movie) which was pulled to pieces covered in fake blood and hung up in the house. The house would be dubbed 'Eviloution' and be built in the then attraction of 'Triceratops Trail', with the original animatronic triceratops used at the start complete with strobe affects to make the animal looked like it was in some distress. Further along the house the same animal would be gutted and hung up by the hybrid men (as described above). Dr. Burton the evil maniac scientist employed on the island would at the start of the house warn guests not to enter as the hybrids he had created would be coming for you, by the end of the house the hybrid- monsters had caught Burton and hung him from the neck on the ceiling. Half-dinosaur-half-human monsters complete with the traditional raptors and spitter dinos would fill this house with scares of every nature!

The popular TV show 'Fear Factor' had a house this year within this island; it would eventually relocate as a show eventually full-time to the studio park. Based loosely on the TV show it would feature all the main phobias and fears that the general public holds. The house would be very dark, slimy, sticky, scareactors pretending to be sick, with fake roaches, snakes, spiders, worms, crawling about and all this in the pitch black! Scareactors trapped with creatures like snakes in a glass helmet, a gooey hair room, a bridge dropping 2 inches but making it seem like you are falling far in the complete darkness were complemented by compressed air guns shooting at you.

The next island would house Studio 666, a dance party on the Lost Continent complete with the fountain being used to step up the scares. Next guests would reunite at the Port of Entry via Seuss Island which had been allowed to have a small amount of mist applied and nothing else, as per the strict instructions from the creator's widow, Audrey Geisel. Bill and Ted[5] were also back this year, this time housed in the expansive and under used Toon Lagoon Amphitheater. Topics this year included: The Osbournes from the then popular reality show, the characters from Scooby Doo, Austin Powers complete with Mini-Me, Darth Vader, an Anna Nicole Smith lookalike, the Green Goblin from the Spider-Man movie and Gandalf. The show ended with the assembled cast dancing and singing to Neil Diamond's 'Coming to America'. Rides and attractions open this year included: The Amazing Adventures of Spider-Man, Doctor Doom's Fearfall, Incredible Hulk Coaster, Storm Force Accelatron, One Fish, Two Fish, Red Fish, Blue Fish, Caro-Seuss-el, The Flying Unicorn, Dueling Dragons, Poseidon's Fury, Jurassic Park River Adventure and Dudley Do-Right's Ripsaw Falls.

Other notable events this year include the first time that RIP tours were offered. The park's advertisement offered, "The ultimate Halloween experience - a guided tour including priority entrance and preferred seating to Halloween Horror Nights houses, shows and select rides. VIP Tour - Non-private, 5-hour tour begins at 7pm - $120 per person or exclusive VIP Tour[4] - Private, scheduled tours - $1,700 per group (15 people max). The event was also captured by the Travel Channel's cameras in their film 'The Art of the Scare' which had been filmed to showcase the level of work and detail that went into organizing the event every year. It also marked the first time an interactive website was built to help build the narrative of each island. The website, though primitive by modern standards, was the first time a website had been built showcasing the attractions that would be presented, along with the ability to download wallpapers and send e-cards. Previously the site would just be a holding page with the logo and contact details. The last notable event from this year was a far less haunting event. Presided over by the park 's icon The Caretaker, Regina Herron[3] and Christopher Mygrant of Tampa got married at the theme park on October 13th. The marriage took place inside the soundstage where the icon's house had been built. The couple decided to get married at their favorite event as they had held their very first date at the event some years prior. Cast members and crew acted as witnesses, but they had other reasons to celebrate too…

The park's creative team along with the various other departments had all worked together to pull-off the maximized event. Though the odds had been stacked against them and the objectives ambitious – they had succeeded. The event had returned attendance numbers that were back to where they had been. The Sentinel reported that, "On the Saturday night before Halloween, some employees said, attendance equaled the previous record of between[1] 45,000 and 46,000." Most Saturdays[10] at the event sold-out and reached capacity. This was music to the ears of the hard working people of the park, with park bosses, crew and the 600 scareactors[2] employed that year could not be happier. The event that year would go down in Halloween Horror Nights history as one of the best.

Notes:

[1] Orlando Sentinel Nov 4, 2002
[2] The Art of the Scare film, The Travel Channel, 2002
[3] Orlando Sentinel Oct 24, 2002
[4] Park map 2002
[5] Bill and Ted Fan Club

[6] Orlando Sentinel Oct 16, 2002
[7] The Art of the Scare film, The Travel Channel, 2002
[8] Orlando Sentinel Jun 13, 2002
[9] Orlando Sentinel Oct 15, 2002
[10] Orlando Sentinel Apr 26, 2002
[11] Orlando Sentinel Apr 26, 2002

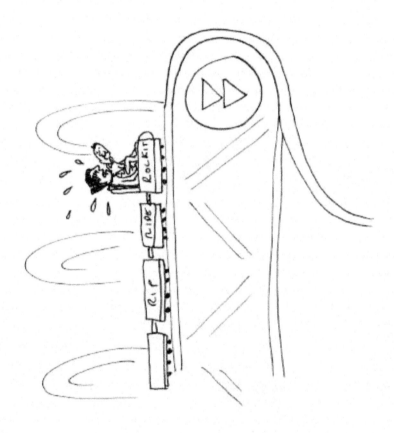

Drac: "I'm on an emotional rollercoaster right now"

Halloween Horror Nights 13

The Director will see you now

"You oughta be in pictures!"

An extreme year needed an extreme house; least that was the plan for this year. Building on the successful move from the studios to Islands of Adventure, the resort wanted to increase the scares, increase the suspense, as well as the tension and the spine-chilling creepiness of the whole event. This could be done by building another park-owned and created icon that could be tailored to embody all these attributes and reflect them at the event. Various designs were undertaken before a combination of input from marketing and the park's art and design department created Paulo Ravinski or, 'The Director'. Fitting nicely in with the resort's overriding movie theme, the Director would be an embodiment of the evils that would await unsuspecting guests within the event. Officially cranking the dial from downright scary to extreme, Universal knew they would be playing with fire and thus would court some controversy. The icon would be bounced off the idea of 'snuff-films, a relatively obscure film genre that had been going as long as cinema but had become more well-known due to the advent of the internet in recent times; those movies being where someone is filmed actually dying. So the Director would be a movie director who needed victims for his latest snuff-films, where he would not just kill unsuspecting victims but also horribly torture them too. During this time a niche genre that was starting to break out to be mainstream (albeit for a short duration) was torture-horror;. Later movies of 'Saw' and 'Hostel' would go on to encompass this niche and have reasonable box-office success. Building on this emergence of a new genre, Universal was quick to add this into their character so as to keep the event as relevant as possible. Gone were the campy monsters of the past, as this event was squarely re-building its brand around the demographic it attracted, despite running the risk of making the event too extreme which could isolate their audience or upset the wider audience. It would be a gamble that would ultimately pay-off but there would be bumps along the road.

The backstory that was created by Universal was a twisted tale of evil: "Paulo Ravinski was born in Eastern Europe. Aspiring to be a filmmaker, he initially started out as a snuff film director, capturing actual human suffering, torture and death on his movie camera. His first project was a controversial feature known as The Widow's Eye. The film shocked so many of his country population that Ravinski was forced out, which is when he came to America. Law enforcement agencies and film critics call his work snuff cinema. The Director prefers his work to be referred to as 'art'."[11] Combining many connotations of popular horror with the new wave of horror movies that were hitting cinemas at the time, Universal had created an icon that could have the event built around them, much as they had with their past icon of Jack, but unlike how the event had been planned in the last two previous years where both respective icons had been scrapped at the last minute.

It was August 6th of that year when news broke in the local media that Universal were not just trying to make the event more extreme overall but that they wanted to make their first extreme house. The press reported that an 'inside-source' had informed them that the house was being designed for construction, you would have to be 18 years old and must sign a full waiver before entering. The local paper went on to describe the house that was in full-planning, "No word on exactly what this horror-to-the-nth degree will entail or if, as some suggest, it will require an additional entry fee. One site said the stout of heart will wear a harness while the floor drops from beneath them - and that's before they spend some time in a casket."[10] Rumors at the time said that the house would be built inside a soundstage, with controllable temperatures and management of footfall could be better monitored, along with the space required for this rumored up-charge house. In fact, closely surveying the park maps of the time, it can be seen that one of the soundstages and attached path is seen on the map but contains no number. It goes some way to show how close this house was into production and marketing before it was subsequently cancelled. The Jurassic Park area of the park managed to squeeze three houses within its boundaries, yet the use of the soundstages (which have always been popular haunt locations) would go underused; this adds to the theory. Despite the rumors then and now, the house would never come to fruition. It was also rumored at this time that Universal would be building a 'ghost ship' house along with the extreme house; the former would be seen though it is said that the extreme house was likely pulled due to concerns from higher management and the legal team, but this milestone in the history of the event goes to prove how serious the park was about organizing an event that was definitely aiming to increase the scares.

It was around this same time in early August that the park began advertising the forthcoming auditions for the event. Some 1,100 people were needed to fill the positions in the houses and scarezones, which would be a significant increase on the previous year's record of 900 scareactors. This was combined with early projections that the event would be attracting some 40,000 visitors on the busiest nights with another 21 nights of fun to be had[9]. These projections reinforced Universal's attempt to make the event more extreme and added to the need to hire more people than ever before. The move to the Islands park had also been a good move too, as industry experts had estimated that the park had received a 10% bump in attendance overall for the year, just by moving the event to the Islands park away from the Studios[6]. So the decision to keep it at the same park from last year was made very early on.

The TV commercials began and the billboards were put-up, and along with their release, so did Universal receive a trickle of complaints. Many complained about the 'graphic' nature of the tortured victims in the 'snuff-film' advertisements that were seen and other complained about the general creepiness of the google-eyed monster from above the highway. Though surprising the complaints were not as frequent as had been seen in past years. Maybe Central Florida residents and visitors were getting used to the annual event? This year also marked the first use of media gifts, small bespoke handmade horror props sent to the select few in the media in the interest of providing further coverage of the event and boy did they start in style! The first small number sent out were to named people within the media that were photographs of the recipient but had been altered by means of 'photo-shop' to appear to be in various levels of distress and torture, as though the Director had cast the recipient in one of his latest 'snuff-films'[8]. "It's kind of disturbing to see yourself looking like that," said Bob Opsahl, anchor for WFTV-Channel 9. "I mean, I don't go see movies like that." Though most of the media took it well and saw the funny side of the gift, others were less happy. An anonymous anchor was reported as saying "With what is going on in the world today, and with the sickos Halloween Horror Nights attracts, this is all some borderline psychotic needs to think he has a message from heaven to knife one of us at a public appearance." Though Channel 6 was quick to close-out these complaints, "I take security as seriously as the next guy," said Bob Frier of WKMG-Channel 6. "But you've got to be thinking way outside the box to think this thing is a safety risk. This was funny." Co-anchor at the time Jacqueline London followed Frier's sentiments by explaining that being a news anchor they would both see some pretty serious and horrific things on a regular basis, "but a promotion for Universal is hardly one of them," she said. London then quipped in reference to these comments that "they wouldn't want to pry my mouth open. They'd want it closed."

The commercials frequency on TV were increased as the event drew closer and as more of the media than ever before were talking about the 'gifts' they had received, the Travel Channel played re-runs of their documentary filmed at the previous year's event 'The Art of the Scare'. This all led to pre-event tickets sales increasing significantly. In fact by October 1st, just days before the event, advance ticket sales were running 8% ahead of advanced sales for 2002[5] from the same period. Universal knew that as long as the buzz maintained and the event was delivered to expectations (with the vastly increased number of scareactors), the gamble would pay off and the event be a hit.

The house number would be increased to six and would begin with 'Scream House Revisited' and would reunite guests with the previous icon, The Caretaker', back in his dilapidated manor house built inside Soundstage 20. In fact, the house was left from the previous year and was redressed to look more decrepit and evil. Roaming the house were partially embalmed creatures and scattered about were decaying corpses with tortured souls of the evil operations that the caretaker undertaken in the house. Along with the victims, the Caretaker roamed about in a menacing fashion lurking with mummified corpses and caskets galore. Though the layout of the house was similar, some alterations had occurred and the house generally was presented in a more terrifying manor, the addition of burnt out rooms to indicate a level of trauma had been suffered to the building that mirrored the horrors faced by the occupiers. It was also worthy of note that last year this house had been built for Cindy and not the Caretaker, it had only been repurposed at the last minute, so this year the house was a full-fledged house of evil for the maniacal Caretaker, where more time had been taken to tell his twisted story.

The next house and one that adjoined inside the same soundstage was 'All Nite Die-In' and was this year's icon's house. Entering into a large deserted drive-in movie theater that was showing various horror movies projected onto the big screen, guests would be taken on a twisted journey through some of the most horrific movies in history. Though many horror movie franchises were represented here, albeit in an unofficial capacity, guests could recognize the horrors even if they weren't exactly authorized for use and were used based on the principle of 'fair-use.' Each room represented a scene from a famous horror movie with the Director inside lurking in each house to usher guests through the house.

The next house was 'Funhouse of Fear in 3D' which would be this year's only 3D house but not the only comical house. Located in the Thunder Falls Terrace area the house was filled with clowns in every sense and in every room. Universal billed the house as "Nothing is what it seems in this mind-boggling maze of optical delusions and maniacal clowns that will have you running for the exit. Too bad there isn't one." Gorey scenes were interspersed with disorientating illusions of scareactors jumping out to guests and crazy mirrors used to show faux exits. And although the house was filled with clowns, Jack was completely absent from the proceedings.

Though the previous house was relatively small in comparison, the other two Jurassic Park houses were quite large and the first one was an extension of the scarezone in this area. 'Jungle of Doom' located in the Triceratops Discovery Trail area and in Camp Jurassic, the house would be filled with jungle people and zombies performing ritual killings and human sacrifices. This combined with cannibals eating human flesh to distractive attractive males and females wearing not much more than loincloths. The main difference in the house over the streets was the use of more blood and gore, with scares coming from the darkness that was seen within the area and the great deal of shrubs and plants that lined the area.

The final house in the Jurassic Park area would go on to become a Halloween Horror Nights staple, and would feature a house that would return time and time again, such was the popularity of the house where scares and stomach-turning sensory delights were provided in equal measures. 'Psycho Scareapy' would be located in the Jurassic Park Discovery Center and take up most of the ground floor, the house was huge! Entering into the house from the rear of the building, guests would be taken into a ghoulish and nightmarish insane asylum of the murderous kind. Demented ghoul like inmates had overthrown the facility, killed all the guards, nearly killed all the doctors and were now running free in a world of unfettered craziness. Padded cells and electricity pulse treatment chairs were scattered about in the various rooms along with one very memorable scene in the bathroom where fake human excrement had been scribed over the walls with the park's art and design pumping in smells to match the visual delights. The aim to terrorize your person along with your sense of smell was hand-in-hand in this epic inaugural house.

The final house and the one that had been most talked about prior to the event was 'Ship of Screams' located in the Popeye and Bluto's Bilge-Rat Barges queue housing. The house would follow the HMS Friday that had been launched January 13th 1913 and had reappeared some 90 years later with no souls on board merely adrift in the open seas. Ghostly crewmembers in full uniform and suitably attired passengers were hidden lurking in the misty shadows of the ship[4].

There were five scarezones this year. Port of Entry became 'Port of Evil' and mixed gale force winds, bright lights and loud drumming music to push guests into the park. The Opening Screamonies was also back this year and featured in this location. The Director complete with his minions tortured various people with glass helmets filled with snakes, spiders and rats. This ended with a sound-off of fireworks before the event was officially open. Marvel Super Hero Island became 'Toxic City', and had hordes of mutated, melted faced mutants running around in a foamy environment. The foam machines from the previous year had been redeployed to great effect. The original idea was to reimagine the scarezone that had been undertaken the year before, due to its popularity, however rumors at the time dictated that Marvel were less than impressed with what Universal had done to their characters, so stepped in to kindly request that the zone and house of 2002 was not repeated.

'Hide and Shrieeek'[7] was located in the 'Toon Lagoon' area of the park. Various sets had been built to line a path through the area that would act as various backdrops from scareactors to actively hide within but hide within plain site. For example, black backdrops were used along with black clad actors so hiding like camouflage could be undertaken, before the scareactors could jump on unsuspecting guests. Though this was a technique that had been used before, it was the first time it was used to such success in the streets. The next scarezone was 'Night Prey' and was located in the Jurassic Park area, as previously described. Podium dances and fired torches lit the path between scares from various locations including from the hedges and shrubs where the raptors of the previous year had been based. The next scarezone was on the Lost Continent renamed 'Immortal Island', it would see an epic battle between fire versus ice, settled only by a ride of then Dueling Dragons ride to see who the winner would be. The Ice Queen who had been within the scarezones on the previous year in a smaller capacity was now back and located in this zone up against the Lord of Fire. Various battles would be held nightly and the various minions of each side would pull guests into the action and ask for their cover. Complete with the battles of the area guests were also greeted by the Chainsaw Drill Team who were dressed as orcs with very elaborate makeup and costuming, complete with a reappearance of the fabled Rat Lady complete with medieval monks once again located within her glass coffin; deployed back on street as she had been in houses in recent years. There was a final scarezone 'Boo-ville' but this was merely a bit foggy and acted as a welcome reprieve for most guests.

The one common thread that all the scarezones had in common was the use of the number '13' throughout. Purposely deployed into every house and street, the number would be a reflection of the old superstition and would be used to great effect throughout. The other attribute that tied the streets together well was the use of music. 2003 marked the first time that the creators had used music from 'Midnight Syndicate', who are an American musical group that work mostly within the gothic genre of music, starting in 1997 and based out of Chardon, Ohio. Music from their 'Realm of Shadows' album was used to enhance the streets and provide a knitted together experience that was unlike previous years. Universal would go on to use their music frequently in the years that followed.

The attractions that were open this year include: The Amazing Adventures of Spider-Man, Doctor Doom's Fearfall, Incredible Hulk Coaster, Popeye and Bluto's Bilge-Rat Barges, Storm Force Accelatron, One Fish, Two Fish, Red Fish, Blue Fish, Caro-Seuss-el, The Flying Unicorn, Dueling Dragons, Poseidon's Fury and Dudley Do-Right's Ripsaw Falls.

Expanding on the Opening Scaremonies show of the first night, a new show called 'Infestation' would be located near the entrance to the Enchanted Oak Tavern. Universal billed it as "Here's your chance to 'audition' for The Director's latest film, as you get to interact with a host of creepy, crawly, co-stars. You must be 18 or older." Members of the public would be doing basically Fear Factor tasks where glass helmets with spiders, snakes, scorpions etc. would be poured on the volunteers (real volunteers too!). The Director hosted the event and a wheel of misfortune where your fate would be randomly selected to have various creepy critters poured over you[3].

The other show this year was a marked return for the time-travelling due of Bill and Ted. This marked the occasion where J Michael Roddy had ceased writing the show and had now given the reins fully to Mike Aiello, who had co-writing the script last year with Roddy. Mike said at the time, "This year a challenge because we went about writing the script a little bit differently. It was a team effort by a group of people with lots of different ideas and viewpoints. Universal had a basic idea that they wanted a little more music in the show this year and we (myself and Kenny Babel) wrote first based on that. Gregg Birkhimer (this year's director) gave us many points and ideas for his vision of the show. It was a fun process and a great learning experience." The show marked the first time the opening announcement of 'switch off your phones and do not record the show' was done in a tongue-in-cheek video manner much to guest praise. It also featured a return of satirical gags featuring then Iraqi leader Saddam Hussein (which was actually played each night by Aiello) and various members of the Busch administration. The show also featured a return for Aaron Bailey playing the part of Bill, as he had not played the character for a few years but it also marked the start of a new actor, Scott Stenzel who took up the part of Ted for the very first time. This time being located at the Toon Lagoon Amphitheater, the show would feature: characters from 'The Matrix', 'The Lord of the Rings', Captain Jack Sparrow from 'Pirates of the Caribbean: The Curse of the Black Pearl' which had been released a few months prior to the event along with various stars from popular music. The show this year also coincided with Universal closing the Wild West Stage Show in the Studios Park to make way for the Fear Factor show, though this had no bearing on the event or the Bill and Ted show that year[2].

This year marked a few firsts. The first being that express passes were sold in strict quantities for the very first time. In fact they had sold out on nearly all Friday and Saturday nights during the event marking their return an absolute given for the event's managers. The other being that donors of actual blood (rather than the fake stuff at the event) were being offered discounted tickets to the event if donated during the month of October at any of the Central Florida blood banks. At the time blood donation levels had reached their absolute lowest for many years and the local hospitals were demanding something to be done about the decrease. Incentivized donations with event tickets were just one of many drives that occurred at the same time that year[1].

Notes:

[1] Orlando Sentinel Oct 29, 2003
[2] Bill and Ted Fan Club
[3] Park map from 2003
[4] Orlando Sentinel Aug 6, 2003
[5] Orlando Sentinel Oct 1, 2003
[6] Orlando Sentinel Sep 10, 2003
[7] Orlando Sentinel Oct 3, 2003
[8] Orlando Sentinel Sep 21, 2003
[9] Orlando Sentinel Aug 6, 2003
[10] Orlando Sentinel Aug 6, 2003
[11] Universal Studios Orlando released character info

Halloween Horror Nights: 14th Annual

What's your breaking point?

Twice the fear!

In the formative years since the atrocities of 2001 the parks of Central Florida had greater struggled to attract tourists and push for growth. A real slowdown in the market was seen from 2002 and continued into 2004, though Universal had an ace up its sleeve and that ace was Halloween Horror Nights. Despite the bad headlines of visitor numbers down and takings being slow, the event was growing and seemed to build bigger and better for each year. In fact many analysts at the time directly attributed Universal's visitor number bump in 2003 to the Halloween Horror Nights event; this one event that had been held on various dates for one month could attract so many people that it could effectively push the overall yearly total of park guests up on the previous year – which was music to the resort bosses' ears. Building on what had been in the previous year and knowing that the event needed to grow with the visitor numbers it was enjoying, the park's management decided to put on the biggest event that they had in the event's history.

This year would feature: 7 houses, 1 show, the parade would be back, 4 heavily themed scarezones with 12 rides/attractions open most nights, but not only was the level of entertainment increased but so was the geography, as for the first time in the event's history they decided to utilize both parks. A detailed plan was drawn up whereby the best locations for scarezones and houses could be presented but to also maximize footfall flow and the marketing that could be attributed to a two-park-one-ticket event. Pinch-points like the Jurassic Park area could be fenced off and expansive between park areas (not open to guests) could be opened up to move guests between the parks. Logistically it would be a large undertaking but if Universal could pull this off at a time when visitors were needed it could really benefit not only the event but the resort as a whole.

News of the plans came in July that year, when the local press ran articles of what was in store, "Aficionados of fright can experience twice the chills this fall when Universal Orlando expands its popular Halloween Horror Nights to include both of its theme parks. It's the first time in the event's 14-year history that it will take place in both Universal Studios and the newer Islands of Adventure." The article continued, "Universal said this year's

Halloween Horror Nights will include seven new haunted mazes, bigger and more intense 'scare zones', a Halloween parade and a haunted cornfield that is currently being grown on one of the park's back lots."[6] And it was the latter that Universal was aiming to intensify like never before. Once the plans early on in 2004 had been decided to undertake a dual park event, the organisers wanted to maximize the space on the 'backstage' areas to create large and detailed scarezones that they couldn't create in the usual guest areas. The usual scarezones were located in high traffic areas that could not be closed off during the day to park guests, so all props and stages need to be relocated after the event finished each night; though some larger props that aren't too gruesome often remain if no parades are on that specific route. Knowing that areas could be managed better as they were backstage it afforded the park's creatives to build scarezones that were as detailed as the houses in these select areas.

The largest scarezone built to date would be 'Field of Screams' and would be over 2 acres in size. Located between the parks behind 'The Cat in the Hat' attraction the scarezone would use real corn, that as mentioned earlier, was being specifically grown on the backlot. 'Welcome to Hillside', the fallen down dilapidated sign read at the entrance to the scarezone. Rotting trees, bales of hay and straw stuffed scarecrows lined the route. Lurking in the actual corn was scarecrow scareactors combined with chainsaw toting farmers, that were selected for their ease of movement between the corn. Chants would ring out from the scareactors of, "Stay off the path that is twisted and worn. Where stalks all grow tattered and torn. For all those who do, stay lost and forlorn. Singing forever the Rhyme of the Corn." The scarezone was so large and so detailed that people were mistaken in believing that the whole installation had been a permanent attraction.

There was however one issue that the scarezones had to combat this year, and none more so than that of the cornfields of this scarezone - the hurricane season. Florida had received a battering that year from various weather events from the season, though not all reached the shores of Florida, the Atlantic area did produce: 15 tropical storms, 9 hurricanes and 6 major hurricanes over category 3. And by the time the event had started, the Central Florida area had received four hurricanes which had pummeled the parks and affected visitor numbers, especially those from the local area and neighboring states. Great effort was placed to attract this important demographic as some 100,000 Florida residents registered with the Orlando/Orange County Convention & Visitors Bureau[5] website were offered specially priced tickets in an aid to get the locals back in the parks, due to the storm issues of the time. And although the storms battered the cornfields in the first few weeks, and a lot had been damaged during the summer, the scarezone was repaired before a welcome reprieve was seen when the storms eased off in mid-October.

The next big scarezone was 'Fright Yard' and it was located again between the parks behind the Poseidon's Fury attraction. Universal billed the house as, "An ominous industrial landscape of rusty trucks, stacked freight containers, and burning buses, The Fright Yard is infested with the worst society has to offer. You suddenly find yourself caught between "survivor clans" where The Demented lie in wait for The Twisted and both tribes are waiting for you. Armed with chainsaws and flame-throwers, they hide, lurk, and stalk guests in this heavy metal maze. Even with police choppers hovering above, this is a twisted and terrifying turf war that has no rules." The area, though slightly smaller than the cornfields of the other dual park scarezone, was in fact much larger than most of the scarezones that had been seen up to this point; it was also extremely detailed. Large faux-buildings and fake train overpasses were erected and then partially burnt down, covered in graffiti or broken-down to show the chaos of a town where mob-rule was in existence. Burnt out cars, industrial waste and civic infrastructure items were left scattered and broken in the streets. Again affording its unique location, the park's creatives could build sets and props that could be left in situ ready for detailing to be added. They also, for the very first time, decorated certain props within the scarezone with the usernames of the fan communities from the various fan websites for the event; a sort of nod to the fans for all they do in helping to publicize the event online (they also added the names in discreet locations within the website). Effectively these two scarezones were like additional houses, such was the level of detail and the ability to explore them that had been created by the Art and Design department.

Two other scarezones were seen this year, including a return of 'Midway of the Bizarre' located this time in The Boneyard of the studios park and 'Port of Entry' located as the name suggests at the front of the Islands park. The former was very much like the scarezones that had been seen in the Amity area of the park at past events, though some new additions were seen. The latter zone was a mixture of lighting props and electrical devices that were removable and thus suffered no damage in the storms. Fake bolts of lightning were played out where scareactors would collectively run and hide; a tactic that seem 'all too close to home' considering the battering that the Central Florida residents had received at the time.

Seven houses had been constructed this year, with rumors of an eighth extreme house surfacing again, this as in previous years proved to nonexistent. The seven houses however would prove to be very popular with a knitted together theme of 'bad luck' and 'Friday 13th' attached to each house. Anticipation for the houses was built via the internet this year where the houses could be presented and unveiled like never before. Building on the feedback from the previous year, a website with full 'Flash' based animations was constructed to highlight the backstories of each house, to show the characters that might lurk within and the stories that had brought them together. Early on in the development of the event it was always key to the Park's Creatives to create detailed and sometime elaborate back stories to enable guests to be taken into the worlds they were presenting, and no better way of starting this journey then by releasing tidbits and clues via the site to build this anticipation. As the event unraveled to highlight the houses, so did the media receive information for publication, the billboards were put up, posters were released and for the first time elaborate house specific queue videos were made, all designed to tell the respective story and move the narrative on. The latter in fact proved very popular, as in the previous years' queue videos had been just collections of clips to ready guests before entering whereas this time specially created videos were made teasing guests as to the impending doom that they were about to meet. And it was the first house that had the most detailed video which would quickly grow to be the most anticipated.

'Castle Vampyre' was built in Soundstage 23 which is a large stage for a large house. The house was so large, that it actually had staircases and elevators installed. With such an asset built as this the park's creative set about creating a 'Blair Witch' like documentary that could be screened in the queue for great effect. The video which is about 8 minutes in full length shows a frightened woman accessing the forgotten castle before ultimately facing her doom just as the camera's film would and by burning-up. Inside the various rooms were decorated to represent every popular vampire from folklore and movie history (though not specifically tied to any franchise). The gothic castle façade would lead to rooms filled with caskets to areas where humans were being surgically farmed for their blood, to a 'fang-tastic' disco rave with scantily clad vampires, to more well know vampires such as the vicious Nosferatu vampire, to the black and white gothic Dracula, to a leather clad 'Blade' looking vampire squad to just gruesome man-monster bats hanging from the ceiling. In total there were exactly 22 different types of vampire lurking within the house. The backstory being that every 13 years the various sections of 'vampire-dom' meet to literally hangout at the castle, whilst guests are drafted in to explore the goings on. The tag line of the event had been 'What's your breaking point?', for which Universal and its 22 selected types of vamps were eager to find out, in a house that pulled no punches.

The next house up was 'Horror in Wax' which was located nearby in Soundstage 20. Universal billed the house as "The classic monsters themselves are all here... carved in wax, sculpted in resin and frozen in paraffin... perfectly preserved at the very moment tragedy struck. But this twisted enterprise was not abandoned - instead it became home to a deranged menagerie of the bizarre who lure guests inside for purposes that will become terrifyingly clear." The website of the event also told the tale of Gunter Dietze[7] who had mysteriously died shortly after creating the wax museum that was to be explored at the event. The house contained various mutant wax like creatures, the classic Universal monsters in wax form and various past guests to the attraction which had been partly covered in wax thusly suffering various burns and deformities.

'Horror in Wax' shared its soundstage with 'Hellgate Prison', which was another house which utilized the queue video technique to great effect. Universal billed the house as, "Warden Robert L. Strickland's monument to himself where paying visitors suddenly find themselves lost and alone inside the penitentiary's cellblocks, corridors, and secret chambers... alone with a prison population of insane inmates, crazed convicts, and convicted criminals with nothing to lose before they walk the 'last mile' to sit on top of Old Smokey, the world's most excruciatingly painful electric chair." It was this chair which had been made into the centerpiece of the experience, where a prop chair, sparks, bangs of light and a fake electrical current would be violently injected into a faux scareactor to give the appearance of electrocution; the sight was horrific and proved that Universal was keen to keep pushing the boundaries further and further.

Hellgate Prison featured a storyline of a prison out of control, prisoners run amuck and guards were left beaten and bruised throughout. The house included: a visitation room where prisoners behind glass threw phones at the glass and taunted guests with abuse, a demolished sick bay, a laundry room, a toilet scene (which was similar to the gross-out scene from Shadybrook in the previous year), and a boiler room with burned remnants of former guards and prisoners. The house concluded with guests entering into a multi-pathed labyrinth of chainmail fences where people often got lost and separated from their respective groups. Angry and aggressive inmates would shout abuse and throw items at the fences, combined with search lights and sirens which disorientated people. The house courted controversy due to its adult themes and use of simulated death, but it wasn't the only aspect which received criticism.

The event's mascot this year was a bald inmate of a mental health facility that had been put into a straitjacket due his possible murderous intentions or his lack of ability to handle the horrific aspects of the event that had been presented to him; either way, the mascot which was featured in nearly all the marketing depicted a man suffering from mental health issues. This generated a fair amount of controversy at the time where people were quick to point out Universal's insensitivity to the issue of mental health. "Universal's public-relations department calls the promotion "lighthearted" and says it never meant to offend anyone. But we are offended and angry. Kate Hale[4] was the president and CEO of the National Mental Health Associations of Florida at the time and she was quoted as saying, "Universal's public-relations department calls the promotion 'lighthearted' and says it never meant to offend anyone. But we are offended and angry." Towards the end of the event on October 30th a small silent protest was conducted outside of the studios park. The media made light of the issue and brushed it off as 'they should be protesting at the increased ticket prices' rather than the innocent use of this mascot. Regardless of the impact that the mascot had made on the event, the character would not return as mascot or event icon ever again.

The next house built at the event was 'Ghost Town' and it was located within Soundstage 22. Universal billed the house as "Strangled by gold fever, the violent town of Lightning Gulch disappeared in a fierce thunderstorm that swallowed up the settlement and all its ill-fated souls. Today there is no trace of the Gulch... except when vicious storms rage, once again revealing all of the buildings and the tortured ghosts that lurk in its streets, saloons, and alleyways. Still desperate to protect long lost treasure, these wretched spirits remain blinded by the lust for gold and enraged by greed."[3] A first for the event in that the house featured a western setting which the park creatives were eager to build. Universal on the West coast had a long tradition of making western movies, so-much-so that sets built for the classic westerns of the past are still sitting on their backlot to this day. A miniature town of worn-out timber clad buildings was assembled with gun-toting zombie-like cowboys with mummified call girls spread throughout the knitted rooms and scenes.

Located in the former Hercules attraction building, Universal built 'Horror Nights Nightmares'. A series of rooms were created showcasing the popular recent past icons that the event had created. Jack, the Caretaker, the Director and Eddie were all presented within the house. Jack had his infamous photo booth contained with the house, likewise the Director had a newly reimagined morgue to experiment within and Eddie finally had the lion share of the latter part of the house where he could chase guests in a mini-mockup of the 'Run' house corridors that had been built for him (but not used by him) in 2001.

The next house offered this year was 'Deadtropolis' and it was located in the Earthquake Queue building. The house was Universal's first full zombie house which unofficially tied into the events of the Universal remake movie 'Dawn of the Dead' which had been released in March of that year, where scenes from the movie were actually played in the queue to ramp up the anticipation for the horrors contained within. Entering via a quarantine guests were bombarded by zombies at all different levels of zombification, much like in the popular movie. Soon guests would be exploring streets lined with crashed vehicles, to domestic settings like houses and garages with hiding and distracting zombies (like the vomiting one in the house). Moving on guests enter onto the openness of the streets where dead homeless people minus their brains lay in the streets, soon guests enter into China Town before an escape alley leads the guests out of the house. TVs and monitors line the house detailing to guests to not get infected that just one bite or scrape could infect you instantly; so with one fine cheeky scare the event's creatives installed a dripping water pipe above that would drip water onto each guest's heads. A final scareactor would announce to guests that they had survived the house but were now unfortunately infected!

The final house offered this year was 'Disorientorium' and built within the underused Carnage Warehouse. The light-hearted house this year which featured a series of scary yet comical scenes that were a welcome reprieve compared to the horrors of the other houses. The house's story was that it was supposedly a side-show carnival like fun house that had been built by an outside company. The first scene was a return of the spinning tunnel filled with stars and moons which led into an area where camouflaged scareactors in black and green costumes were lurking. This would be followed on by a house of mirrors where the popular 'Treaks and Foons' characters from the past year had returned to jump out on guests. The house would end with a return to the tunnel effect where guests would have to crouch down to exit whilst scareactors would reach out from all sides of the walls and ceiling.

The parade was back this year. It had also been completely overhauled to contain new floats. The floats along with the houses had been designed this year using state-of-the-art computer aided design programs (CAD) which allowed the event's creative teams to build the houses on the computers and then simulate walkthroughs. So proud of the addition and the its ability to aid in the business of designing the best scares, Universal released a video to the internet this year detailing how it aided in house and parade design. The parade had a castle and ship float designed that were extremely detailed, like never before, when some had hypothesized was due to the use of CAD. Bill and Ted[2] were also back this year, with popular themes and characters including: the Olsen twins, the Austin Powers characters, Michael Jackson (with lampooning his issues of the day) and Paris Hilton. There was also a showing of 'The Rocky Horror Picture Show' (the movie) which was projected continuously onto screens on one of the streets of the New York area, which marked the first time the popular movie had been seen at the event.

Though occurring this year but not about this year, the event became award winning for the very first time. The local press ran articles of the event's success, "Remember those creepy television advertisements for Universal Orlando's Halloween Horror Nights, the ones that featured Caretaker, the skeletal mortician, inspecting an assortment of scalpels and other painful-looking instruments? The chilling ad campaign has received an Effie Award from the New York American Marketing Association." The Association named the park's brave step in moving the event from one park to another and in attracting guests when other park's nationally had struggled since 9/11. The association also noted the resort's fortunes in increasing attendance, which had risen a huge 64 percent in 2002[1].

'The Crowds are back' read the headlines in the local press[8]. Overall attendance figures for the year showed that the Central Florida area attracted an additional 8% more visitors than it had in the previous year. The newly constructed 'The Mummy' ride which had replaced 'Kongrontation' that year and the highly successful Halloween Horror Nights event had been directly attributed to the overall increase in attendance. Todd Pack in the local Sentinel wrote, "Revenge of the Mummy and an expanded Halloween Horror Nights helped lift its attendance 14 percent to 6.7 million." The gamble for Universal to spread the event over the two parks and increase the scares had paid off. At a time when most parks and resorts around the country were only seeing small and modest increases in their attendance, Universal was significantly beating the local figure. Universal's addition of a new ride linked to a highly successful multi-million dollar franchise and the expansion of the popular event were directly attributed to this third and fourth quarter success. Noticing that anticipation could be built with a detailed story, which could be presented and teased to the audience through marketing (though specifically through the website), Universal decided that next time they would push the narrative even further and take the event where it had never been before.

Notes:

[1] Orlando Sentinel Aug 9, 2004
[2] Bill and Ted Fan Club
[3] Park map for the event
[4] Orlando Sentinel Oct 15, 2004
[5] Orlando Sentinel Oct 13, 2004
[6] Orlando Sentinel Oct 27, 2004
[7] Halloween Horror Nights website 2004
[8] Orlando Sentinel Dec 14, 2004

"We've now permanently installed a door to the globe in case of anymore future downpours of sharks…"

Halloween Horror Nights: Tales of Terror

No one will live happily ever after…

The mission statement for Halloween Horror Nights 2005 was to present an event where guests were taken on a journey into a new world where every show, zone and house would be linked and knitted together, like never before. However, this endeavor would not be plain sailing and would ultimately be presented differently from how it was planned originally.

The dual-park situation was extremely popular and helped to ease crowds from the Islands park, that in places did bottle-neck and cause operational issues with public footfall flow. So the idea to retain the dual-park use was kept, at least areas of the backlot not open to guests could be opened up and the massive soundstages could be used. Initially two icons were planned, one that would represent each park. 'Fate' would represent the studios where games of chance would be installed and a variety of different paths would be offered. The character would be a blind woman who would be clutching cards and dice to empathize the point. The other icon would represent the Islands park and be called 'Darkness', where a turn-left only sign would be deployed where guests would follow a darkened path with a more straight forward story-like experience would be offered. Unfortunately, due to a variety of reasons, the concept was dropped early on.

The next concept, which ultimately was accepted and used at the event would tell a tale of 'Terra Cruentus'. Terra Cruentas would be a land ruled by the Terra Queen, who was planned to be the event's icon. In this newly created world, human blood, bones and flesh would be the world's only source creation, so a never-ending cycle of sacrifice would have to be played out around the park, but particularly at the Port of Entry. A show named 'The Terra Throne' at the entrance to the Islands park contained within a scarezone called 'Terra Guard Run' would collect and gather members from each house and zone to partake in the sacrificing show. Blood from the victims would be taken for distribution in the Gorewood Forest area of the park (around Jurassic Park) where it would be given to the ground in the aim of producing iron. Likewise, the bones would be buried for this purpose too and the flesh would be collected to feed the demons and minions of the land. The iron that was created would be collected nightly to add to the Terra Throne, an evolving throne where the Terra Queen would sit to rule her empire and for more victims to be held and sacrificed, thus creating a cycle that would be needed to be undertaken to maintain the strange world.

The above tale was presented to the bosses of the resort and accepted for use. Unfortunately it was a little later on and full development was underway when some of the same executives who had green-lit the overall thematic left the organization[1]. New executives came in and knowing that the event was now responsible for year-on-year attendance growth, they wanted to ensure the overall theme was sufficient for the expectations they had. The new executives decided to leave the planning that had been undertaken as it was but requested that a new park icon was selected. Fearing that the Terra Queen was perhaps a little too sexy (and not creepy enough) or not sufficient to build an event around for the purposes of marketing, a new icon would be selected. So as to not ruin the carefully planned story that had been developed, the Terra Queen would remain as the event's mascot but a new icon would be developed. Various ideas were considered when the event's creatives decided on creating a character named, 'The Storyteller'. The new icon that the marketing would center on, would be an evil old lady, almost witch like, that could be presented as the narrator of this whole world's story and as the story takes places within different dimensions and different times, having a character like that would generally add to the knitted together thematic that the park wanted to go for this year. As well as appearing in all the marketing for the event, she would also appear in one of the houses and at the Port of Entry and not anywhere else. The website was built around her and her stories, it teased the audience of the site every week with the frequent small updates that started in the summer and gradually unraveled all the stories before the event commenced in October.

It was then in August of that year that the New York Times and Orlando Sentinel ran mutual articles about the up-coming event and the need to fulfil the 1,000 vacancies that were required for the event. The largest story ever told by the event, required the largest influx of cast and crew which had ever been seen up until this point. The Sentinel reported, "Think you have what it takes to be a professional in the scare business? Then Universal Orlando might be looking for you. Every Tuesday through Sept. 13, the theme park is holding casting calls for 1,000[3] performers to frighten visitors during Halloween Horror Nights 15." The articles in both papers stated that the park was looking to recruit stilt-walkers, celebrity impersonators, scareactors and street performers for the month long event. Anticipation really grew at this time, knowing that the event was once again making national headlines for the right reasons.

The opening night began and the opening scaremonies began where the Terra Queen and her minions were presented to the audience. Additional pyro-effects and fireworks were used to celebrate the fact that the event had started. The show would remain nightly and alter slightly, with the main purpose of the show to tie the aspects of the event together and to show a 'live' human sacrifice on stage. The final show of the event would see the humans replaced by the Terra Queen herself, where she would be sacrificed. The sinister monks would proclaim as part of the legend of the Queen that she would return in 15 years' time to present her world again (so expect to see her in 2020?). As well as setting up the narrative for the event, the show would tease and highlight to guests as to the horrors that awaited.

The first house that most guests this year attended was 'Demon Cantina' and was located in the Carnage Warehouse behind Marvel Superhero Island. The house would be one of the most popular for this year. Loosely inspired by the legendary 1996 movie 'From Dusk till Dawn', the house would be the guests' own adventure into the cantina of this world, where instead of vampires, demons of all kinds would come to feast and drink within the bar setting. Feasting on the flesh provided by the Queen and drink the blood of foolish mortals who had stumbled into their realm. The website billed the house as, "Mankind tempts fate if anyone is foolish enough to step inside the Demon Cantina, flagrant trespass on the turf of the ferocious Bone Choppers of Ironbone Gorge. Celebrating their own last Season of the Queen, the meanest of the Queen's Black Guard enlist chainsaw-wielding maniacs to provide entertainment and seductive creatures to supply amusement... and all take one last taste of sweet warm Bloodberry wine." The faux-wine in fact would actually go on to be sold at the event in specialty glasses, available at various re-themed outlets for the event. Something that Universal had never done before but would visit again once more when Hogsmead would open where they would sell the ever popular 'Butterbeer' – was this an early inspiration for the popular drink? The theme was diesel-punk and it featured various victims in various states of distress where demons aplenty would appear to make even the sternest of guests jump-out-of-their-skin. The house ended with the puking drunk fake scareactor placed outside the house. The same prop had been seen in past houses.

The next house on the journey would take guests in to a forestry setting (Gorewood Forest) on Jurassic Park island where 'The Skool' would be presented. The house would be a boarding school for the new demons, monsters and mutants that were being bred and trained to take over the processes at the other houses at the event. Smaller actors were used, all with masks on as the Halloween was not just celebrated on the one night but the whole of October at this ghoul school. No teachers were seen in the house, as guests followed a path around all the various classrooms and dormitories. The house would again like the opening show of the event, be a teaser for the monsters that were about to be presented in the other houses.

The next house in this area would also prove to be extremely popular and would ensure the creatures contained within would be back at the event time-after-time. The house located in the expansive Jurassic Park Discovery Center was 'Body Collectors' and the house was huge. Set in a Victorian-like industrial environment, the house would serve as a warehouse for processing the victims of the opening show. Various rooms would be presented showing the victims being dismembered and their organs, flesh, bones and other items being harvested for movement to the areas of the park where they were required. Filling the house were these silent white faced, smartly dressed creatures that had fixed grins on them as they worked on the victims. The creatures were called 'The Collectors' and they were directly inspired characters that appeared in the then very popular TV series 'Buffy the Vampire Slayer'. They appeared in only one episode entitled 'Hush' where the voiceless monsters were called 'The Gentlemen'; they had been deployed within the episode to cut out the tongues and murder anyone that spoke to them, so the episode became very popular for the quirky use of no talking throughout the episode. One fan-favorite house had the Collectors ripping a backbone from a victim tied to a table to great theatrical effect. The popularity of the house and the regular 3 hours+ that the queue maintained on most nights ensured that the characters of the house would be surely back for future events.

Both scarezones on the island of Gorewood Forest would be supported by 'Cemetery Mines' scarezone that would see a collection of mutants scaring guests as they chased them from hiding in the entrances to the many mines that were scattered about.

The next house on the journey would be 'Terror Mines' and for an event first, it would be placed inside the 'Poseidon's Fury' attraction. Walking the same path as the attraction, guests would be taken into a mine setting where mutants called gnome-rats would be lurking around every corner. The house also had the first novel use of lighting. The park's creatives had explored the idea of giving guests the use flashlights to use in the houses, though fearing they may unwittingly be used as weapons (by accident) by guests or being stolen outright, the idea was never implemented. Instead the idea of giving every 12th guest a helmet with flashlight attached would be brought into play within the house and little other lighting would be used (the helmet could also be counted out as they were handed to guests to prevent theft). The effect worked well for guests who had the helmet or who were with the guest with the helmet, though less well if you were that 11th person since a helmet had been given out. The helmets would then be controlled by sensors that would automatically switch them off at certain points or back on to heighten the scares. The extremely dark house took guests around the various areas of the mine where the effects of the house had been altered to accommodate the mine theme. This also concluded at the water vortex tunnel where light and water were used in equal measure to disorientate guests. Outside, the scarezone of 'The Fire Pits' saw the entrance to the ride and surrounding areas transformed into a medieval village complete with peasants, knights and some-how, the Chainsaw Drill Team.

The next house would be 'Cold Blind Terror'[2] and it would be located inside Soundstage 20. The house would feature a polar landscape that was both extremely cold (the air-conditioning had been ramped up) and the lightness of the house strongly controlled, this created a cold deep and dark house. Universal billed the house as, "Bone-chilling cold and blind terror numb the senses as one cannot see, one cannot hear… and one cannot escape. In and out of total darkness, mankind find themselves shivering from both fear and the icy cold blackness. Strange sounds split the darkness, but one cannot be sure the source… one cannot be sure what lurks behind… one cannot be sure of what lies ahead. One cannot be sure if they'll ever see light again." Many complained that the house was less themed than the others but instead of a gory backstory it was the use of the cold air and lack of light presented in a confined space that was center stage for the use of scaring the guests.

Around the corner from the above house was 'Blood Ruins' in Soundstage 22. Universal billed the house as, "Still ruled by defrocked monks, the ruin at the old Blood Abbey serves as prison, hospital and asylum to a population of fresh mankind "donors". In centuries before its walls began to crumble, the Blood Abbey was the place where terrible tools of torture were invented. Now these instruments have found new use as Ore Mongers fanning the flames of Dragon Forge demand a never-ending supply of blood for the tempering of the Blade." The house was originally planned to be located in the 'Dueling Dragons' attraction's queue building. Pre-Harry Potter expansion, the queue building was a gothic setting that had been highly themed to build expectation for the ride ahead; a medieval dungeon like setting located within the bowels of a castle deep in the forest would hold guests before they chose sides and rode the dragon. This was all changed and re-themed to Harry Potter in 2010, however back in 2005 the area would have served as a perfect location for a house (much like the Poseidon's Fury attraction building). However, when the executives changed, so did the use of the building. Park bosses were not happy that one of the most popular rides of the park would be offline for the duration of the event when empty soundstages were sitting there waiting to be used. And although it cost more to move the house to the soundstage (originally much of the original queue setting would have been untouched), the house had to be hastily redesigned from the ground-up. Creatives countered this issue of sets that weren't as detailed as originally planned by ramping up the level of makeup to the scareactors within. As the story unfolded it told a tragic tale of a rampant bubonic plague that was spreading amongst the villagers and monks alike. Makeup artists from the park attached fake buboes and ulcers to the characters and created deformed mutant like appendages to increase the gore factor of the house.

The final house presented was 'Where Evil Hides' located in Soundstage 18. This house would act as the newly appointed icon's house with the character of 'The Storyteller' appearing at certain times throughout. Universal billed the house as, "Beyond Maldaken Pass lie the very places in mankind's worst nightmares where night terrors are real. The places where the monsters live, the skeletons are stored and the bodies are hidden. The places in the imagination where terror plays hide-and-seek with the unfortunate dreamer. Once inside, one faces all of those dark hallways, passages and doors that open to exactly what one had hoped they did not." The house told the tale of a psycho-killer on the loose within the setting of a suburban house. A white faced, boiler suit wearing killer would be seen jumping out at guests throughout (from cupboards, under beds, through windows etc.) whereas 'The Storyteller' would pop up at times to move the narrative along.

The attractions that were open this year included: The Amazing Adventures of Spider-Man, Dr. Doom's Fearfall, Storm Force Accelatron, Incredible Hulk Coaster, The Cat In The Hat, One Fish, Two Fish, Red Fish, Blue Fish, Caro-Seuss-el, Dudley Do-Rights Ripsaw Falls, Jurassic Park River Adventure, The Flying Unicorn and Dueling Dragons. The following attractions operated on peak nights (mostly Fridays and Saturdays): Twister...Ride it Out, Revenge of the Mummy, Jimmy Neutron's Nicktoon Blast and Shrek 4-D. Bill and Ted were back this year and the show featured characters from 'Family Guy', 'Star Wars' and the new Tim Burton movie 'Charlie and the Chocolate Factory' which had been released in July of that year. There was also a very memorable moment from the show where Ronald McDonald and The (Burger) King have a fight scene.

This year was also memorable for the staff of the event as it received no higher praise than winning the inaugural best Halloween event for 2005 from 'Amusement Today's' Golden Ticket Awards. 'Amusement Today' had been running the celebrated awards since 1998 but had only until this year added the category of Halloween. The judges of the event were extremely impressed with the level of detail within the houses and streets and how the whole event was tied together under one narrative.
Notes:

[1] Orlando Sentinel Oct 12, 2005
[2] Park map 2005
[3] Orlando Sentinel Aug 22, 2005
[4] Orlando Sentinel Jul 25, 2005

"At the Monster's Café: "I'll have the spare ribs please…""

A new era was coming…

A final area of note occurring during 2005 was the possible acquirement of rights to certain characters that would eventually make a big impact on the event. A small article[1] in the Sentinel ran on July 25th with the headline, "Big-screen horror characters come to life; Orlando firm teams up with New Line Cinema to create film-based haunted houses." The article told the story of how New Line Cinema was starting to look for licensing partners to utilize their recently obtained 'fearsome threesome' of Freddy Krueger, Jason Voorhees and Leatherface and their respective franchises of 'A Nightmare on Elm Street', 'Friday the 13th' and 'The Texas Chainsaw Massacre'.

Many discussions were held on a plethora of ideas, from video games to clothing, though New Line Cinema was very keen to bring the icons to a theme park or haunt attraction. Later on in November the company showcased a number of prototypes at the annual conference of the International Association of Amusement Parks and Attractions in Atlanta, where real costumes and latex masks had been made using profiles of Robert Englund's actual face. And although nothing was to be seen of the characters in 2006, it wasn't until 2007 that the characters would finally be released on the world…

(Author's note: but please don't skip the next chapter though!)

[1] Orlando Sentinel Jul 25, 2005

Halloween Horror Nights: Sweet 16

"Horror comes home!"

Halloween Horror Nights 16 was planned as the event's first ever retrospective event. All the best and brightest from the previous 16 years would be showcased in all seven houses, three (well four) shows and (four) scarezones. Official news of the park's intentions came in July of that year when the media was trip-fed tidbits of information and that the event would be a celebration of the overall event's brand. Slightly before that in June of that year Universal altered the archives and placeholder website in favor of a new teaser site which would over the coming months build anticipation amongst the viewers by releasing small background stories, faux press clippings and the like. Tickets for the event officially went on sale on July 14[1] for $59.95 plus tax[1]; hoping that select days may sell-out again it would be a direct aim to get the tickets out there very early once more (in fact it was exactly 11 days earlier than when they had launched the tickets in the previous year).

Along with the various pieces of information released over the summer, it was also officially announced that the event would return to where it began, dubbing the new event as "horror comes home!" It was also around September 1st that the resort began to start adverting for new recruits to join the army of scareactors needed for the event. Like previously at the Islands park where numbers had increased to a new record of 1,000 members of the cast, it was decided to maintain that number to ramp up the scares for this anniversary style event. Needing people to do the scares in lieu of just relying on props or technology to do the scares (something that Universal's competitors at various locations around the country had done) was something that Universal wanted to highlight. "The scares truly come from the performers," TJ Mannarino[2] of the resort's Art and Design department said. "They can be relentless, or they can be subtle, and you can't get that from technology." Along with the 1,000 performers, the park would utilize hundreds of backstage crew and artisans along with 60 persons to man the makeup and prosthetics department for the month long event. Their driving focus was to bring back the event's icons from the past events, bringing them together to celebrate all that truly scared the most and provided the most chills. "The icons will dominate the entire event from haunted houses to shows," said Mannarino. "It's their world."

An elaborate stage was constructed outside Mel's diner at the top of the

Hollywood section of the park. The stage would provide the opening show of the night called 'The Arrival' and it would play on and off all evening with the aim that at least everyone who was in the park would catch a glimpse of it at some point. The show featured the horned beast himself 'Darkness' from the movie Legend and although not an icon of the event, he had previously featured heavily in the event's parades. As master of ceremony he would bring forth and summon the icons to take center stage, introducing each one. His minions, made up of vampires, weird monks and mutants selected from various scarezones would be on hand to assist. Darkness raising from the ground to the center of the stage would first bring forth the Storyteller who would quickly introduce herself and her house before pulling out a tongue of a victim tied to a chair. Each icon would follow a similar route of introduction before torturing an actor with an elaborate staged magic trick; they would get more gruesome as they went on. Next would be the Director who would promptly electrocute a lady in a bathtub, followed by the Caretaker who would rip the prop organs from a man's chest, a man lying conveniently in a coffin at high level. With the final and most elaborate gruesome act of Jack the Clown placing a man in a giant blender before then switches it on to very bloody and splattering consequences. Once the introductions had been made, a series of fireworks were let-off and the event was officially open.

"Pain is temporary, but film is forever". Which is the creepy catchphrase that ran out of the first house on our journey, that house was 'All Nite Die-In: Take 2', located Sound Stage 23, a sequel house to the Director's popular house of 2003. Incredibly similar in style but with different movies, the Director would take guests on a journey through a drive-in movie theater to visit some of the scariest scenes from motion picture history. One of the first scenes took guests right into the living room and kitchen from the opening scene of the 'Scream' movie with popcorn on the stove ready to explode, with an actress who was extremely similar to Drew Barrymore followed by the relentless 'Ghostface killer' who popped up with knife in various locations within the sympathetic recreation of the set. Other rooms within the house included scenes recreated from 'Hellraiser', 'The Ring' and 'Silence of the Lambs', with the final room being an ensemble of various killers from the previous scenes and other movies to chase the guests out into the street.

'Dungeon Of Terror: Retold' would be the next house and just like in the years past, the original Fright Nights house would be located once more in the Jaws queue building. The house was billed as[3], "In its day, it would lure tourists by the thousands. Now, it is only visited by the occasional lost traveler. Enter the Dungeon of Terror, where mysterious whispers call you deeper into hell. A place where the Teller of Stories demands the undivided attention of her 'guests'. Once you make the mistake of entering the Dungeon, you'll wish you had not because no one can leave until Her story has been told." Introducing the house in her typical rocking chair manner, the Storyteller would collect tickets before sending guests onto a murderous tale of a roadside attraction gone wrong. A souvenir stand, followed by various exhibits and then motel-like rooms saw a gang of mutant inbred weirdos (complete with pig masks) torture and kill various passing travelers, all headed by a buxom lady in a flannel skirt complete with chainsaw. And although the house was pretty unlike the original house of the same name, it fitted its location perfectly and provided some really good scares.

'People Under The Stairs: Under Construction' could see a return for the event's 2nd originally built house from the 1991 movie of the same name and it would be located in a wholly new location for the event. Located in Sprung tent 1 or its official name of 'World Expo Warehouse 1' would see the event construct two sprung tents just for the purposes of Halloween Horror Nights. Utilizing what remained of the original sets plus creating more sets to fill the tented environment, the house would see guests come face-to-face with the freaks of the original movie. Utilizing the same gimmick of the previous year, where every 12th guest would be provided with a helmet with flash light the house would try to pull off the same technique to marginal success. Unlike Poseidon's Fury building where the light could be strictly controlled, the sprung tent would be too illuminated for the effect to work properly throughout, with some guests reportedly leaving the helmets behind half way around the house. One memorable scene from the house, and one that received much praise was a scene where guests where shot with a shotgun that had been filled with water, adding in the special effects, smoke and sound-effects to make the impression that they had actually been shot like in the movie.

Neighboring next to the above house in Sprung tent 2 would be 'Psycho Path: The Return Of Norman Bates'. Which was incidentally the third house ever created for the event back at the start. The original house and motel had long since been demolished to make way for expansions to the Kids' Zone area of the park, and although nothing remained from storage from these large sets, Universal's craftspeople set about recreating an impressive façade that would look wholly reminiscent of the original motel set. The house was billed as "There is a vacancy once again at the legendary Bates Motel. Unlocking the door reveals a portal into the darkest depths of insanity. Your eyes prove to be useless as your mind takes over and leads you through the macabre nightmares of a pathological killer. A killer named Norman Bates." The house used elements from the previous

142

houses that had been presented from the Psycho franchise whereby guests would enter into the motel, see the office and cabin room 1 before descending into a mad world of Norman's mind. Rooms filled with mirror knives and huge eyeballs floating from the ceiling portrayed guests' descent into the mind of Norman Bates. This amalgamation of both respective Norman Bates' houses made for good scares throughout, building up to the final room where disorientating projections, music, soundbites with rows and rows of showers lining the walls filled with knife wielding mothers!

Although the above façade was impressive, nothing could beat the façade and setting of the next house. 'Psychoscareapy: Maximum Madness' was an amazing house that would be Jack's own house this year. The set which was so impressive that many fans of the event petitioned Universal to leave it in situ to remain as a year around attraction and although this didn't happen, no one could deny that it was one of the most impressive sets ever built for the event. Located in huge Soundstage 22 the house was billed as "Shady Brook Hospital has been plagued with rioting inmates off and on for years. These small incidents of chaos have always been resolved quickly and contained with minimal casualty. However, Shady Brook's newest resident is about to change all that. If you think you know insane you don't know Jack. Step inside an asylum where the sideshow is death and the "big top" has padded walls." Setting the house back in Jack's time before he was murdered around the early 20th Century, the designers at Universal studied hospital architectural styles from this time to build an 'Art Deco' looking façade whose design would be seen throughout every room of the house. Rows of padded cells and inmates running amok would lead guests to Jack, complete with straight jack. The inmates would slowly transform into disciples of jacks with similar makeup styles and speech before guests would be inevitably guided to the infamous toilet scene once again.

The next house would see a return for the icon that was never really an icon, that of Eddie. 'Run: Hostile Territory' would be located in the Earthquake queue building and would see our titular host chasing guests chainsaw in tow around tight chainmail corridors within a warehouse style facility for torture. Reminiscent of the recent spate of horror-torture movie that had been released recently, such as 'Hostel', the house would actively portray scenes of deviant acts in the aim of distracting guests before Eddie popped up to chase them into the next room. A booming soundtrack of drum n' bass music combined with orchestra accompaniment with manic laughter was pumped into the house, along with no air-conditioning; this created a house that was hot, humid and loud but was filled with chainsaw chasing maniacs.

The final house would see a welcome return of the Caretaker back in his experimental mortuary in 'Scream House: Resurrection' located in Soundstage 23[8]. The house was billed as "Through blood, bone and ash, evil has risen again. Abandoned for years, this gothic mortuary contains the eternally tormented souls of the Caretaker's victims. Aided by a cultish group of Followers, the Caretaker assures that you will enter on your own two feet, but leave sealed in a casket." The story of the house knitted together the theme of loss and bereavement that played on the main character of the house. Guests were informed that the reason behind his killer ambitions was his searching for a means to bring back to life his departed daughter Cindy. For the first time Universal acknowledged the existence of Cindy and rewrote her backstory to fit in with the character of the Caretaker. No longer portrayed as a crazed torturing killer, the Caretaker was seen as a father struggling to cope with the loss of a loved one – he was still terrifying though! A cemetery was presented near the end of the house, complete with this amazing lightening effect that made guests and scareactors a like jump! Both he and Cindy were seen throughout the house, which was very much like but not the same as the mortuary presented in previous years.

The four scarezones this year consisted of 'Blood Masquerade' which was located in Shrek Alley. The main premise of the scarezone was that the vampires from Castle Vampyre were assembling for a masquerade party and to "renew their vows to a darker power". The zone was nowhere near as brilliant as the previous house and nor was the makeup as intense but it did fill the wide alley well and present some good scares.

Next up in the New York area was 'Deadtropolis: Zombie Siege'. The house was billed as, "A greenish fog crawls in pockets along the streets. Hunched forms cut through the haze slowly. These silhouettes appear human, however the moans and cries they sound chill you to the bone. This is the new reality. A new dynamic has evolved for the phrase "us" and "them": Us being the living and them being zombies. View the haunting sites of a new metropolis populated by the undead. A Deadtropolis." This scarezone was intense! Firstly, Universal decided to increase the total number of scareactors within this zone, they packed it with broken vehicles, disorientating smog and sirens with a very loud soundtrack but secondly, the makeup, the cast had been made up exceptionally well. The disorientating effects combined with the sheer number of zombies per guest was amazing, it was a very well done scarezone. And if the zombies weren't enough there was another huge beast waiting for you at the back of the scarezone...

'Harvest Of The Souls' was located in Central Park and was a repeat of the scarezone that was a sequel scarezone (like the Vampyre scarezone) from the previous year's 'Field of Screams'. The sets were not as detailed as had been the previous year (where acres of corn had been especially grown) but this was met with increased scareactor numbers in this tight winding path. Demented corn-kids and scarecrows lined with the paths with pumpkins and dead trees placed strategically.

'Horror Comes Home' was the final scarezone on our list and was located on Hollywood Boulevard. The park map declared, "Take a macabre walk down memory lane with the haunted sights and sounds of previous Halloween Horror Nights. Keep your camera handy as some of the most infamous characters prowl the streets, looking for prey." Banners lined the street here depicted every year of the event in anniversary, selected scareactors from the past 16 years had been selected to line the streets and provide the scares. All the major characters were there, with the exception of the Cryptkeeper.

The dynamic time travelling dudes were back again in 'Bill & Ted's Excellent Halloween Adventure', this time taking place for the first time in the newly refurbished 'Fear Factor Stage'. Popular references this year included: the highly popular (at the time) TV series of '24', 'Deal or No Deal', 'The Da Vinci Code', 'Mission Impossible' and a remarkable lookalike of David Hasselhoff[4].

Rising from the ground at the back of the New York scarezone like a mechanical phoenix from the ashes was the myth and monster himself, the 30 ton Robosaurus, who had return for this year after a 12 year absence. Although the show and location were also exactly the same as years past, it did for the first time tie into the scarezone's narrative. The story presented in the show, was that to stop the zombie uprising the plucky robot with marines team had been sent into the area to wipe away all the living dead. So as well as the chaos of the usual show whereby several cars are crushed and the like, it also went onto breath fire and move around to show its clearing of the gathered zombies. It was actually the best performance of the robot at the event and was incredibly popular most nights. Show director J Michael Roddy[5] said at the time, "Robosaurus was a big hit in the early '90s, in the infancy of our event, I think people love Robosaurus because it's something real. It's not a trick. It's a 40-foot-tall, mechanical dinosaur that eats cars. There's no trickery. No illusion. When we were looking at the things that we could bring back, Robosaurus was at the top of our list."

Another show that was presented this year, though not officially as it was going through some tests at the time was the newly installed Universal 360 globes that had been placed as various locations around the lagoon. The nightly show was started this year as an aim to keep guests in the park until closing to see the special show. It was these giant orbs that were used at various times during the event showing clips of the event's icons and various clips from recent horror movies. The orbs standing 30ft tall by 36ft wide would present a whole 360 viewing screen that could be seen from many of the location around the lagoon. Combined with lasers, pyro-effects and fireworks the film introduced by The Director (of course!) was a fascinating use of this technology.

Though RIP tours of the park, where guests are guided in both exclusive and non-exclusive groups around all the shows and attractions each night had been introduced in the previous year, this year Universal introduced for the first time the fan favorite tour of 'Unmasking the Horror Tour'[6]. Originally costing just $35 and limited to 15 guests, the tour would see two to three of Universal's great tour guides taking guests for a 'lights-on' tour of three selected houses (usually two from the soundstages and one from the backlot or 'hacklot' as it was known this year). The two hour tour, held not during the event's nights but during the day, would lead guests around the three houses where guests would be imparted with all the back stories and shown all the details that can easily be missed in between all the carnage and scares. Often members of the resort's Art and Design department would be on-hand to answer a few select questions and guests would very often see workmen fixing-up the houses from the previous night's damage. The tours were so popular that they were promptly brought back for the following year.

Also premiering this year was a new pass for passholders to the park[7]. The 'Premier Pass' was rolled out for the mega fans of Universal. There were aspects to the pass, including all the benefits of the other annual passes along with two-park freedom, select valet and no additional charge, free entry into this year's Halloween Horror Nights on all of the nonpeak nights. Although the pass was not as popular as management had hoped for, it did increase the park's attendance for non-peak nights.

Notes:

[1] Orlando Sentinel Jul 17, 2006
[2] Orlando Sentinel Sep 1, 2006

[3] Park map 2006
[4] Bill and Ted Fan Club
[5] Orlando Sentinel Oct 12, 2006
[6] Orlando Sentinel Sep 29, 2006
[7] Orlando Sentinel Oct 2, 2006
[8] Production die-aries from original event 2006 website

Hitch: "I rode that ride by going North by Northwest from here, it made me go into a Frenzy, causing me to get Vertigo and now I feel like a Psycho..."

Halloween Horror Nights: Carnival of Carnage

Choose Thy Fear!

The year 2007 was for many a year of change for not only the event but also the resort. Two iconic rides ('Earthquake' and 'Back to the Future') would both close within 14 months of each other to make way for new attractions. Both the addition of brand new lands for Harry Potter's universe and Springfield USA (from 'The Simpsons') would be announced this year, along with executive changes and other organizational changes. Most of these revisions and reinvestments were due to the fall in attendance that had been seen overall for the year 2006 for both parks, however this did not reflect on Halloween Horror Nights, which actually increased its attendance and managed to again create a bump in attendance for the fourth quarter of 2006. The local Sentinel reported at the time, "Last year, the company reported a record gate of nearly 500,000 visitors for those Halloween Horror Nights, accounting for almost one of every 12 visitors to Universal Studios"[7]. Universal Orlando President Bill Davis also said at the time, "We're very pleased with our fourth-quarter results and will do everything we can to maintain momentum, we're seeing increases in attendance from Florida, our overall U.S. market, South America and the Caribbean. And, like the rest of our industry, we're hard at work creating aggressive marketing programs we expect to help us in the UK." And everything he could do, he did, as the resort announced that the event would again be bigger and better than it had ever been before.

New Line Cinema, founded in 1967 by Robert Shaye, is an independent film studio owned by Warner Bros which had started out distributing art-house and educational films to colleges and schools across the country. It later went on to undertake less distribution and therefore concentrate on more of its own productions. The studio focused on lesser known talent and allowing them to experiment and flourish to mixed success. This business plan remained much the same through the 1970s and 80s where one movie even went on to receive a coveted Academy Award. It wasn't until 1976 that the company began making full-length major motion pictures, their first was a movie called 'Stunts'. The action thriller did mildly well and allowed the company to invest in three further motion pictures all based around the horror and sci-fi genres, which again all under performed to company expectations. It wasn't until 1984's release of 'A Nightmare on Elm Street' and its subsequent sequels that proved to be highly successful at the box-office, conferring the title of 'The House that Freddy Built'. This continued into the 1980s when the third film in the Freddy franchise managed to make nearly 10 times the budget for the movie back for the studio. It was also around the late 1980s hot on the success of this movie in 1987 that by 1988 the company had acquired the right to use the characters from the 'Texas Chainsaw Massacre' films[1]. Leatherface was later joined by Jason and co when the company acquired the rights to the popular 'Friday 13th' franchise in about 1989. The company went on to continue the same lucrative mix of reasonable budget sizes to these cult franchises releasing them to good box-office returns for many years.

Long before New Line had acquired the rights to use Jason, they had tried to get a 'Freddy vs. Jason' movie off the ground. Many fans, particularly those who regularly attended the various horror and fantasy related conventions wrote to the respective owners of the icons to register their approval for such a move. In fact due to various owners of Jason and varying degrees of success for subsequent sequels, it would take 15 years of 'development hell' before the project could be realized; New Line buying the Jason franchise was the true catalyst to the whole project. During these 15 years it would see $6 million spent on eighteen unused scripts and over a dozen writers all working on it. But the toils of the past productions were not in vain as the movie was finally finished in 2003 when the movie went on to make $114 million at the box-office[2]. Also during this time the 'Texas' franchise was fully rebooted by New Line in 2006 which also went on to make solid box-office returns. The three characters were exceedingly 'hot' during this period and had made a real comeback from their earlier successes of the 1980s to draw in popular audiences around the world by 2007. And as mentioned in 2005's chapter of this book, New Line, a progressive forwarding thinking company was also looking to expand the popular characters' appeal to not just movies but to other mediums; at the time licensing agreements for: toys, comics, video games were all considered and some were put into production. It wasn't until 2006 that the company officially licensed the use of the icons to Universal Studios for use in Halloween Horror Nights.

The official announcement came on June 27th, 2007 that the three icons of horror would be officially joining the event on both coasts[3], with the event taking place in Orlando in the Studios and not at Islands of Adventure[5]. It would be the first time the cinema had officially granted the rights to use the characters in a theme park (though many had tried to bring them to events and park before). "We're obviously extremely excited about it. It's going to be a great addition to what is already a great event, we're thrilled!" Jim Timon, Universal's senior vice president of entertainment had said at the time. Universal promised at the time that they were extremely excited about taking the three characters and exploring where the park's creative minds could take them. It was also around this time and just before, that the website for the event updated to show a random field in the middle of nowhere where a coming carnival was about to take place…

Slowly over the coming weeks various vehicles and trucks assembled on the field with some becoming 'clickable', once clickable visitors of the site could work out various puzzles and games to unlock secrets about the upcoming event. It was around this time that various fan websites started to notice increased numbers in memberships to their forums, especially hhnvault.com (which is no longer running). Plucky fans trying to decipher the clues and find solutions to the puzzles would discuss solutions and what the possible items on the site would mean. This ramped up the anticipation from the online communities which combined with the increase of social media interactions at the time (Facebook had reported a 178.38%[4] increase in signups during this period from the year previous!), all led to further conversations and marketing for the event as the online community for the event 'started to explode' in popularity.

Eventually, via the website and various press releases the event's official icon was revealed to be the ever popular Jack the Clown (though unofficially various stores had put out marketing posters before the 'big reveal' date). The story behind the event was fully unraveled and was to be 'The Carnival of Carnage'. The story went that the cold October winds were bringing a dark and sinister carnival to town. Jack, now your ringmaster, has taken hold of the event as he brings together the most diabolical combination of sinister sideshows, a midway of carnage and the most maniacal movie madmen ever, featuring Freddy Krueger, Jason Voorhees and Leatherface, three of the most modern and current horror icons that the silver screen had at the time. It was released that the freakish foursome would be unveiled at a special 'opening scaremonies' show before their official deployment to their own individual houses at the event. They would not however feature on the streets, together (other than in this opening night show) or in any of the other shows; though they did feature together in all the marketing, particularly in a number of popular commercials that showed a man entering the carnival and getting literally accosted by the foursome along with a short sequence showing 'gory-getaway' guests getting attacked at the onsite hotels.

The house count would also be increased this year to eight and instead of having a number of carefully allotted scarezones, this year would feature the park being plunged completely in fear by being one giant scarezone (though technically four to five set scarezones were seen with roaming characters).

Halloween Horror Nights: The Unofficial Story & Guide

The move to increase the street scares and increase the house number was a direct result to crowding within the park and the excessive long queues for the houses that would be expected. Timon went on say, "We're making a good step forward with the lines and the waits. We have added a haunted house, so we have one more haunted house experience to help absorb some capacity. We're also opening up the show stadiums, which will help absorb thousands of people an hour in show capacity."

Along with the scares came five shows. The first of which was the 'Opening Scaremonies' which only ran on the first night of the event. The show featuring a carnival announcer who warmed the audience up by listing the various scareactors who would be present this before introducing our new Ringmaster Jack. Ever the showman, the character jumped on the stage, complete with ringmaster jacket and cane to announce "I'm back", much to the gathered crowd's cheers and clapping. A disheveled looking woman was then pulled on stage, named "Jill" (which is ironic as originally Jack's girlfriend would be called Jill but she was dropped at development stage for this event). Complete with her torn jacket and hastily applied clown makeup, Jill remained frozen on stage in freight as Jack introduced the three icons that everyone had gathered to see. Jill now turned assistant under Jack's instructions turned a number of giant playing card posters to reveal the pictures of the three icons. Once fully revealed, Jack announced "welcome to the carnival of carnage", the crowd cheered and a number of fireworks were let-off. Then suddenly the lights were killed, and a spot light focused on the shivering Jill, with a buzz of chain sounds coming from off-stage, Leatherface himself burst through his poster onto the stage to face Jill. Taking a large swipe at her, she ducked for the monster to disappear into the darkness. Still trembling she ran stage left towards the Jason poster, from which with a burst of energy the 6ft 8 tall Jason came bursting through the poster to the sound of Jill screaming. Swinging his large knife at her, she falls back to the center of stage away from both posters before the chilling Freddy rhyme is played out. Looking on in terror, she is quickly grabbed from behind from Freddy and taken off-stage. The lights go up, the crowd cheers as Jack re-appears to announce that the carnival is now open. Though only appearing on opening night, the show was massively popular and remained online for years after the event for all to see.

The first house inside the event was 'Dead Silence – The Curse of Mary Shaw' which was located in Soundstage 22 and the house would replicate the movie to exacting details. The Universal picture was released in March of 2007 and for many was a commercial flop due to limited success. Released domestically but not in many foreign markets, in fact it didn't even get made into a DVD in the UK until 2010 when reasonable Blu-ray sales in the US prompted the move; the film for many was seen as poorly conceived so nobody expected it to become a haunted house attraction. Created by the same people that brought us the 'SAW' franchise[6], the movie tells the story of a man named Jaime who after receiving a weird package with a doll named Billy inside, witnesses his wife's murder, for whom he believes is caused by Mary Shaw. Destined to find out the truth, Jamie goes to the town of Raven's Fair where the ventriloquist Mary Shaw used to perform and is buried. Shaw had been buried years prior due to cutting the tongue out of a boy who booed her on stage. The psychological chiller starred Ryan Kwanten as Jamie, Amber Valletta as Ella and Donnie Wahlberg as the Detective Jim Lipton. And although the movie was considered a flop by many, the movie would actually be a perfect example from which a truly brilliant haunted house could be devised.

The house began where the main character travels to the town of Raven's Fair at the very cemetery where Shaw was buried. Standing by the gravestone was Walberg's character complete with trench coat and flashlight informing guests to not go any further, to turn back now. Eventually guests made their way through into the mortuary and then into the basement from the movie before eventually following the path through to the theater where it all started. A neat cat-walk trick was played on guests whereby the illusion of being much higher and then suddenly falling was played on guests. Soon guests were in rooms filled with dolls, some with moving eyes (there was also a cameo of the puppet from the SAW franchise (Billy) located here, passing here various Mary Shaw's would pop up in bursts of lightening as guests passed paintings and photos of people which as you pass turned to them looking like tortured souls. The end of the house featured one final scare of clown puppet suspended at high level that would swoop at guests. A clown that people inadvertently thought was Jack, but it wasn't. The house was so detailed that many guests who had gotten hold of a DVD of the movie (or who had seen it at the cinema) remarked how well the house was at recreating all the main scenes from the movie. DVD sales did increase for the movie after its release and how many could be directly attributed to this event is uncertain but I would estimate quite a few, as I would never have seen it without it being featured at the event!

Next on the tour of the park was 'Psychoscareapy: Home For The Holidays' located on Soundstage 23. The popular Psychoscareaphy crew would be back in an entirely new house that would be themed around a possible breakout of inmates to terrorize a small mid-western town during the Christmas festivities. There would be some confusion about the name of the house where some outlets and merchandise carried the former name

152

for the house of 'Silent Night Psychotic Nights'. The name had been changed at the request of Universal's legal department so as to not possibly impact on third party movie franchises of a similar name from the 1970s ('Silent Night, Bloody Night' etc.). The house would be exceedingly bright and represent various buildings within the small town with inmates providing various levels of comedy and scares in equal measures, as the house would be one of two comedy houses for the year. Along the snowy journey through the house, guests would see people of the town stuffed into turkeys, people wrapped into Christmas trees with lights tied around them to other towns folk having cookies cutters pressed into their flesh. This combined with the scents that were pumped in again including fern tree scent and cookies to 'burnt human flesh' smell from some unfortunate person stuffed inside the oven. This was all finished off by one inmate complete with Santa outfit and chainsaw, like some demented and evil mall Santa, to chase guests into the streets beyond.

The neighboring house (sharing the same Soundstage) would be that of the first of our icons and would feature Freddy in 'A Nightmare on Elm Street: Dreamwalkers'. Like all the other houses, the house would feature a specially developed narrative but would also add in scenes from the movies to act like a mixture of recreation and sequel to the popular franchise. From the website and queue videos, guests would piece together that they were about to become 'Guinea pigs' for a new experimental drug that had been developed to aid in providing a good night's sleep. The drug would be applied by guests walking through a tunnel lined with black vinyl where fans would deploy the drug via misting vents that would spray a fog within the tunnel (really just dry-ice!). Once applied sleep would be induced by a chanting woman announcer, telling people to "sleep", "sleep", "sleep"… As the fog would lift guests would find themselves inside the soundstage facing the infamous house on Elm Street, lovingly recreated to exacting details. "You'll definitely feel like you're at 1428 Elm Street," said J Michael Roddy, manager of show development, of the Freddy house. "Universal presents Freddy's surreal dream world, including a sleep clinic, a steamy boiler room, a gallery of his creative kills, and a hallway where you can't tell what's Freddy and what's merely one of his many, many reflections."[8]

Once inside the house within a house, guests would pass the stairs into the first room. It would be the stairs where the first scare would come, as guests 'conga-line' into the house awaiting the first room, a quite boo-door would open under the stairs with a Freddy popping up behind selected guests to whisper quietly in their ears' "Freddy's gonna get ya!" before quickly disappearing quietly back to the stairs. Once inside the first room, a recreation of the Johnny Depp dream sequence (site note: Depp's first ever movie role), guests would be entering the room on its side where a recreation of the tortured Depp is lying on the side. As guests look on in horror, a boo-door would open up (now to your left) with a loud bang with a snarling Freddy complete with pronged gloves scratching through to welcome guests before loudly disappearing into the loft-hatch once more. Confused as to where to go next, guests would eventually see the bed on its side, and like in the infamous scene, guests would have to pull their way through the bed sheets to enter into the next scene. Not knowing exactly where the next step would be would be a continuing attribute of this house, where it was presented more like an actual maze than a house.

Once through the bed, guests would see other guests suspended on tables being doped with the drug from before, having nightmares, twisting and turning in their sleep all having the same nightmare as you the dreamwalkers. Soon after guests would be within the boiler room scenes of the house that would feature various paths including a mirrored section. Originally, some of the walls were to be electrified in this area to give guests a mild shock for touching the wrong walls, this was however pulled before opening by the safety inspectors, fearing possible complaints. Likewise another addition was pulled at the last minute, whereby originally the house would feature Jason in the boiler scene before being suspended behind bars (like Freddy vs Jason, but Freddy winning) and although the prison cell remained it stayed empty with guests wondering what should have been in there. It was later revealed by the event's creatives that New Line had stipulated that the icons remain separate in all the houses. Regardless of this feature, the house would prove very popular and would consistently have one of the longest queues for the event.

Next up was 'Vampyr: Blood Bath' located in the Nazarman's area. Nazarman's had originally been the first place on property repurposed just for Halloween Horror Nights, however this venue would have a different future from after this year, marking this house the last to ever be held here. Soon after the event, the areas used for the house were cleared and created into storage space. Dividing into two, the Nazarman's back area would by early 2008 become a Starbucks and Ben & Jerry's stores, respectively. Unfortunately, the final house would not be the greatest of send-offs as the house in many fans eyes' failed to live up to the house franchise it had drawn from. Taking the idea from the original (gangs of different vampires meeting up to feast) and now moving the setting to a New York nightclub in the present day, guests would be taken into the nightclub where unsuspecting dancers would be spirited away by flying vampires for their blood to be drained. The house was notable for presenting a number of 'sexy-vampires' of both genders on podiums dancing with little on that mixed into the horror of vampires feasting on humans and animals in the processing area. Unfortunately, the house did utilize outdoor portions of the Nazarman's area that with sunlight or rain became a breadth of scares. One neat attribute that many fans witnessed in this house was the use of scareactors pretending to be members of the public, who would either react more to the scares around them or would become victims inside the house. Though not unique to this house, it was also witnessed at the Texas Chainsaw house, the Friday 13th house and throughout the scarezones. It is unknown whether Universal ever continued this method of ramping up the scares.

The next house would be 'The Texas Chainsaw Massacre: Flesh Wounds' located inside the Earthquake queue building, a building that would have a name change after the event to fall in line with the attraction altering to become 'Disaster'. There had been some very minor controversy over the name of the house as various fans had thought it was called 'Fresh wounds', instead of 'flesh wounds'. It is likely that as Psychoscarephy's name had changed it could be that this house had a slight name change at the last minute (for reasons unknown).

The house was themed to the remake of the original movie which had been out in cinemas in the previous year, though much of the house was similar to that of the original movies. Starting on at the family manor (complete with sliding door), guests would enter into the strange depraved world of the Hoyt family. Passing through the basement of the house complete with dining table with all assembled family members, guests would soon pass the school bus complete with the shouty Sheriff Hoyt from the remake before being chased for your life through runs of bedsheets tied to washing lines as Leatherface himself chased guests through the area and onto the street. It was exactly like being in the movie of 2006.

The next house would also transfer guests right into a movie, with guests entering into scenes from 'Friday 13th Part 2' in 'Friday The 13th: Camp Blood' located in the Jaws Queue. Scoring highly with fans and public alike, the house would be perfectly suited to timber framed fishing huts of amity, making this house so authentic to its original source material. Jason was everywhere in this house with only the largest of scareactors being deployed, with their towering presences intimating guests further than just the makeup. Windows in the house (yes windows!) were formed to allow views of the Jaws Lake to act as the infamous lake from the movie, with various Jason's popping up to scare guests. Decapitated camp councilors would be mixed with councilors thrown in body bags and tied from the ceilings to two very detailed show-scenes; one where a victim was decapitated 'live' as guests passed to another where the shrine to Jason's dearly departed mother had been recreated. The house ended with huge splattering's of blood where guests were sprayed with water to simulate the effect.

'Jack's Funhouse in Clown-O-Vision' would be next in one of the Sprung tents and would be the final comedic house of the event. Using the popular 3D technology that had been used to great effect in the past, the house mixed scares and comedy in equal measures. Universal billed the house as "This Jack'd up funhouse plunges you laughing and screaming into an oversaturated world of color that leaps at you with more crazed clowns than you can shake a kid at. Before its over-you will know Jack!" Playing on all the five senses the house mixed visual gags with smells and dynamic colorations to present a fun house gone wrong.

The final house would be 'The Thing: Assimilation' located next-door in the other Sprung tent building, the house would be a direct sequel to the popular 1980s movie and directly tie into the 25th anniversary of the original release. The original Universal picture from 1982 had actually been a revamp of the book and 1950s movie of a similar movie, which took the main premise but transferred the action to the North Pole. Kurt Russell starred in the original as the main hero and one of the sole survivors of the events in that movie, who would be recreated in the Orlando house. All the mutating creatures and special effects in the movie had been created by Rob Bottin and Stan Winston. Using these as a template, the Universal creatives set about creating monsters that would be in keeping with the creatures of the original but in a modern setting. The detailed makeup and animatronic characters would be throughout the house and if Universal had slipped in the design, it could be argued that they spent more time on creating the monsters than actually worrying about the scares in the house; whatever your opinion the house would go down as one of the most unique in recent years.

Other than the Opening Scareamonies, the other shows that year would feature 'Bill And Ted's Excellent Halloween Adventure' back in their new Fear Factor Stage home. Along with the time-travelling duo there would also be a Freak Show at the Animal Actors Stage that Universal billed as, "This year, Brian Brushwood will appear with his world-renowned magic show. Stuffed full of the most intense, riveting, and disturbing feats you've ever seen performed live." A show featuring Jack and introducing his girlfriend 'Chance' was held outside Mel's on a large temporary stage that featured various park guests (6 in total) succumbing to various means of torture and magic tricks. This was all completed by the first appearance of

'Rocky Horror Picture Show: A Tribute' located on the Beetlejuice Stage (which was very befitting as the stage required very little redressing). The show would go on to return on select years thereafter.

The scarezones were not officially separated as select scareactors were allowed to roam between zones. The roaming scareactors included weird biker clowns on motorbikes with carnival horse heads attached, the Chainsaw Drill Team and various clowns in bumper cars. The fixed scarezones were located in five areas, they were: Killer Carnies located in New York with circus acts performing, Motormaniacs located on Hollywood Boulevard & Plaza Of The Stars, Treaks & Foons were back and located within Shrek Alley, Troupe Macabre located within the main path of Central Park (this featured turn of the century French circus performers in black and white garbs chasing guests up and down Central Park), followed lastly by a large Ferris wheel erected by the lake outside the Men in Black ride (the wheel had appeared on the website and it could not be ridden). The various tours would again be offered this year, with the behind-the-scenes tour again taking place during the day where guests could explore the soundstage houses and the Vampyre house.

Notes:

[1] Nightmare Movies: Horror on Screen since the 1960s book by Kim Newman
[2] Box Office Mojo website
[3] Orlando Sentinel, June 28 2007
[4] Zuckerberg, Mark (August 26, 2008). "Our First 100 Million", Facebook Blog
[5] Orlando Sentinel Sep 7, 2007
[6] imdb.com
[7] Orlando Sentinel Sep 24, 2007
[8] Orlando Sentinel Sep 28, 2007

Halloween Horror Nights: Reflections of Fear

I Dare You to Say it One More Time...

Halloween Horror Nights 2008 would again be a bumper year for the event, and much like last year this year would go down as being one of the absolute fan favorites. Much of the reason behind this informal accolade is due in part to the incredibly detailed backstory that was created for the event, which was probably the most detailed of all backstories ever given to the event, along with the high level of fan and public interactivity that was created especially for attendees of the event, something that had not on this scale occurred before. And although this year would be a solid favorite, it would not be a smooth ride, with many challenges presenting themselves along the way so Universal could hold the world's largest Halloween event.

As we know, in the recent years at the resort, Halloween Horror Nights had been wildly popular, so popular in fact that it had helped tremendously hike up the overall visitor numbers in the final quarter of each respective year. Building on this solid foundation and continuing with further investments in the parks and better, more targeted marketing, Universal Resort posted some of its then best financial results. In February of that year the resort posted a $92 million profit for the preceding year, which had doubled from the previous year to that[1]. This included an overall visitor number that was up 3% from the following year, a jump which had not been seen since 2004, a lot of which was directly attributed to the success of the event in the final quarter of 2007. Building on this legacy, the park's creatives decided to set about creating another immersive world that would start long before the event, via the website.

Another in-house designed icon would lead this year's event, a decision that was taken early on. The story would focus on the mysterious Dr. Mary Agana and her transformation into the urban legend of Bloody Mary. There wasn't any official backstory for the urban legend, rather, a series of comparative tales had been told and written about for many years; some included the Tudor Queen Mary I and others about a tortured soul from Normandy. Whatever the tale you had heard, most people knew how one would go about summoning her urban legend or had at least heard of her. Universal decided to ignore the tales of the past and create their own unique tale of how the character was created. "We take that which everybody knows and we build the whole part that everyone doesn't know," said Jim Timon, Universal Orlando's senior vice president for entertainment[2]. "And then turn it around a bit: What happens when you get pulled into the mirror?" And once pulled through the broken mirror, guests would expect to be taken into a world filled with urban legends, fantasy, fairy tales and myths.

The backstory for the icon would be one of the most detailed ever created by the event's creatives. "We wanted a unique tonality to her. What does the inside of a mirror sound like?" said J Michael Roddy, Universal manager of show development. "It's a combination of underwater sounds, some echo chambers, and we hired three very talented actresses to combine three different elements of her voice so that there's a similarity to it, but also something supernatural about it[3]." Mary would not just use sound to ramp-up the creepiness, she would be a first truly sensual icon that can get under your skin and affect all your senses. Roddy continued, "You can't connect with her because she doesn't have eyes. That is the connection people look for immediately," he said. "So now forcing people to look up at something and it's looking back at us and there's no way to relate to it. I think that's really effective." Along with her creepy sound, glassy stare and extreme anarchic power there would be something truly disturbing about her, that would affect and attract people like no icon has before. Jim Timon continued, "It's a trace memory. It's reminding you of something you'd rather not remember," he said. "I'm thinking that's where we're getting them is on a sub-psychological level!"

She was officially introduced as Dr. Mary Agana on the event's website on July 1st, 2008. Viewers of the site would enter into her office and read her journal. The setting was 1958 at the time, but the overall story would take guests through time and eventually through dimension. The office was very tidy and had a desk abutted to a large wall mounted mirror. Items would eventually appear and become clickable revealing nuggets of information about the new icon; eventually a journal appeared which informed us who she was and that she was a psychiatrist. On a day-by-day basis to tie into events that were presented as happening in real time (events of July 18th 1958 were released on July 18th 2008 for example) and with each journal entry about her patients or experiments it became clear she was slipping slowly into some kind of insanity herself, the possible catalyst being a rejection letter to National Association of Mental Health (NAMH).

Slowly as the weeks went on and the updates came, it appeared that Agana was not just trying to cure her patients fears or anxieties, she was trying to see where they manifested from, a process that would often require her to torture her patients to better treat them, or so her deluded mind thought. This level of immersive therapy continued to until one patient was killed during the process. The very next entry in her journal was then filled with her excitement for what she had done, rather than her remorse; this was paired with the office becoming increasingly disorderly. As the next case came her style of writing changed with far more doodles and pictures being drawn within her journal, several patients were then killed before she started to question her own sanity. Finally she began treating one of the doctors who rejected her, who she later killed, and finally a local detective named Boris Shuster. During the buildup to the event, Shuster would actually have a real window redressed as his office, which looked exactly how it had been on the website. A testament to the popularity of this character (for who we as fans never actually saw!), the window is still there to this day and can be found in the New York section of the studios park.

In her last journal entry on August 27th it showed a dilapidated office and broken mirror where she had become Bloody Mary. Later a paranormal investigation society created by Shuster (called the Legendary Truth), investigated the office in 2008 on the anniversary of the events revealing definitively that she was the inspiration for the urban legend we all know. It was later revealed that Agana herself was brutally murdered, supposedly by Shuster on discovery of the shocking acts she had committed, though during the event it was revealed she had been murdered by another man, an ex-convict who was either an assistant or patient of hers.

The story was powerful, it was detailed and it became a must-watch for many fans of the event. The story was so strong that literally ever day fans of the event found themselves rushing back from work/school to refresh the site to see if there had been any updates; the suspense was as effective as a Hitchcock movie. Bit by bit the story revealed itself until the full reveal of all information (when Agana became Bloody Mary) around early September actually crashed the event's website, such were the high numbers of fans, locals and tourists trying to access the site at the same time to see what the conclusion to this summer long epic was. It was a truly great time to be a Halloween Horror Nights fan.

However, whilst the story played out on the website, things behind the scenes and in the fan community were not as smooth running. The first issue of the event came in August of that year when the plans were leaked for the event. Though not displayed publicly, and only spoke about in exacting circles, the house names were also leaked at the same time. One fan realizing that Universal, unlike Disney, must seek permission for any building permits from the City Orlando, as long as you can travel to the City and complete the associated forms, any members of the public could at that time access the drawings submitted. This lead to five of the eight houses having their actual titles known, with three left for speculation. This process would later have petition from Universal to the City to be changed to prevent these leaks, this was emphasized when Universal began the permit process for the new Harry Potter land that was going to be built at Islands of Adventure. To prevent leaks of this super-secret addition to the resort, the City agreed to not disclose the drawings for the purposes of themed entertainment in that disclosure may be used against the resort's intentions. This minor law change that came into effect could be later be nicknamed, 'The Potter Law' by the fan communities.

Not only had the drawings and house names leaked, but so did the title of the event, when Universal inadvertently included the name of the event on the event's website before the big reveal. Then the official commercial was leaked, though not in its entirety. The company that had been contracted in to make the commercial had placed a number of screen captures from the commercial and the making-of on their website. And lastly, some of the billboards were erected early by accident. The largest number of billboards had been placed around the state that year (over 80 in number), the huge boards contained the logo of the event with a glassy eyed Bloody Mary starring down at the passing traffic. Though little was made of this minor mistake, the billboards would go on to draw criticism from the local communities of Central Florida for their 'graphic' appearance[4]. One local mother said at the time, "Each year, I grow more frustrated and disappointed by the choices Universal makes in advertising this event, which glamorizes violence and human cruelty. This year, I find the billboards truly unacceptable to our community." Though as you can see from this book, the billboards seem to draw complaints every year.

Building on this expanded and immersive event theme, it would be 23 nights in duration, feature: 8 brand new houses, larger sized and quantity of scarezones with less shows but with the hiring of the largest number of scareactors ever with records detailing that the record of 1,000 in the past had been exceeded this year. The first show would not be an Opening Scaremonies this year but rather a media preview show that happened before the event in September located at the Horror Makeup Stage. A Legendary Truth operative introduced the show that included a terrifying sequence where Bloody Mary burst bloody and torn through a mirror live on stage, much to the gathered crowd's surprise and delight. The show would later be posted online for everyone to enjoy in lieu of any formal Opening Scaremonies.

The first house of the event would be 'Body Collectors: Collections of the Past' and was located within Soundstage 20. The theme was that some of the most awful crimes of our history were not in fact created by the persons the history books define but rather by the demented Body Collectors. The Victorian theme was heavily influenced by Jack the Ripper and Sweeney Todd. Heavily detailed London Victorian streets were met with coaches, London fog and East-end Prostitutes "hello guvnor, how's about a good time?" one would say near the entrance. Walking down the first alley guests would be confronted by one of the grinning collectors floating in midair before, a similar knife swinging collector would come at guests from the side. Streets had their original street names from the infamous case (such as Mitre Square), along with the scents and smells of Victorian England, one façade even had "Aiello & Roddy" barbershop written above, as a sort of Easter egg to fans (both men are well known Creatives for the event). Eventually guests would be lead into the demon barber's shop before witnessing a man having his leg chopped off with spraying blood effect (just water) before entering an area that looked like a factory. One other memorable scene included a scantily clad prostitute on the street corner waving and chatting to guests before a collector jumped out from the shadows behind her, then grabbed her, pulling her backwards before slicing her throat there and then. The gore and the effects were staggering in this house and were worth many repeat visits in order to see how they actually created those effects to such brilliance.

Next door would be 'Creatures!' in Soundstage 22, Universal billed the house as, "Creatures straight from the cover of Atomi Comics' "Strange Tales" burst forth to rampage and massacre the backwoods locals. Join Johnny, Cleet, Jim Deedle and the rest of the gang at the Butchered Buck as they fight off this terrifying invasion of creatures from who knows where." This house told the story of a sleepy back water which was being attacked from an alien that had landed in the area. Various Southern locals doing battle with giant prop aliens were seen, including recycled pieces of 'The Thing' house that were taken from the previous year.

Over in the Sprung Tents the first house was a very experimental means of presenting a house, that house was 'Dead Exposure'. The story was that of a plucky photographer who through the use of photography captures the moments his town becomes over run with flesh eating zombies. The special effect, which had not been used before or since included a completely dark house that was only illuminated via a number of camera flashes. Entering in via a photograph, guests would see the use of blacklight strobes timed to camera clock in every room that created the flashes of light, this was paired with illuminous paint on costumes and sets that created the sensation of capturing the moment with very timed and rehearsed zombie scareactors. The tie in to the narrative was that the main protagonist was one of Agana's patients whom she wrote about in her journal.

Next to this house in the other Sprung building, 'The Hallow' delighted crowds. A combination of different phobias and legends were presented here. Universal billed the house as, "Where do the traditions we observe each Halloween come from? It is said that every Halloween within the blackest parts of the forest, Samhain, The Lord of the Underworld, lives again and the souls of the damned beckon you. For if you journey deep enough, you will see that Samhain's traditions are trapped within The Hallow.[5]" An impressive forest environment was created for the house complete with large façade, inside witches, ghouls, skeletons and demons acted out demonic practices that terrified audiences.

Next up would be the sole movie based house this year. 'Doomsday' was held within the newly created 'Disaster!' queue building which had opened with the newly refurbished ride in January of that year. The queue building had not changed much with only alterations to maximize use of the space for the event with easily moveable props for the ride that could be wheeled out to make way for Halloween Horror Nights. The movie of the same name had been released in May of that year to mixed success. Capitalizing on the same thought process of last year with 'Dead Silence' (a movie that didn't perform well at the box-office but would create a good haunted house attraction that may well increase DVD sales) the park's creatives went about creating an exact detailed environment that was reminiscent of the movie. The story was that of a post-apocalyptic Scotland, where they have bred a virus that ravages the population, leaving those left behind after the plague to survive by any means necessary. Punks and chainsaw guys filled this house to mixed responses.

'Interstellar Terror' would be presented in Soundstage 20 this year. The story was that of a scientific community based on board the first space ship to leave our solar system. Reappearing after some time later orbiting our moon, the guests of the event were sent in to investigate the strange reappearance of the ship and what might lurk inside waiting for us. Despite several houses being presented over the years at the event that feature aliens or spaceships, this was the first house that took guests into space. Slowly the story is revealed to be that after leaking the solar system, the crew discovers a mysterious relic that makes them all go insane and become murderous. The house used the space setting to great effect creating houses that contained low-gravity to airlocks showing crewmembers being pulled out into space.

The next house would be the icon's house located within the Jaws queue building and was called 'Reflections of Fear'. The house was an exact replica of the website and used details from it to create the sensation that guests had now entered the world of Bloody Mary. The only downside of this house was that if you hadn't been on the website, little in the house may have made sense to you, though most people had. Mirror effects were used throughout the house to create now only the story but also the scares. Guests were transported through time to various versions of the office as seen in the journal as she treats and then tortures her unsuspecting patients. A neat cameo in the house was her desk where a bottle of 'Sleepwell', the drug from the previous year's Freddy house had been placed there by the park's creatives for sharped eyed fans of the event.

The final house and one of the most popular from that year was being held in a new building to be used for the event for the third sequel in this house's franchise, that of 'Scary Tales: Once Upon a Nightmare', located in the Parade Warehouse (B-79). The building, located right at the back of the staff only areas of the studio, was built to house parade floats when not in use. The floats had been wrapped in cellophane and moved to a new location for the duration of the event. The house was required as the Nazarman's area was now out of use (as previously mentioned in the last chapter). The house had a huge façade built that took guests on a twisted journey featuring strange versions of Cinderella, Alice in Wonderland and The Wizard of Oz.

The seven scarezones this year would be many and plentiful with an exceptionally high level of detailing. The first would be 'American Gothic' located on Production Central. It was billed as, "Some legends allow a simple man or woman to remain immortal. Some deeds, so dark, take a simple person and transform them into lore. America's past has been filled with these dark deeds, sorted characters and unbelievable acts of horror. Reflect upon your own mortality as you venture through history with the infamous Lizzie Borden as your guide." It would be a reimagining of a scarezone that had featured before in the early days of the event.

Tying into the nearby 'Scary Tales' house, 'Asylum in Wonderland' would delight guests in the Hollywood Boulevard area of the park. The zone featured highly decorated and designed characters that had been lifted from the original text but with a contemporary spin. Borrowing the same theme was 'Fractured Tales' located nearby in Kidzone, with fairy tale recreations around every corner from some of your best loved children's tales that had been twisted to horrific proportions. "The stories that we created are familiar, so you play that same kind of game where people kind of know a little bit about what they think it is," says T.J. Mannarino[6], director of art and design for entertainment at Universal. "But then when they come and see it, it's a whole different slant to it."

'The Path of the Wicked' was located on Plaza of the Stars near the entrance to the park and toyed with the simple idea of 'What if the Wicked Witch had actually won?' The Land of Oz had been presented like never before with flying monkey men, tortured characters and witches everywhere, with guests singing out "Toto, I've a feeling we're not in Kansas anymore!" After the carnage of this area guests would often find themselves in 'Streets of Blood: Body Collectors' in the New York Streets area. Tying into the house that year that also featured the grinning ghouls, guests would witness New York re-dressed to simulate the terrors of 1888 London when the "Ripper" struck (or was it the collectors?). This neat house and scarezone played on people fears for 120th anniversary of the terrible real-life events of the then Victorian England.

The final scarezone would be 'The Skoolhouse' located outside Mel's Drive-In, the scarezone would see the largest ever set built for a scarezone. Universal billed the area as, "Mr. Renshaw's class has always been good. Mr. Renshaw's class has never broken the rules. Mr. Renshaw's class has always been perfect little angels. All of that changes when the kids from the Skoolhouse "cut" class. The children of the quaint town of Carey, Ohio are out to teach everyone that their version of Trick or Treat may be the difference between your life and death." Along with the school house that had been built as a set within the zone the area was complimented with a high number of scareactors all dressed as murderous school children dressed in Halloween costumes with distinctive masks. The characters interacted with guests all evening every night to create a truly great scarezone.

There would also be an unofficial eight scarezone in the park this year that although not on park maps would return nearly every year since. Located in the main path outside the Gardens of Allah that run through Central Park, the event's creatives installed exactly 500 jack-o-lanterns throughout the trees that had been individually lit by LEDs which had been timed to flicker and dance to the music that was pumped into the area. At points in the specially chosen soundtrack, a 'wind' would blow through with them all flickering out[7].

Brian Brushwood was back again this year, again located at the Animal Actors Stage to bring his unique show of magic and wonder. The 20 minute show would be altered slightly from the previous year and would contain more tricks that Brushwood would perform himself. The main five routines would be intercut with punk music numbers where the popular cell phone trick from the previous year was carried out much to the guests' delight.

Along with Brushwood, the time-travelling duo, Bill and Ted, were back again with their ever popular show. This year it featured many political gags, as the presidential election was in full swing. References to 'Indiana Jones' were made as his new movie had just been released that summer, along with 'The Dark Knight', 'Hellboy', 'Predator' and a lookalike of Miley Cyrus, this was all topped-off with a cast dance-off to the Aerosmith vs Run DMC's 'Walk This Way'. The final show that year had returned like Brushwood from the previous year, that of 'The Rocky Horror Picture Show' tribute. The popular show featured such classics numbers as 'Dammit Janet', 'Sweet Transvestite', 'Touch-a Touch-a Touch Me' and finished off by a rowdy and rambunctious rendition of everyone's favorite the 'Time Warp'. Other attractions open this year include: 'Men in Black: Alien Attack', the newly opened 'The Simpsons Ride', 'Revenge of the Mummy', 'Jaws' and 'Disaster! A Major Motion Picture Ride... Starring You!'

Notes:

[1] Orlando Sentinel Feb 23, 2008
[2] Orlando Sentinel Oct 15, 2008
[3] Orlando Sentinel Oct 15, 2008
[4] Orlando Sentinel Sep 4, 2008
[5] Event map 2008
[6] Orlando Sentinel Sep 26, 2008
[7] Orlando Sentinel Sep 26, 2008

At the park gates: "I'm sorry but we have a strict no makeup and masks policy!"

Halloween Horror Nights: Ripped From The Silver Screen

"It's Showtime!"

This year's event theme would be a year unlike any previous year. The event would not just dedicate a house or two to a particular movie but the film based studios park would play host to an event that would see every house and scarezone based on either actual movies or would be inspired by different movies. It would an ambitious project but it was handled by one man synonymous to fans for his dedication and knowledge of movies, that lead creative was J Michael Roddy, for which unbeknown to fans, would be his last year of working on the event. The man who had started way back in 1991 as a Norman Bates scareactor[7], now Show Director and creator of Jack the Clown, would ensure the event would see him leave in style by putting on the largest event to date. "We're turning the front gate into the facade of the Universal Palace Theater. There will be a box office, there will be a movie screen showing trailers," said Roddy, then show director for Universal Orlando Entertainment. "And then once you walk in, all these environments, all these movies are ripped from the silver screen and come to life[2]." Due to the size of the event and the level of complexity, planning for the event this year started earlier than it had ever done up to this point. Roddy said at the time, "We've been working on 2010[event] since July [2009], so it's starting to actually be more than a year-round process. There's not a time where we're not in some capacity working on Halloween Horror Nights[7]."

The event which had begun its mammoth marketing for the event starting in April of that year with the highly detailed website that slowly unraveled until June when more and more information for the event had been issued via the website. The website over the many months told eight different tales, all of which alluded to clues about the houses and scarezones that would feature that year. The clues didn't stop there either, as like in the previous years, fans had gotten hold of the blueprints for the various permits issued by the City of Orlando right before the 'Potter Law' came into force. Universal's Art and Design team knowing of the leak from the previous year had already issued the paperwork to the City referring to each house in code names rather than their actual names (as had been the practice before). With the obtainment of these names and clues from the website it brought fans into an absolute frenzy trying to decipher them and work out which horrors were coming for us.

The event opened on September 25ᵗʰ with queues clogging up the I4 with eager guests excited about entering the park. The first house up was 'Silver Screams' and would be the icon's house this year which was located at the back of the park in the Parade Building. Once inside, guests would enter in via the front of the Universal Palace Theater, which had turned into a dilapidated state. Greeting guests at the front, complete with flash light was The Usher, he would stare at guests within the line and whisper, "tickets please". Once inside the house would act as corridor then room, corridor then room setup, then repeat. The corridor would not only act as the respite between the horror but it would include posters of the film you were about to enter, this way it ramped up the anticipation, as prior to the event no guests knew which movies would be presented.

The first movie, and quite aptly would be the first true Universal horror picture, was 'The Phantom of the Opera'. Guests would enter in a stone built vaulted ceiling basement where the illusive phantom is playing his impressive organ. As he plays the organ, various pipes and bursts of air can be seen while the gothic music is blazed out in full volume. As guests delight in seeing him play with such a passion, another phantom (without mask) appears at the end of the room to give the maximum scare. The next corridor leads to the set of 'My Bloody Valentine 3D' which had been released that year in theaters. Entering into the famous hospital scene of the movie guests are first confronted with a blood stained wall that reads, "Happy Valentine's Day", and as guests ponder this message the gas mask wearing pickaxe man would come running down the hall; he then pops up again until guests move onto the next scene. Whereas in 2007 the event took guests on a sequel of 'The Thing' (1982) movie, this year we would not be back within the first movie with various creatures in varying states of mutation attacking, before heading to the next room where the 'Evil Dead' franchise was represented. Guests here witness Ash doing battle with chainsaw against a large ghoul like creature. In the next room we witness the original death of our icon before moving the next scene to see the popular 'Shaun of the Dead' movie. Guests are now back inside 'The'Winchester' pub right at the climax of the movie when the zombie hoards are attacking the boarded out windows. Both our hero Shaun and a zombified Ed are seen inside as various popular 'Queen' hits are played on the jukebox. The final scene of the house is from the 2008 movie 'The Strangers' before guests head out as The Usher provides one last final scare.

The next house on our tour would be highly anticipated. 'Saw' was brought to the event inside the Jaws queue building, though this wasn't the first 'Saw' attraction as there had been one open in the UK a few months before the event. Our event's 'Saw' would lead guests on a tour of the greatest hits from the popular horror franchise. Saw's Producer Oren Koules[3], who actually at the time lived in Tampa, said during the event, "Having people experience the Saw films live, not just on the screen, but to have people walk through it, taste it, touch it and feel it - is amazing for us." So impressed with Universal's dedication to detail, the Producer was actually spotted with colleagues attending on various nights. Roddy went on to say, "I think Saw is the most popular of our brands this year, I think it will be one of the major draws. It's prevalent, it's contemporary, people know what that is." He continued, "You're actually going to walk into Jigsaw's lair. As you walk in, it's an industrial building, almost nondescript. And as you enter, you're immediately in his workshop. You'll see all of the TVs and the cameras, and you'll come face-to-monitor with [puppet] Billy, who'll give you your task, which is to make it through this maze[4]." "For us, it's a big, big challenge that we replicate this 100 percent," said T.J. Mannarino, director of art and design for Universal Orlando. "Saw will have to match that intensity, that excitement." And meet the intensity it did!

The queue for the house would feature clips from the past movies in the franchise and posters for the upcoming Saw VI that was released during the event. Guests would enter into a warehouse environment before being confronted by Billy the puppet who asks "do you want to play a game?" before sneakily throwing a burst of air at people's ankles as they walked passed him. Various scenes from the movies were depicted throughout the house including the infamous head-bear-trap sequence, a man in barbed wire and even a medical scene with Jigsaw. The creators had actually used a high number of props from the original movies, where no less than Billy the puppet, which had been given to Universal from the last movie's production, along with Jigsaw actor Tobin Bell who had recorded new dialogue especially for the event[5]. The house was finished by an effective scare where a circular row of Jigsaws complete with pig masks were all waiting for guests where five of the six would be dummies and one human; but which one? They would rotate the dummies so guests would enter for repeat visits would not know which one of the six would be jumping out at them. They also deployed scareactors into the queue for this house, where they would queue and chat to people in character in the queue lines, but once inside would be grabbed and tortured by Jigsaw to increase the intensity of the house.

The next house and possibly one of the most immersive ever built was 'The Wolfman' located inside Soundstage 22. The house had been built with cooperation of the Universal production staff who were working on the movie at the time of the house's design. The aim was for guests to experience the movie and then experience the house. However, due to production setbacks the movie's release date was delayed until after the event, with the new ethos being, 'enjoy the house and then enjoy the movie' (guests had to wait until January 2010 before they could see the movie). Regardless of this issue with timing, the house was exceedingly impressive. The first area guests encounter was a gypsy settlement who provide foreboding stories about 'the beast' before we are led into the forest. The forest was possibly one of the most detailed scenes ever created with guests having to stare in wonder at the immersive level of detail the park's creatives had designed. Real trees, moss, grass, hills, fog, gravel, even a moon(!) etc. were combined with the sound of pounding feet as the mysterious beast was drawing closer and closer before a inexplicable howl rang out within the area. Guests could be forgiven for thinking they had actually been transferred to the moors of England! "We were basically given access to all their designs, and this is a big-budget version. A lot of amazing production value has gone into it." Roddy said. "Although the house is built inside a soundstage, it has an outdoors feel with a gypsy camp, a forest and the sensation of being chased by a lycanthrope. This is the only place you're going to be able to see the Wolfman (at the time). It doesn't open until February, so that's pretty cool for us," Roddy said[6].

After exploring the moors guests enter into the village, the mansion and the crypt from the movie before the beast actively targets us the guests. Eventually we are led back into the woods (a different scene) whereby the Wolfman is chasing us and jumping between hills and hedges as he chases us down. Finally we reach a mound where the Wolfman jumps onto a large natural plinth howling at the moon above. Just as we stare in fright, having been caught, a hunter emerges from the side complete with blunderbuss and silver bullets to fire the beast, which sends the scareactor flying back to the hill below (he must have been wearing a harness for such a stunt), before guests make their final run for the exit, the Wolfman now scared and battle damaged attacked guests for one final scare. Despite the movie being released after the event, it did not dampen the house, for which in this author's opinion was one of the most immersive ever created.

The next house would be the event's comedic house and was presented in Sprung Tent 2 as 'Chucky: Friends till the End'. The house was a funhouse created by Chucky with toys in various states of play combined to scare guests witless. Quirky sets of freakish teddy bears or scareactors whose costumes were hundreds of plush dolls knitted together ambling around would lure guests into false senses of calm before a knife wielding Chucky would pop up from a boo-door complete with large butcher's knife. This was the first official house to feature Chucky in the Orlando event, whereas he had been present in both shows and houses at the Hollywood event for some years.

Next-door in Sprung Tent 1 the park presented 'The Spawning', an original house created by the resort's creatives that had been sponsored by the media company 'Fangoria'. The house had been based on the concept of mutant creatures living in the sewers below a town that were emerging to attack the water plant workers who maintained the tunnels. The mutants were named, 'sculders', and were presented as freakish scaled monsters with huge claws. The name of the beasts along with the setting led many to believe that the house had been inspired by various episodes of 'The X-Files' though no official tie-in was given.

The next house would be 'Dracula: Legacy in Blood' and was located in Soundstage 23. The setting was Eastern Europe around the turn of the last century with a huge façade built within the stage of a mysterious castle perched on the side of a cliff, complete with speared heads and foggy atmosphere being pumped in. The house featured Dracula and his many, many brides through the claustrophobic stony areas of the castles, seemingly popping up at every turn. The house was epic due to the high number of brides in various states of vampirism from beauty to feral to beast like those that were seen jumping out and feasting on poor unfortunate souls throughout. The house was so popular that it was awarded in-house as 'house of the year' for 2009.

Also sharing the above Soundstage was 'Frankenstein: Creation of the Damned'. Universal billed the house as, "It has been a fortnight since his creation caused the castle to be engulfed in flames. Doctor Frankenstein now continues his work to perfect the art of resurrection and regeneration surrounded by his creations. The Creature has also returned to make the Doctor pay for the pain and suffering he has had to endure. The Creature will destroy everything in his path to gain redemption, and you are now caught in the middle of the epic battle."[1] Completing the lineup for the big three from Universal's classic horror monsters, the house would feature another huge castle façade where Dr. Frankenstein is seen experimenting on various body parts before guests are confronted by the legendary beast. Various laboratory and dungeon scenes were depicted in pure steam-punk fashion and featured the Doctor, the monster, Fritz, the bride and various other characters. The house was impressive for its use of electricity effects, pyro and smells. It left guests reeling from the sensory overload that had been thrown at them, to make this house outstandingly popular.

The final house would be one of the two original concept houses for the event that were sponsored by 'Fangoria', that of 'Leave it to Cleaver' located in the Disaster queue building. The house told the sad tale of Sam Meetz, a butcher who owns and operates 'Meetz Meats', in Carey, Ohio (who was actually played on the website and queue videos by park creative Mike Aiello). The house featured guests on a tour of the factory where various Meetz Meats mask wearing employees with undertaking varying cannibalistic activities for the processing the flesh for human consumption. The house had been inspired by various B-Movies from the 1950s and 60s.

The scarezones this year included 'Lights Camera Hacktion' located on Hollywood Boulevard. The concept was that the Chainsaw Drill Team of the event is being included in a movie about a murderous chainsaw wielding mad gang, the problem is: production has hired the original murderous chainsaw wielding gang from the event. After action was called the team has set about setting about all of the production staff whom are in various degrees of injury while the gang chases production staff and guests alike throughout this zone. Next up was 'Cirque Du Freak' located in Kidzone Plaza. Inspired by the Universal movie of the same name that was released during the event, the zone featured characters and sets from the movie that spread into Central Park and onto the edge of the new Simpsons area.

The scarezone 'Horrorwood Die-In' located outside Mel's Drive-In, was presented where a big screen had been erected with parked cars to simulate the appearance of a drive in movie playing. The screen would play clips of Universal horrors movies from the past and present whilst characters from the movie world of horror would prowl the streets (mostly for photo-opportunities). The monsters included: Norman Bates, The Barlow vampire from the made-for-TV movie 'Salem's Lot', characters from 'The Strangers', 'Saw', 'The Exorcist' all ushered (excuse the pun) by the main icon himself, The Usher.

Next up would be 'Apocalypse: City of Cannibals' located in the New York area of the park. Where various scenes of destruction were witnessed with hordes of cannibals running around creating mayhem. Nearby on the Plaza to the Star would be 'Containment', a small scarezone that featured a misty green fog with various scareactors in medical overalls in varying states of mutation; this was abutted on Shrek Alley by ' War of the Living Dead'. This noisy scarezone featured WW2 zombie soldiers of different armies fighting a battle to the death (well they're already dead, no?). Gun battles and fog played host to this popular scarezone.

The above six scarezones were the official scarezones of the event but in the final week of the event the park's creatives decided to use the Sting

Alley area of the backlot to showcase an additional scarezone which would act as the preview for the coming year. This additional scarezone was named 'Shadows from the Past', and featured nearly all the past event icons, including: The Caretaker, The Director, Eddie Schmidt, Jack the Clown, The Storyteller and The Usher, plus various other characters including Alice and The Terra Queen. The Frequent Fear Pass was also extended towards the end of the event to encompass additional nights for fans desperate to see this later addition to the event[10].

Two shows were offered this year, these were 'The Rocky Horror Picture Show: A Tribute' which was presented in the same way as it had been in the previous years, along with another version of the popular Bill and Ted show. This year's show featured references to the new Terminator movie, Avatar, a lookalike for Britney Spears, all topped off with a medley of songs to commemorate the passing of pop's Michael Jackson which had occurred a few months prior to the event. Rides open for this year's event included: Men in Black: Alien Attack, The Simpsons Ride, Revenge of the Mummy, JAWS, Disaster! A Major Motion Picture Ride... Starring You! and Hollywood Rip Ride Rockit. There was also the opportunity on select nights to attend special signings with various celebrity guests. Steve and Tango[9] from the popular 'Ghost Hunters' TV show were on hand various nights, including Tippi Hedren[9] (from Hitchcock's 'The Birds' and other movies) who had been happy to sign autographs and pose for photos and also, John C. Reilly[8] who had been there promoting his movie 'Cirque du Freak: The Vampire's Assistant' with other members of the cast onsite. Along with the unique popcorn prop that had been sent out as media gifts, there was a special rare prop given out to select guests this year. These were specially created beads for guests booking on the 'Gory Getaway' packages this year; these black and red beads would feature medallions of the main house icons from the year and are now extremely collectable.

Notes:

[1] Event map 2009
[2] Orlando Sentinel Aug 27, 2009
[3] Orlando Sentinel Aug 27, 2009
[4] Orlando Sentinel Sep 25, 2009
[5] Orlando Sentinel Sep 25, 2009
[6] Orlando Sentinel Sep 25, 2009
[7] Orlando Sentinel Oct 11, 2009
[8] Orlando Sentinel Oct 18, 2009
[9] HHN's official page at Facebook.com
[10] Orlando Sentinel Oct 29, 2009

Halloween Horror Nights XX

Twenty Years of Fear

"A New Era of Darkness Begins!"

The event in 2010 would be the second ever retrospective anniversary year but unlike the 'Sweet Sixteen' event, this year would seamlessly mix everything that had been from the past with new horrors in an interesting way. "It's not just this big Carol Burnett special of Halloween... It's not a clip show," said Jim Timon[1], senior vice president of entertainment at Universal. "That would have been the easy thing to do - a let's-rest-on-our-laurels Halloween. There was no desire creatively to do that." And although the park would present horrors from the past 20 years of back catalogue, the emphasis would be on setting the event up for future scares. "We want to make sure we touch on, in some sort of house form, some sort of street form, something that bases us in the 20 years of Horror Nights, but then that's it," says Mike Aiello, show director. "Everything else about the event, we want to make sure we are pushing this event forward, establishing a groundwork for the next 20 years." They also had to pull something out of the bag as the economy had been bumping along for a while and this impacted Universal at the time; no so much on ticket sales, as they were steady, but definitely on room sales. Around this time, hotel occupancy across Central Florida was down to 57.5%[2], which was a fall of 6.7% on the previous year; so a real push was seen at Universal to sell hotel occupancy, by means of discounts and special promotions. This trickled on for most of 2010 as the economy started to grow and newer attractions came online such as 'Hollywood Rip Ride Rockit' (2009), 'The Simpsons' Ride (2009) and 'The Wizarding World of Harry Potter' (Hogsmeade) on June 18, 2010. These efforts lifted attendance through the spring and summer of 2010 but it would be Halloween Horror Night's job to continue this increase into the fall and through to the holiday celebrations.

Starting to plan the event for 2010 as far back as the summer of 2009, the park's creatives originally wanted to go with a Halloween tree theme where the roots of evil are never quite dead. In fact the scarezone that was hastily brought in for the final weeks of the event in 2009 ('Shadows from the Past') had a tree theme as its icon when it appeared on the official website at the time. There had also been the inaugural 'Entertainment Designer

Forum' held in April of 2010 where various props and costumes from year's past were showcased, along with the event logo surrounded by tree branches. The initial idea was to bring Cindy back[3], the un-used icon from the past who had morphed over the years into The Caretaker's daughter. The concept would be her destroying the Halloween tree and what had been seen before in favor of new horrors that she would unleash. It is not known why she was replaced with the new event icon of 'Fear', but it must have been late in the planning phase as a whole house had been developed for her inside the Jaws queue building which would remain for the event, whereas, the new icon did not have his own outright house.

It was around this time that the website started to update, bring forth the now annual consumption of rumor and anticipation making for the fandom of the event. The Legendary Truth website that had started in 2008 also became live again and worked hand-in-hand with the main website. Various charred photos and symbols were released with the fan community spiraling into a frenzy trying to connect all the pieces together to work out who would be the icon and what houses etc. we were likely to see coming up. Soon the items assembled to create a lantern with branch like pillars creating the roman numerals XX on the side. Soon after the icon of 'Fear' was unleashed, when the icon left the first message on the website, "Nineteen years... Nineteen cycles... What has been decades for some has been Eons for me... On the Twentieth cycle... I shall be revealed!" It was soon presented on various media outlets, where it was claimed that Fear had possessed the staff of the resort's creative departments to bring about more terrifying scares than ever before. Soon the lantern became clickable on the website whereby the various past icons would be seen in the fire. "Fear is going to show himself this year," Aiello said at the time. "The one thing we've been growing and bringing to the guests every year is going to physically manifest itself this year and be that sort of puppet master or string puller. He's been the one entity that's been pushing this event year after year to create fear to feed him.[4]"

Fear would be prominent within two scarezones that abutted each other, one on Hollywood Boulevard and the other at the top outside Mel's Drive-In. The former being a collection of all things Halloween Horror Nights from the past 20 years, presented in the warehouse style from the commercial that also ran at the same time. A fake warehouse reflected the event's own actual warehouse that had housed the horrors of past events for over a decade now. The scarezone was named 'Twenty Years of Fear' and directly tied into the Parade housing building's house of 'Horror Nights: The Hallow'd Past' where guests were taken into a replica of this warehouse to face the creatures of the past brought back to life in a sort of 'greatest hits' for the event. The Mel's Drive-In scarezone was more of a meet-and-greet with the icons. All the past icons were present, excluding Bloody Mary (due to a copyright discussion that was occurring at the time), they all appeared with the mark of Fear (war paint or a scare etc.) across their persons to show their creation from Fear himself. "These icons were a piece to the puzzle that all had to exist physically in order to bring fear, to open that lantern and bring Fear into existence," Aiello said[5]. Another interesting fact was that the Cryptkeeper from the early days of the event was seen not with his fellow icons in this scarezone but rather in the former scarezone sitting on a throne right at the start of the zone; in a way saying, here's the original icon at the start of the event and the scarezone.

The former icon of the event's house would be 'The Orphanage: Ashes to Ashes' and was located in the Jaws Queue building. The house was billed as, "Ashes to ashes, forever now dust. For years she has existed in the shadows, never getting her due. Misunderstood by all around her, she has had enough of her playthings at the Good Harvest Orphanage - now is the time for vengeance. This burned out shell contains the souls of the forgotten and the lost who all scream one name: Cindy[6]." The Jaws building lent itself well to the development of this house, much like it had in 2007 for the Friday 13th house. The charred remains of the orphanage complete with burning embers, smoke effects and 'burnt flesh smell' was complemented by the first ever use of real fire inside a Halloween Horror Nights house. Towards the end of the house, located outside of a window aperture was a gas powered fire effect behind a pyro-glass panel that added the effect that the fire was still ravishing the building with now being the time for guests to exit. Complete with the burnt out environment of a building still on fire (yes Universal used actual wood they had burned themselves to maximum effect) was the occupiers of the orphanage who jumped out at various points with the maze complete with Halloween masks and fire damaged costumes.

Next up was 'Legendary Truth: The Wyandot Estate' located within Soundstage 22. This huge house was constructed to resemble an actual house inside the enormous soundstage. The house directly tied into events taking place on the sister website to the main event website that of legendarytruth.com, where online guests had again been appointed field investigators for the event. Entering into the soundstage, guests would be amazed at the 1:1 size of this temporary haunt attraction, something that was enforced by the use of an actual parked vehicle outside the house where the LT investigators had setup their recording equipment. Guests walking passed the vehicle could study a number of monitors of 'rooms inside the house', where various haunting experiences were taking place.

Though not actual CCTV footage, the vehicle acted a means of heightening the anticipation for a house that would go down in the event's history as one of the most chilling.

The house would be like a grown-up version of the haunted mansion, where ghosts would come at guests from all angles. It was also the first ever exclusive ghost-only-house[7] that the event had created, something that seems unfathomable in the event's 20 year history but it's true. The backstory was that the house had been constructed in the 1920s by the then Wyandot family for the purposes of a family home and guest house. The father of the family, Malcolm Wyandot then became possessed at some point and by October 30th 1929 he had murdered his family and the 13 guests that were staying at the time. The house would then take guests on a journey showing the tortured souls that had returned. The house actually utilized more special effects than any house had ever used before with ghosts using not just the campy pepper's ghost effect but also misdirection, lighting effects to open up areas that were presumed to be something. It was the later of these which produced a great scare where a ghost is seen charging at guests but would then 'jump' into the floor, another scareactor timed and dressed like the former would then appear under the floor and would be dragged on a pulley system screaming under the guest's feet and disappear into the wall ahead; lighting was used to show that guests would actually standing on clear glass, when the light went off the appearance of floor boards would remain. This scare combined with a creepy bed scene with exact timings and a ghost chair to terrify and delight guests in equal measures. The house also had a cameo by the Storyteller, she like all the other past icons would make cameos in each respective house throughout the event.

Next was 'Havoc: Dogs of War' and was located in the Sprung Tents. The house was billed as, "Ten years ago, the Shadowcreek Enterprise was tasked with developing an elite corps of soldiers. They succeeded. Through an inhalant that includes a compound of testosterone, adrenaline, and other anesthetics, Shadow Creek's latest run of volunteer test subjects are ready for inspection. The project name: HAVOC. The subjects are known simply as Dogs of War." This noisy house was completed by security/army officials trying to secure the deranged misfits that stalked this house, the sound of their firepower would ring in guests' ears as the very jumpsuit clad mad-men and women would come at guests from all angles.

'Hades: The Gates of Ruin' was located within Soundstage 23 and was an impressive mix of horror and myth where the ancient Greek god of the underworld was presented along with all his terrifying minions (no not them minions!). Guests were taken through an impressive cave façade (that resembled a demon-like face complete with nostrils and smoke effects) directly into the underworld of his controlling, where guests were confronted with impressive sets and equally impressive detailed scareactors. Notable scareactors of the Cyclopes, Medusa, a Minotaur and a Kraken were all seen. The Medusa was particularly notable for the extensive detailing to her costume complete with her unabashed insistence for staring down guests to give them the ultimate spooky experience. The house was also notable for being the first house to feature ancient Greek mythology as the sole theme of the house.

Also located inside the same soundstage was 'PsychoScareapy: Echoes of Shadybrook', another house from the popular event franchise. This time guests would be returning to a boarded-up Shadybrook some 15 years after the infamous asylum had closed its doors for the last time. Left behind remaining in the padded cells are a collection of residents that time forgot, who were equally as menacing and maniacal as they had ever been. It happened to feature one of the most psychologically terrifying scares ever showcased at the event, this was 'the corridor of hands'. Half way into the house, a corridor of cell bars ran down both side of the walls, complete with the bars were hundreds of hands grasping the bars, where 90% were fake with that creepy 10% left to reach out and grab at guests (though no intentional touching was seen), the only problem was, which hands were fake and which were the real ones? It was noted at the time, that this scare terrified people, some holding the lines are up to allow enough people to have passed before hand so particular freaked-out guests could run ahead. The house also used the relative new function of 'red-buttoning' which had come into use several years previously, though the button in this house was very prominent; once pushed, a boo-door would open to reveal Jack the Clown who had been an inmate of the original asylum.

'Catacombs: Black Death Rising' was another house located in one of the Sprung Tents. The house was billed as, "In 1534, an undisclosed outbreak plagued thousands of citizens in Paris and Marseilles. As a group of doctors quarantined the most infected against their will, the townspeople turned and sealed them to their doom. After almost 500 years, they remained without escape. Until now... they are rising, ready to take vengeance on any living being that dares to enter the Catacombs." The house started in a mausoleum with crypts containing rotting flesh and skeletal remains. The guests would then travel through a labyrinth of catacombs with doctors (complete with bird like breathing appendages) was attempting to work on the plagued victims. The final area of the house was a construction site of sorts within a museum where various corpses had been unearthed and were now poised to attack.

The final house was 'ZombieGeddon' and it was presented in the Disaster Queue building. The house was billed as, "It's Zday +6 months. The US government has taken back the continental states while clearing the remaining Canadian infestations. They license and sanction private companies to capture 'un-live' subjects for target training. Dozens of independent training 'companies' appear, promising the best training that money can buy. Then there's ZAP...The Zombie Awareness Program." The house would also act as the sole comedy house this year, a spot usually reserved for the 'PsychoScareapy' houses, though this year as noted previously; it was far more horrifying than usual. The house had zombies of all ages throughout and linked directly into the neighboring scarezone of 'Zombie Gras' which had been located right outside the exit to the house. The idea had been that many of the zombies being tested by 'ZAP' inside the house had escaped and had decided to crash a Mardi Gras that was happening within the town of the same setting. Outside smashed-up carnival floats were seen with zombies now in full Mardi Gras costume whilst chewing on pieces of human flesh would jump out at guests both exiting the ride and guests walking through this pinch point to the rest of the studios. This was particularly heightened when the nearby Bill and Ted show would kick-out after each performance.

The all original line-up of houses was complemented by an all original line-up of scarezones. The next scarezone was 'The Coven' on Shrek Alley where witches both aesthetically pleasing and haggard witches were present to jump out at guests. This was flanked on the Plaza of the Stars with 'Esqueleto Muerte' where technicolor skeletal scareactors were hired to jump onto entering guests from their black caskets; a particular scare filled zone when the sun had set. The final scarezone would be located within Sting Alley, entitled 'Saws N' Steam' it would house the now steam-punked Chainsaw Drill Team within a wet misty environment that would petrify anyone who chanced their luck down the dark side street.

Returning shows this year would be 'Brian Brushwood: Menace and Malice' located this time on the Beetlejuice stage. The popular show returned for the last time and took up the stage that had usually housed 'The Rocky Horror Picture Show'. The other show that returned this year was the popular 'Bill and Ted Show' located again in their new home of the 'Fear Factor' Stage. Notable topics for lampooning this year included: Tiger Woods, 'The Jersey Shore', Justin Bieber, the 'Twilight' movies, the 'Kick Ass' movie and the 'Black Swan' movie (all of which had been released that year).

Rides that were open this year included: Revenge of the Mummy, Men In Black: Alien Attack, Jaws: The Ride and The Simpsons Ride. The Hollywood Rip Ride Rockit rollercoaster, the park's most recent ride addition had been due to be open for the event but had been since September 14[8] closed[8]. The unique 17 stories tall ride complete with 90-degree lift hill had opened to much fanfare in the August of that year but had been down periodically due to maintenance. "The overwhelming majority of guests who ride Hollywood Rip Ride Rockit rate their experience as 'excellent.' Our maintenance programs are intense and thorough, with guest safety always the most important priority," Universal Vice-President Tom Schroder said at the time. "We don't share specifics about this kind of work, but I can tell you it is something we don't rush. Each attraction is different and requires its own schedule," he added. "We will reopen Hollywood Rip Ride Rockit as soon as we can do so, but only after we are satisfied all our work is complete." It was therefore decided that as the ride would be worked on during the event, and that queues would be directly below much of the ride's path it was decided to close the ride for the duration of the event. Eventually, the problems would be solved and the ride would re-open to day-guests on October 27th, 2010[10]. Despite the ride being down, Universal routinely surveyed guests on exiting the park on their overall experience of the event[9]. It had early on pulled the highest guest satisfaction level ever, even without the new signature ride, the decision was therefore taken to keep the ride closed throughout the nightly event but open for day guests from 27th.

The level of satisfaction was not the only performance indicator that was ranking high during the event; the level of hotel room sales had drastically improved, something that the Universal management were keen to secure for the final fourth quarter of 2010. New came during the event[11] that room sales were up 12.3% from the previous year for the Central Florida area. "Things are hopping at Universal. And it translates into occupied hotel rooms," said Scott Smith, a lodging instructor in the University of Central Florida's Rosen College of Hospitality Management at the time. Reports that a combination of the recent opening of the new Harry Potter attractions and Halloween Horror Nights had made the resort's hotel room occupancies increase more than the local average to a rumored 16.5%[12].

The positivity of the event was not just seen in the statistics and figures of the resort's accounts but also the romantic-yet-horrific competition that was seen at the time. For the first time ever, Universal began marketing the chance to get hitched at the event. The event had held several weddings previously but this was the first time that Universal had marketed via their

Travel Company the ability for couples to marry. To mark the occasion Universal was going to celebrate this gruesome additional by offering the first marriage for free via a bloodthirsty competition[13]. A press release was issued that read, "Couples can enter by e-mailing a Halloween-themed picture of themselves to hhnwed@universalorlando.com. Photos must be accompanied by a description (no more than 200 words) of why they want an HHN wedding. … Among the grand-prize benefits are food and beverage (including wedding cake) for 20 people and access to a haunted house for the ceremony with 10 scare actors in attendance - including the famed chainsaw drill team.[14]" The winners of the competition were a couple from Vermont, April Richardson, a graphic designer, and Adam Cochran, a pharmacist[15]. The wedding was held on Friday October 15th inside Soundstage 22 at the Wyandot House. The couple who had been engaged since May of that year won a prize worth more than $11,000, which also included park tickets, a hotel stay and other perks. The worthy winners who had been dating for six years were also lifelong fans of the event who would regular throw Halloween parties back in Vermont. The ceremony had been attended by all the main icons and street scareactors, after the ceremony the couple boarded a hearse and were driven by The Caretaker himself to their reception, whilst flanked by the Chainsaw Drill Team. Driving through the park, much to the delight of guests, the couple escorted to their reception which was located backstage in Soundstage 33 (which is used exclusively for special events); whereby the couple was presented with a tiered and cobwebbed cake before enjoying the rest of sights and sounds of the popular event.

Another final first this year was the addition of a VIP Lounge for the fans of the event. For an additional upcharge of just $9.99 guests could enter inside Cafe La Bamba Cantina for not just a drinks bar but also a museum of props from the last 20 years that had been gathered from the actual Halloween Horror Nights warehouse. From select nights various icons would come into the lounge from the neighboring scarezone for photo-opportunities with Thursday nights reserved for exclusive lectures from the event's creatives. Popular topics were alternate icon discussions, alternate themes, further backstory of the developments of both Dr. Mary Agana and 'The Thing', along with houses and scarezones that never quite left the drawing board. Popular with fans of the event, the lounge was positively packed on these nights.

Notes:

1 Orlando Sentinel Sep 24, 2010
2 Orlando Sentinel Nov 24, 2009

[3] Halloween Horror Nights VIP Lounge discussion 2010
[4] Orlando Sentinel Sep 24, 2010
[5] Ibid
[6] Event map 2010
[7] Orlando Sentinel Oct 1, 2010
[8] Orlando Sentinel Oct 14, 2010
[9] Ibid
[10] Orlando Sentinel Oct 28, 2010
[11] Orlando Sentinel Oct 21, 2010
[12] Ibid
[13] Orlando Sentinel Sep 18, 2010
[14] Ibid
[15] Orlando Sentinel Oct 13, 2010

Drac: "At least I only suck the life out of people for 1 month out of every 12!"

Halloween Horror Nights 21

Are you in?

As in the previous year where the event's icon became a personification of emotion, this year it would be a fellow intangible aspect with Lady Luck herself being brought forth to terrify guests. She came about when the park's own fortunes were going great where hotel occupancy was up and so was attendance; though this wasn't luck, this was forward planning and heavy investment by the corporation. To continue this success, it was around early June that the website updated and the public was informed of the event dates, prices, tickets etc. though no word yet on which houses and street scares would be enjoyed. June 28th came and the official event site updated to reveal the overall theme. Pictured throughout were two playing cards, an ace and a queen of spades, which totaled 21, next to a severed and bloody hand[1].

June 19th came around with the first announcement[2] of which house we would be experiencing, 'The Thing' based on the new movie that was going to be released during the event. The Universal picture was a prequel of the 1982 movie of the same name. The basic premise of the movie being that a team of American and Norwegian scientists discovers an extraterrestrial being buried deep in the ice of Antarctica, the movie would end with a direct setup for the 1982 movie by showing the escaped and affected dog running away into the night (soon to be discovered by the characters from the Kurt Russell movie). The star studded premiere would actually be held on October 11th 2011 at Universal Studios in Hollywood during their Halloween Horror Nights event. The synchronicity of the premiere and house with the joint marketing had been deployed very successfully, despite the movie not performing to expectations at the box-office; a process that had been planned in 2009 for 'The Wolfman', that due to production issues had resulted in the movie being released after the 2009 event instead of during. Cinemagoers had been asked that once they had seen the movie, it was now time to experience the movie in real life with houses developed at both coasts for the event.

Located in Soundstage 23 the house did bring guests right into the heart of the action. Beginning their journey guests would travel to the South Pole and find themselves in a snowy environment where they would approach the research station from the movie. With the soundstage's actual thermostat cranked down to the minimum level, guests explored the base from the movie where various scenes had been recreated to show the scientists and inhabitants mutating into the alien creatures. This is later combined with the non-affected scientists doing battle with the aliens. One interesting scene had a human-alien mid-transformation doing battle with a scientist whilst they were suspended on a harness timed to move with the gunshot from the ground character. Soon after guests would find themselves entering into the actual alien ship when the iconic flamethrower is used to dispatch the mutating alien.

Shortly after the announcement, the tickets went on sale via the event website, this was followed by a number of games becoming available throughout the month of August. Week by week new and exciting games would be released that would ultimately reveal clues to the other possible houses that would be forthcoming. More games, along with leaderboards, became available on the 1st September along with the full reveal of all the planned event activities. There was also around this time the first ever fan 'tweet up', where fans of the event were asked via social media to attend a park get-together; though similar events had occurred for the reveal of the Bloody Mary story in 2008. Anticipation was at its highest when the event officially opened on September 23rd that year. The tone for the event had been set when Jim Timon, Vice President of Entertainment announced, "None of our past is here. This is truly - by every aspect and by every design and by every costume, every house, every prosthetic, every scare zone, every piece of makeup --absolutely new. Everything.[5]" And new everything would be, with no more Jack and co, guests would be brought into a new era where new franchises and themes could be explored.

During the buildup to the event a fast spreading rumor started that the old Hard Rock Café would be used to house one of the event's mazes. The Café which had opened with the park back in 1990 was at the time the largest chain in the world. The café which had been shaped into the size of a giant guitar would subsequently close in 1998 when the new café built in the new City Walk would come online. 1999 saw the neck of the restaurant become demolished (this acted as a walkway from the carpark where guests could formerly access the park via the restaurant). The building had been left for storage and occasional staff training, with the entrance to the building inside the Kidzone area of the park. It was around the summer of this year when fans of the event started reporting a great deal of activity inside the building, when various containers and furniture were cleared. Speculation soon ran rampant that the venue would be a perfect location for a house. Speculation was soon quashed when the event opened and no such house had been constructed inside the impressive venue. It was then around early October that Universal issued permits for an 'accelerated demolition' for which by the middle part of the event the building had been fully demolished. It is unknown whether the rampant speculation at the time caused the building to be demolished, possibly fearing trespass in this vulnerable location or whether the building was just removed to make way for future expansions.

The next house in the lineup would be 'Nightingales: Blood Prey' which shared the same soundstage with 'The Thing'. Universal billed the house as, "Within every war, the Nightingales have appeared. Able to transform themselves to fit any setting, these savage banshees feed on the weak and the helpless. Patrolling WWI era trenches, you discover that you are more than just at war…you're being hunted.[3]" The house took guests right into another battle for survival, right into the trenches of the Western Front of World War One. Guests would explore the labyrinth of trenches where the nightingales (a freakish combination of Edwardian nurse meets a toothy, winged demon) are picking off their prey. This noisy house had these demon nurses from hell coming at guests from all angles, including again from above like the preceding house.

'Nevermore: The Madness of Poe' would be located inside Sprung Tent 2 and would take guests through the warped imagination of writer Edgar Allen Poe. The house would begin with guests entering into the writer's own parlor before beginning the journey into his works, which had been presented in chronological order. Pushing giant pages of his literary works aside guests enter first into a diabolical scene from 'The Tell Tale Heart' before quickly stepping into 'The Raven' where the feathered ebony devils would attack from all angles, this even included an interesting special effect where a broken window would smash onto guests (though this was just sprayed water timed to go off with the sound effects and visuals). The house would end with various characters from all his books and poems seen in the house would attack en massse.

Next-door in Sprung Two would be the event's 3D house, 'The In-Between in 3D', which would be the first 3D house since 2007. It happened to coincide nicely at about the height of the fad for 3D glasses at the cinema. Building on this tradition, Universal decided to use more distorting effects that would affect the wearer's perceptions of distance, substrate and depth perception rather than the use of fluorescent paints. Telling the story of two college students who get sucked into a wormhole it took guests into an incredibly unworldly domain filled with demons and ghouls which utilized the distorting effects of the 3D glasses to great effect.

'Winter's Night: The Haunting of Hawthorn Cemetery' would be presented in Soundstage 22 this year. Again another snowy and exceedingly cold environment had been created in the cavernous soundstages that took guests through a creepy graveyard at midnight. Event designers had taken great inspiration from London's creepy Highgate Cemetery, where overgrown grave stones and crypts were presented in this first ever house to be solely based in a graveyard. A ghoulish caretaker of the grounds (not The Caretaker), a number of zombies and ghosts torment guests throughout the house that mixes psychological scares with jumping-out scares to great effect. The elaborately detailed house could be seen as one of the most detailed the event has ever been produced.

The last ever house to be presented in the place where it all started would actually be the first house that had ever started as a scarezone. That house was 'Saws N' Steam: Into the Machine' presented in the Jaws queue building. "It's the very first time that we've decided to take a former scarezone and turn it into a haunted house," said show director Patrick Braillard at the time. "We've never done that before and in that way it becomes a new product.[6]" This hot, wet, humid and steamy house would be perfectly suited to the nuances of the Jaws queue building. The house had been billed as, "Spinning blades and massive, crushing pistons await you around every corner as you are forced deeper into the bowels of a mechanical nightmare. Give yourself to 'The Machine[4].'" This steam-punked workhouse environment would utilize the steam (or dry-ice) very well in that it was used throughout to present some great scares that combined nicely with the gory splatterings of blood and guts in the various fake machines that had been setup. It was a great house that would ultimately send-off the house that started it all in great fashion.

The next house would be 'The Forsaken' and it would be presented in the Parade Building. The house told the story of the four ships that left for the Americas with Columbus, and as we know from history only three made the journey. The forth would be the main subject of the house and would show the crew of that ship die in a watery grave before rising from the depths to attack a Spanish fort. Passing through the ship, a church on the main land and then through the fort, guests would witness the zombie crew doing battle with the Spanish soldiers. The house would prove popular with guests for its imaginative use of narrative and scare but would ultimately prove difficulties off-stage for the management. The special effects had been difficult to manage from the outset, which did not help matters when in the first week the set allegedly flooded from one of the effects. Custodians were deployed hourly to mop up water, clean down the backstage components and ensure the house was checked thoroughly to prevent it from occurring again. This combined with the tremendous floods that were seen in the opening weeks, where the floods were initially thought to be the cause of the water damage; though like in 2012 the area had been known to management for the ceaseless flooding that has occurred in this area during the stormier months.

The final house would be 'H.R. Bloodengutz Presents: Holidays of Horror' and would be the event's comedic house this year. Located in the Disaster queue building, the house would have a lengthy queue video that set guests up for the coming horrors. Introducing the titular main character of H.R. Bloodengutz, the house would represent successive scenes from various holidays dressed as scenes from his latest TV show. Similar to the cinema/drive-in movie houses of the past (corridor-scene-corridor-scene) the house mixed comedy with scares in equal measures.

There would be six scarezones this year. The six would be highly detailed and a real step change from previous years with more money spent on them to create new experiences that had never been seen before. The first would be 'Nightmaze', not only the first time an outdoors maze had been presented at the event but also the first time that park creatives had decided to move walls to change constantly change the layout of the maze each night, this made for a different experience for regular event goers. "When you enter it, you might see dividers and openings ... but once you get in it, those things are constantly moving it," said T.J. Mannarino, director of Entertainment Art & Design. "We're always going to force you to the place you don't want to go.[7]" This foggy and creative scarezone was presented in Production Central.

The next scarezone would build on the previous theme of showing guests something that they had never seen before by literally bringing the house down. 'Acid Assault' located in the New York area of the park would use state-of-the-art projection equipment to show the buildings in the area crumbling to dust. Using similar technology to that use by Disney for their various projection shows, the effect would show the buildings being pelted with acid rain that would eventually leave the buildings to appear to collapse right in front of your eyes. The neat effect had never been used before but had been mixed to time effectively with the scares of the area.

The next scarezone to offer something completely new would be located in the Hollywood area and be simply entitled '7'. The scarezone was again doing something completely fresh by altering to prescribed parameters throughout the night. Featuring various female scareactors that started each night off with impeccable attire dancing to popular music that would over the duration would morph into hideous demonic sirens with rock music ramped up. The sirens would represent the seven deadly sins and would morph periodically throughout the night into their final ghoulish presence.

A smaller scarezone of 'Canyon of Dark Souls' was presented at the front of the park that mixed stilt walkers with hooded monsters and static sets to great effect. 'Grown Evil' was presented in the Central Park area of the park at the event, and would feature a number of animals that were morphing into humanoid monsters. The overgrown area was combined with various sets and props to afford scareactors the best chance of jumping out at guests. The final scarezone would be 'Your Luck Has Run Out' and would feature the event's icon (as she had no house to call her own outright this year). Located on Sting Alley the theme of change was heavily presented where the main icon would again morph inside the alley from fresh-faced Vegas Queen to hideous monster.

Only two shows would be presented this year, one old and one new. The old being the return of the popular Bill and Ted dudes to packed audiences. The highlights of the show this year included references to: The Marvel Cinematic Universe, 'Scream 4' (which had been released earlier in the year), the latest 'Mission Impossible' installment and the newly revised 'Planet of the Apes' franchise. There had been some controversy this year, not with the content of the show, but with the fact that select performances early on at the event had to be cancelled due to the flooding around the area. Sewers being overwhelmed with downpour from the late September storms caused a number of early shows to be cancelled.

The other show presented at the 2011 event was 'Death Drums' a high octane musical performance and dance group which would delight guests in the area outside the then Hercules building. Presenting three different shows each night, the shows would combine drumming performances with glowing sticks to popular dance tracks while an assembled cast of performers danced right in front of the gathered guests.

Setting out to present a different event for a new era, Universal had been highly successful in their mission, which resulted in an experience quite unlike any that any guest had ever experienced before.

Notes:

[1] Orlando Sentinel Jun 30, 2011
[2] Orlando Sentinel Jul 20, 2011

[3] Official event map 2011
[4] Ibid
[5] Orlando Sentinel Sep 23, 2011
[6] Ibid
[7] Ibid

"He is gonna have a right headache tomorrow!"

Halloween Horror Nights 22

Once you're inside, there is no way out!

The buildup to the 2012 event would actually begin in 2011, such was the level of popularity and love for the event by this time, with the inaugural exhibition held at the Orange County Regional History Center with 'The Serious Art of Make-Believe'. The exhibition would run into December and would showcase all the artistry that had been created in the past 20 years of Universal Orlando's history. "There are some things in here that even the rabid fans have never seen. They never saw the light of day," said Andrew Sandall, assistant director of the history center[1]. Everything from the Terra Queen's motorcycle to oil paintings of Jack the Clown, right down to concept art for attractions that had never been built were all showcased at the event. The event was topped-off by a final Q and A session on December 8th that featured many of the creative minds behind the exhibition. It was at this very session that Universal started to tease the 2012 Halloween Horror Nights event, when the previous event had only finished a fortnight ago. Promises of "huge announcements to come" and the development of "partnerships" with other media bodies were mooted at the event.

Such was the popularity of the history exhibition, that the resort along with its fellow competitors from the area decided to hold another forum on design at the very same venue in February of 2012. On February 24th representatives from Universal Orlando, Walt Disney World, Busch Gardens and Nickelodeon[2] gathered for a special Q and A session to raise money for the American Cancer Society. The forum, now in its third year also held a special silent auction for various Universal Studios built props, including ones from the most recent Halloween Horror Nights. Much like the preceding design event, fans were teased on the scale of the upcoming Halloween event and that this year, like the last, the new era of entertainment would contain "new ways of doing things".

And new ways they were, when in July 15th an unexpected announcement occurred from a wildly different location that was broadcasted to the world's media (and not just via the event website like in previous years!). The announcement came from the world's largest fan and 'geekdom' event in San Diego that is 'Comic Con'[3]. "For the first time ever, we're tackling a video-game franchise and bringing it to life at Halloween Horror Nights," Jim Timon, senior vice president of entertainment at Universal Orlando said at the event. Universal had considered making a video game based house in the past but had never found the partner or space within the haunt calendar to build such a maze, so this would be their first foray into the very popular domain of gaming. Jointly announcing the event with John Murdy, creative director at Universal Hollywood, the house would be based on the very popular 'Silent Hill' games. The house would be designed to tie into aspects of both the games, the 2006 movie of the same name and the upcoming Universal feature film of the time 'Silent Hill: Revelation 3D', which would be released on October 26 during the event. This would a similar marketing technique that would link both coasts to new movies appearing in the cinema at the same time as the event; this cross-marketing would prove very fruitful for all partners. The house would be exceedingly close to the look of both the movies and video games when guests entering into Soundstage 22 would first be confronted with a faceless nurse walking awkwardly in high heels before being shot at, before the sirens would sound and guests would be literally plunged into the underworld of Silent Hill, complete with all the characters and falling ash. A tall Pyramid Head character on stilts would terrify guests half way through before guests left the town with one final scare from one of the mutants.

Before the next house was officially announced (which would be very soon after), the fandom having been tipped-off from sources unknown, managed to figure out that there was a strong likelihood of a Penn and Teller house at this year's event. The magic performing duo already had strong links to the event and had even designed their own house for the Hollywood event in year's past. Checking the schedule of their shows for the coming months, it appeared that a gap was seen in July and then a larger gap would be seen in the Fall; which at the time was slightly irregular being that the duo were based in Las Vegas performing their trademark show to packed out audiences most nights on The Strip. Semi-confirmation was seen when in the diary gap, Penn and Teller teased followers to their Twitter account by showing pictures of them in Orlando. It wasn't until August 4th[4] that the duo officially announced their involvement with the event. Stating that they had been officially invited to design their own house for the Florida event, Penn Jillette said at the time, "We blow up all of Las Vegas. It goes terribly, terribly wrong." The house would feature a post-apocalyptic world of Vegas but would be presented in the duo's unique and abstract sense of humor, acting as the event's comedy house for the year. "...to take all the lights and the sounds and all the clichés of Las Vegas and turn them upside down into a fun nightmare," Jillette said. The house wasn't just a house designed by the park with endorsement from the duo; this house would be fully designed in partnership with them. Jim Timon, senior vice president of entertainment had brokered the deal to ensure the pair could have complete creative control of the house, he said, "They're not just putting their name on a haunted house, they're actually designing it." "It was heaven for me because I orchestrated that sort of stuff," Teller then said. "Working with the Universal's Halloween Horror Nights veterans has been 'a pure joy,' he said. "These are people with a proficiency level in a very curious art form that is completely staggering to me[5]."

The house would mix comedy with the current day clichés of the entertainment destination with horror to create a very unique house. The house would be located inside Sprung Tent 2 and would be presented in 3D. The official name was 'Penn and Teller: New(kd) Las Vegas 3-D'. Though the pinnacle of the house and what made it exceedingly unique was that Penn and Teller would actually feature inside the house. On select nights the pair would appear in one of the scenes to not only terrify guests but to also shock them, some guests were heard saying, "was that the real Penn and Teller!?" Yes it was and Universal did not use stand-ins when the duo weren't performing, choosing to leave their section of the house empty so as not to confuse guests. Plucking fans of the event who had worked out the house had been in development with Universal had used the duo's website to work out the timings; again approaching the website and seeing when they were performing in Vegas lead fans to almost accurately work out when the duo would be performing inside the house, which was something that Universal refused to publish (obviously fearing the house could get overwhelmed on select nights). The house seamlessly mixed half-naked zombie show girls with a grossly large and bloated evil Elvis to gross scenes of puking inside the human buffet room. The house was a huge hit for the event.

Skipping back before this house's announcement was an altogether larger broadcast which would unknowingly at the time setup and define the event for coming few years. This was the announcement on July 19th that the popular AMC TV series of 'The Walking Dead' would be coming to the event[6]. Much like the previous Silent Hill announcement, the house would be a joint venture with the Hollywood park and would directly tie into the marketing for the third season of the popular show which would air during the event. This would mark another first, in that this was the first time that Universal on both parks had made houses from a TV show. "For fans of the series, we're going to put you in the footsteps of the characters in the show," John Murdy, creative director at Universal Studios Hollywood, said at the time. "You're going to have to try and survive the zombie apocalypse[7]."

The house would be set in the Disaster queue building and would be entitled, 'The Walking Dead: Dead Inside'; making reference to the words scrawled on the infamous hospital doors from season one. The clue would also be in the name, as the house would take guests on the journey that the main character Rick Grimes suffered starting from the hospital but then into the many popular scenes from that opening season. After visiting the hospital another popular show scene would be the shopping center where it seemed 100s of 'walkers' were banging and scratching at the frosted-glassed doors trying to break into the area to get the guests. The attention to detail and the fact that the house made guests feel like they were straight into the series proved very popular for the event on both coasts. This was an attribute that the event's creatives were keen to fulfil, so they worked closely with the actual designers from the series who were based in Georgia (as the show had been shot there), making the chance to work with the TV Producers of the show even more possible. "Having a chance to be involved in a live event is a completely new challenge for me," Greg Nicotero Co-executive producer said at the time[8]. The level of detailing for the house wouldn't stop at the sets and props, the level of goriness of the performers would be taken to the next level to match the aesthetics of the show. "It's the proximity of having people close to you that are kind of hideous and decomposing and gory. It's fun from the performer side of it, and it infects the guest in that kind of fun", said Nicotero[9].

Shortly after the above announcement around late July, the resort revealed that they were working with another media icon from an altogether different media, that being the musical idol Alice Cooper. The house would be based off of a house from the previous year in the Hollywood event that would be entitled, 'Alice Cooper: Welcome to My Nightmare'. The house that was built in Sprung Tent 1 would be showcase various horror scenes that had been aided in design by Cooper himself and then feature an all Cooper soundtrack throughout. Cooper who was a huge fan of the event on both coasts was excited to work again with Universal when he had been approached by Hollywood's creative director John Murdy, Murdy had spotted Cooper enjoying the event as guests with his family back in 2010. Universal billed the house as, "Journey into the legendary rocker Alice Cooper's twisted mind and witness the natural melding of horror and Cooper's four decades-long career. Here you will follow Steven, the iconic character from many of Cooper's works, as you come face-to-face with a myriad of tormentors who threaten an already-decaying sense of sanity[10]." Entering via a huge façade of Cooper's face and through his mouth, guests were taken on a journey through Cooper's mind that mixed loud blasting rock n roll from his various albums to timed scares (some of which were in the pitch black!).

It was also on this very day (the Cooper announcement) that Universal pulled the permit that had been on the Hercules building to have it replaced with another permit for demolition. Speculation then ran rampant over the possible demolition permit, though it was later revealed that the Soundstage would be torn-down during the event to make way for a new ride; that ride later turned out to be Transformers. This effect led to the eight houses that had been planned now reduced down to seven. Little is known about the house that was partially constructed inside the Hercules building, though many believe it to be a house that was later re-constructed for the coming year (2013), that would go on to raise huge praise for its amazing use of puppets (more on this in the next chapter!). We do know that the Hercules building had been cleared out and repaired at some cost, as the Jaws building which had normally been used as a haunt location had also been torn down to make way for the Harry Potter expansion. It was felt that the relatively new majority shareholders of the resort, Comcast had funding to fast-track 'The Transformers' attraction using blueprints from the Hollywood and Singapore iterations of the ride, so the attraction could be built in record time. This was seen as a movie to increase the attraction number of the park whilst the popular Jaws attraction was being moved to make way for future expansion.

This level of construction also impacted on the streets of the event where popular street locations from the past had to be opened up to cope with the level of footfall the popularity of the event was enjoying. It was then announced by the resort that plans had changed in August and the static scarezones of the past would be adapted to make way for the construction. "Scarezones in the past have been defined places and spaces. Now we want to play with that a little bit," said Jim Timon, Universal's senior vice president for entertainment. "The characters and scare actors will ebb and flow and move and change, so you won't always see the same 'scareactors' in the same places as you may have seen them earlier in the night," Timon said[11]. Having to accommodate for the relatively new 'Superstar Parade' that had been showcased for day-guests, along with improving footfall, the static scarezones of the past could not be deployed. "There are some physical realities out there that we have to adjust and accommodate," Timon said. "It encouraged us to do stuff with the scare actors that we haven't done in our program before[12]." Though some physical sets were built for the scarezones, mostly located in areas where the parade did not travel and where footfall couldn't bottleneck. The streets would be entitled, 'The Legions of Horror' and would be the first time the whole park had roaming scarezones and the second time since 2007 that the event would allow all the streets to be one giant scarezone. The roaming hoards would include: 'The Iniquitous', 'The Vampires', 'The Beasts', 'The Warriors', 'The

Prisoners', 'The Traditionals' and 'The Walkers'. The different factions would be based on the various online games that were popular on the event's official website.

The next house would be 'Dead End' and it would be located in Soundstage 22. One of the two original concepts for this year, the house told the story of a haunted mansion overrun with ghosts that would terrify guests. Rumors quickly spread that the house would be one of the most psychologically scary houses ever created by the resort. "It's stuff that people have always fantasized of as 'classic haunted house.' For me, that is a combination not just of the scenery, it's a mixture of the sound design that we have in there and some of the wonderful special effects that we have that really puts this on edge," said TJ Mannarino at the time. "We do houses that are spectacle, we do houses that are comical, we do houses that follow a wonderful story," Mannarino said. "This one is truly scary[13]."

The other house, located in the same soundstage would be 'Gothic'. This house would feature an elaborately designed cathedral setting during restoration. Having never taken guests inside a cathedral, the journey would showcase to guests just how detailed the park's creatives could be by building a full cathedral set using the forced-perspective technique. Throughout the house various gargoyles, a hunchback and statues would attack guests with everyone getting that feeling, 'is that statue a scareactor or an actual statue?', with us all finding out when it was too late! The brilliance of this house was later reflected when it won 'house of the year' by the in-house awards based on the feedback from guests.

The final house would be located in the Parade building and feature 'Universal's House of Horrors', which some believe to be a late addition to the event due to the rapid decision to demolish the Hercules building. The building had at the time been housing the new 'Superstar Parade' floats which had to be hastily removed then wrapped in protective film every evening in a nearby temporary housing for the event. The house was then allegedly constructed very late on inside the building using the footprint of the previous year's house 'The Forsaken' but none of the same sets and props. Instead a black and white world of horror was presented where guests were taken into the classic world of the Universal horror movies. The problems didn't end there though, like in the previous years, the first two weeks of the event were laden with heavy rainfall that periodically flooded the area around the queue location, which had been moved to behind the building to cope with footfall for the other houses.

Bill and Ted were again back this year and featured popular references to: 'Mad Men', 'Magic Mike', 'Ted', 'The Dark Knight Rises' and 'The Hobbit', all topped off with various bouts of the craze that was sweeping the world of 'Gangnam Style' dancing. Complete with this show was a new addition unseen before, that of '20 Penny Circus: Fully Exposed' located at the Beetlejuice stage. The show mixed gross-out humor with magic tricks to delighted audiences nightly.

Notes:

[1] Orlando Sentinel Nov 18, 2011
[2] Orlando Sentinel Feb 16, 2012
[3] Orlando Sentinel Jul 15, 2012
[4] Orlando Sentinel Aug 4, 2012
[5] Ibid
[6] Orlando Sentinel Jul 19, 2012
[7] Ibid
[8] Orlando Sentinel Sep 14, 2012
[9] Ibid
[10] Official event map 2011
[11] Orlando Sentinel Aug 31 2012
[12] Ibid
[13] Orlando Sentinel Sep 21, 2012

Halloween Horror Nights 23

What evil has taken root?

As in the previous year the speculation began with the presentation of 'A Year in the Life: Backstage to Onstage at Universal Orlando Resort' which was held at the Orange County Regional History Center in February this year. The exhibition would showcase all the designs and stories from the past years at Universal Orlando, plus teasing for what would be about to unfold later in the year. TJ Mannarino[1] said at the exhibition, "It's always fun to pull up the archives and start looking at stuff that really was the beginnings of some of the bigger projects. Some of these events have grown to massive size and they actually touch, in effect, the world. Halloween Horror Nights is now in four separate parks, from Singapore to Japan to Hollywood to here in Orlando." As well as the gathered props, blueprints, set pieces and costumes that had been put on display, the exhibition features a huge wall that showed the timeline for planning the events we all love. Halloween Horror Nights was seen to be a now 18 month affair from initial concept through to the execution of every night. Apart from the various showcases at the event, it was highly rumored and teased that both 'The Legendary Truth' (the fan interactive collective experience) would be back and that this year would again feature a high number of outside owned properties for the houses.

This was swiftly followed in March by the Entertainment Designers Forum which was held at the same center, where discussions took place about how the houses are brought from concept to design. This was followed by Spooky Empire's MAY-HEM / Halloween Extreme convention on Memorial Day Weekend of May 23th -25th in Orlando, where the Universal panel again teased the return of Legendary Truth but also that this year would see a massive increase in merchandise. The increased merchandise would also be readily available on the website for those who could not attend the event.

Later on in the year to June and the building permits were issued to the City of Orlando, confirming that again we would all be enjoying 7 houses. This was rapidly met when around the end of that month (June 26th) Universal announced the first house would be based on the modern cult classic movie 'The Cabin in the Woods'; this was combined with the event's website updating to reveal the tree/root them once again with the tag line "What Evil Has Taken Root?" on the following day.

The house would be based on the movie that had been released in the year prior to much success. Officially labelled as a horror-comedy, a genre which had been weirdly absent for many years at the cinema, it mixed tongue-in-cheek post-modernistic humor with straight out gore, culminating in possibly one of the bloodiest finales ever. The movie starts pretty traditionally by recounting the tale of some pretty cliché high school students who eventually end up in a cabin in the woods, little do they know that they are actually a part of a horrible experiment, which inevitably goes wrong and all hell breaks loose (literally). The movie had been produced by largely the same team that had brought us 'Buffy the Vampire Slayer', headed up as executive producer by Joss Whedon. The house would effectively stick to the original storyline and would take guests right through the many famous scenes of the movie, to make everyone feel like they were right there inside all the action. "We are building the cabin completely. You're going to walk through a forest to get there. You're going into the cabin. You're going to go into the cube cells. We're literally taking everything we can in the film and giving you a kind of best-of montage of the film with this kind of linking story," said Mike Aiello[2] at the time.

This was achieved by extensive research by Universal whilst working together with the original filmmakers, which led to the creation of extremely detailed sets that were not only exacting to the movies but were filled with detail. The most notable scene from the movie which led to the most notable scene from the house would be the elevator scene. Guests would enter into a room filled with elevators, then just at the right moment the elevators would 'bing' indicating that the monsters had been selected, thereby every elevator would open to feature a whole array of monsters to terrify guests. There was even the popular merman that would spray blood (water) onto guests inside the control room. Drew Goddard[3] the director of the movie said, "My wish for Cabin was always that it would live on outside the film, that people would take that ball and run with it, and I can't imagine a better fit for what we were trying to do with the movie than to make a maze out of it." The house had actually been one of the largest ever created, having been built inside the enormous Soundstage 21, which had never been used for the event before as this stage was usually occupied by production companies. Fun fact: Both Jack the Clown and the Caretaker appeared as cameos in the elevator scene but only for the briefest of seconds[20].

'The Evil Dead' house would be announced next. The house would not be based on the original series of movies but rather on the recent remake which had been released earlier in 2013. As in previous years, the house would be across both American events at the same time with each coast undertaking their own creative touches to make two unique houses from the same property. John Murdy[4] from Universal Hollywood said at the time, "If you're familiar with what we do with Halloween Horror Nights, we create living horror movies. So we want to make our guests feel like they got up from their movie seat, walked through the screen, and now they get to live through the world of Evil Dead. So we're bringing it to life with movie-quality sets, makeup, costumes and props. It'll be like living the experience for real."

Working closely with the original filmmakers, Universal was keen to build a house that not only featured all the classic components of the movie but also all the best scares that could be created in a way that wasn't predictable so they would be presented totally fresh and incredibly scary. Fede Alvare who directed the 2013 movie said at the time[5], "It was mind-blowing. It was really like walking into the movie and having the chance to witness every crazy, gory moment of the movie firsthand, with people walking next to the characters. So it's amazing. It's so flattering and so great, and I think it's a great way to honor, not just the movie, but the Evil Dead franchise in general."

The event would also tie straight into the release of the Blu-ray for 'The Evil Dead' movie, with copies of it available for sale at the event. Inside the house, all the classic elements of the movie were there, including the initial book reading, to exploring the basement, the tongue splitting scene, right down to the iconic approach to the cabin through the forest. The house was very popular and held regularly long queues on every night of the event.

It was around late July that the announcement came that 'The Walking Dead' would again be returning to the event. Building on the success and level of immersion of the previous year, Universal was to bring the horror TV series back to the park and showcase season 3 in the house and seasons 1 and 2 in the streets where every scarezone would be dedicated to the popular show. The New York area of the park will show the fall of Atlanta from season one. This would be followed by the woodlands in the Central Park area. A Survivor's Camp was setup in the Kidzone area, which had been recreated exacting to the one scene in the series. Mel's Drive-In area would feature the Farm with detailed sets and props built with a mini-show that would be unlike anything seen at the event before where a live disemboweling by various 'Walkers' would take place. This would be attached to Hollywood Boulevard where the Clear would be presented. This would be the first time in the event's history that the entire park would have scarezone based from one single property. And if planned in advance, guests could walk all the scarezones in their order from the two seasons (as though they had been thrown into the actual show!) before enjoying the delights of season three inside the house. It was a hugely ambitious plan which was executed brilliantly at the Orlando event. Across the country in Hollywood they too had a house based on Season three that differed from the Orlando one by adding in a few additional scenes.

Proving their abilities at the last event, the producers of the show allowed the event's creatives to flourish for the planning of the house. "We didn't have any specific characters last year, but this year we're able to use Milton and Merle and Penny," Mike Aiello[21] said at the time. This included recreating the house of Penny from the show, a house that has never been seen on screen but working with the producers the event could provide their version of what it could look like. Working with the Georgia based producers of AMC enabled the event's Art and Design department to build a partnership that would not just last this event but would continue to the next year as well.

The house for the event was presented in the Parade building with the event's creatives again working closely with the original producers of the show. John Murdy[6] said at the time, "it's fabulous to work with partners who are equally passionate and also get what we do." Walking the course back in the Spring of that year the park's creatives and designers from the TV show especially chose the parade building to house the large maze. Mike Aiello[7] said, "We knew we wanted to do the chain-link maze that has the tower as its focus point, that could not have been done anywhere but in a soundstage or B79 [parade float building]." Construction of the tower along with the prison scenes took all year, with the parade floats again relegated to another building. The house was topped-off with the inclusion of the twisted Governor who was seen throughout taunting 'walkers' and guests a like. A neat addition to the house, was a scareactor costumed as a 'walker' who had been chained up to the left, combined with a chainmail pen to the right just outside the entrance. Scareactors working in tandem would work to make guests jump out of their skin as the lines snaked up and down around this area; it provided some entertainment watching unsuspecting guests in lieu of no queue video.

Around August of this year all the other houses were announced via the event's official website and their new Twitter account that had gone live at the end of July[8]. Possibly the most anticipated and best house to ever be constructed at the event (*this writer's opinion!*) was the Universal picture 'An American Werewolf in London'. The one house that Universal had been designing and planning without success for over six years, would now finally be brought to the event[15]. Based on the original British-American movie from 1981, the house would take guests right back to that era for a journey through the moors of Yorkshire before heading down to London. The rumor was that the house had to be postponed from the year previous due to the construction of the new 'Transformers' ride, the house would for the first time replace scareactors with huge puppets that would be controlled by a number of scareactors for great effect. Working in partnership with legendary movie director John Landis the Orlando staff would work tirelessly to recreate the look and feel of the original movie. "It's something we've always wanted to do, and we've finally figured out a way that we'll be able to," said creative director Michael Aiello[9] at the time. "The only way this could have happened as authentically as we've been able to do it was with John's involvement with us." Landis helped in all areas of the house's development, providing original source material and props that Universal could work from to create the scares. Weeks and months of planning were put into the exacting look of each werewolf, where like in the movie, full sized 8ft tall puppets were built. "They are using the exact same - now sort of dated but effective - technology that we used," Landis said. The creative makeup genius that is Rick Baker had originally made the puppets for the movie back in 1980. Spending just as much time back then building the animals and then working them on set as Universal was doing in 2013; Baker's tireless efforts to create the fiendish lycans actually awarded him his first Academy Award for makeup for that actual movie. "The attraction is really homage to Rick's work," Landis said[10].

But it wasn't just the werewolves that would be created to the exact specifications of 1981; the sound too would be directly mimicked from the movie. "We had to go back to the original elements of the soundtrack and break down the tracks," Landis then said. "They used the sound effects from the film and the music from the film... They create a whole new ambience - but it's a new mix for this specific environment." Mike Aiello confirmed the dedication that was seen in creating the sound of the house by confirming the iconic howl of the werewolves had to be recreated to exacting parameters. "Capturing the sound of the wolf was incredibly important," he said[11]. "We didn't want to try to replicate or re-create those sounds if we knew we could have access to them." The only way the house differed from the movie was that an active decision was made to tone the humor of the movie down inside the house and ramp up the scares instead. Starting off on the moors then travelling to the 'Slaughter Lamb' pub, guests were then taken to London to see all the iconic scenes of the movie, including an indoor recreation of Piccadilly Circus and the London Tube. This culminated in one of the most elaborate scenes ever constructed where a scareactor costumed as the lead character from the movie (David) actually slowly transforms before your very eyes into a werewolf. Landis said at the time, "What I've come away with is I'm very impressed with how ambitious Mike is - they're building these very elaborate sets, fully realized reproductions of the Slaughtered Lamb, a bit of the tube station, Piccadilly Circus, the hospital. It's really an attempt to 'recreate in the flesh,' so to speak, an experience for the guests.[12]"

The house took the longest to build that year and was one of the last to be finished before the event. Built inside and occupying the whole of Soundstage 22 the house would combine intimate scenes such as the hotel with larger scenes like Piccadilly Circus where London cabs, double decker buses and even a police box (Tardis maybe?) would be recreated around the carnage of a werewolf loose in London. An impressive team of 60 scareactors would be deployed to work the house including an equal number of operations staff to keep the house alive and moving. It was possibly one of the most ambitious projects that had ever been created at the event. Landis was extremely positive and impressed with Universal's dedication to not only create the house but to painstakingly recreate all the scares from the movie, he said, "First of all, it's a theatrical event, an all-immersive theatrical event. It's very different from a film. What I hadn't considered before sitting down with the team was they have these practical realities of getting a certain number of people through, and just the logistics of the whole thing is complicated[13]." Proud of the team he said finally[14], "These guys really are passionate about this stuff, there's a level of enthusiasm that's just infectious and wonderful. They love it, they really do!" The final touch of the house preparation and for one that Landis was present for, was the final attachment of the long running 'Easter egg' of every Landis movie, that of 'See You Next Wednesday'. This time it would be manifested as a movie poster for eagle-eyed fans upon entering the Soho cinema scene of the house.

Next door to this house was another installment in the park's wishes to bring video games to the event, this was 'Resident Evil: Escape From Raccoon City' which was located inside Soundstage 21. The house was billed as[16], "Raccoon City is overrun with Umbrella Corporation's most terrifying experiments, and the only option is complete destruction. You'll need to duck and dodge Lickers, Hunters, and Nemesis himself if you want any chance of escaping Capcom's video game terrors before missiles send everything back to hell." The event decided to not make the house from the recent franchise of movies that had been released but to rather stick lovingly to the original 'Resident Evil' 2 and 3 video games; this even included a special scene towards the end of the house that included a 'paused screen', as the house was one giant video game that guests were experiencing, with the player of the game pausing it to go use the bathroom etc. Which was a nifty idea but not popular with fans that found the scene interesting but not scary. Working closely with the video game's creators Capcom, the house followed the story from the early noughties, and presented sets and costumes that looked very authentic to the original game.

The next house, located over in the Sprung Tents would be 'Urban Legends: La Llorona', a house that had been at the Hollywood event in the previous year. A house that was so popular it would go on to reach 'house of the year' status on the West coast. The house followed the tragic Mexican myth of Llorona or 'The Weeping Woman' which detailed the story of a mother killing her children before being damned to walk the earth for eternity. The house had borrowed half the sets from the Hollywood version of the house, before creating an entirely new path for the remainder. This noticeably difference saw guests enter into a small Mexican village, followed by chapel and crypt to then descend into the watery made world of the urban legend. The house was chilling and intense that mixed a variety of scares to create a truly terrifying experience.

Next to this house was 'After Life Death's Vengeance' in Sprung Tent 2. The house used the 3D technology again to great effect. Universal billed the house as[17], "Serial killer Bobby "The Blade" is about to meet Ole' Sparky. 2000 volts are going to send him to a horrific realm of pain. His victims have waited an eternity for vengeance. They're bound to turn Bobby's afterlife into an unimaginable, infernal torment." Like the previous house, this one would be one of three that were entirely new concepts for the event and not linked directly to any other movie, TV or video game property. This would be the first house to use the 3D technology without using comedy; in fact this year did not have a comical house at all. The house started where we witness the execution of a serial killer, using a prop from a past year that had been entirely redressed to great effect. Soon guests descended via the turning vortex (used every year) into the afterlife which allowed the 3D technology to confuse and disorientate guests throughout.

The final house of the event this year was a sequel to the popular Havoc house franchise that had been built up over the years. 'Havoc: Derailed' would be presented in the Disaster queue building where actual train carriages had been setup to give the appearance of the misfit maniacs on the loose following the derailment of the train they were riding in. The house design was especially created to allow the event's creatives to experiment on a number of scares that they had been planning for a while. "Although the train cars are not moving, the house features a before-and-after motif. The crash point is accompanied by blinding light and very loud sound effects [to create the illusion of a train crashing]" Mike Aiello said at the time. "The back half was an easier build than the front half for us because building confined train cars is something we've never done before." This experimentation included the use of 'air-bladders' that were installed in the final scene to create a sense of chaos that would be used to push guests towards the exit while scareactors were attacking from all directions. "We're either (a) going to be really good at it or (b) we're going to learn from it," he said. "We do stuff like that every single year because it's the only way this event moves forward with the type of effects we do.[19]" It was truly inspiring to see the event still experimenting with ideas and concepts, which for an event that is over 20 years old is something very special indeed.

The two shows this year would see a return of two of the most popular. Bill and Ted were back with their usual comedy-music fest with references to: 'The Big Bang Theory', 'Les Miserables', Disney's construction of 'Avatarland', 'The Man of Steel' and various lookalikes of Miley Cyrus, Justin Bieber, Anne Hathaway and Kim Kardashian featured in the final dance-off. The other show presented was a return of the popular 'The Rocky Horror Picture Show - A Tribute' located again at the Beetlejuice stage.

Notes:

[1] Orlando Sentinel Feb 1, 2013
[2] Zap2It article June 2013
[3] Ibid
[4] ign.com article June 2013
[5] Ibid
[6] Zap2It article July 2013
[7] Orlando Sentinel Sep 20, 2013
[8] twitter.com
[9] Orlando Sentinel Aug 16, 2013
[10] Ibid
[11] Ibid
[12] yahoo.com/movies article Aug 16, 2013
[13] Ibid

[14] Ibid
[15] Ibid
[16] Official event map 2013
[17] Ibid
[18] Orlando Sentinel Sept 20, 2013
[19] Ibid
[20] Orlando Sentinel Sep 27, 2013
[21] Orlando Sentinel Sep 20, 2013

"So am I in the right place for HHN?"

Halloween Horror Nights 24

You've been warned!

It was late March of 2014 when we first received the news via the official event's website that there would be 8 houses, 2 shows and many street experiences, dates for the event followed soon after. It wasn't until June 10th that we got our first indication of a house. The news websites and papers ran headlines such as "Walking Dead will overrun Universal for Halloween nights[1]", and although it was an impressive feat to see the popular TV show back for a third year, some fans were less than impressed, though these seemed to be in the minority as most fans could recount the excessively detailed and memorable scares from the past two years (live disemboweling for example!).

The new house would feature all the key scenes and plot twists from the fourth season of the popular show. The news promised that the house would feature more scareactors and more elaborate scares than ever before. Guests would enter into the prison, walk through the cell block and then into an impressive scene with a crashed helicopter. In order to encompass the huge number of increased scareactors and massive set pieces, the house would be based inside Soundstage 25 – which had never been used for the event before. The 11,000 square feet stage[2] is one of two specially adapted stages that are just for the use of television production (due to the addition of additional rigs and a high-level gallery control room). Mike Aiello[3] director of entertainment for the event said at the time, "We're bursting at the seams, as far as Soundstage 25 is concerned, by how much we're cramming into that space to ensure we're hitting all the necessary beats that are within season 4." Building the house inside this huge stage would effectively enable the house to be twice the size of any other. This fact was heavily marketed along with the tie-in that the event would begin around the same time as the show's fifth season.

The house started more or less in the queue where an impressive façade (probably the largest ever) had been created, complete with fencing and barbed wire guests queued along the façade until they entered inside. Once inside the house it did not feel claustrophobic as the event's creatives had filled the giant scarezone with a labyrinth of rooms and set pieces. The number of scareactors deployed was very noticeable, there were 'walkers' coming at you from all angles, be they real actors or props. Moving on from the grocery store, guests would find themselves at the Country club and then finally at the walls of Terminus. Two very interesting scares were the use of lighting to make some prop 'walkers' appear to be running down a hall, when in fact they were stationary; the other being the forest scene where there must have been over 20 scareactors dressed as 'walkers' and a similar number of prop walkers disguised with the light effects. It was a hugely impressive house that probably made all the naysayers' jaws hit the floor; such was the detail and expansive size of the house.

It was then announced around July 16th that the next house to be revealed for the event would be 'From Dusk Till Dawn' and would be located in Soundstage 22. The house would be based on the recent TV show and not on the movie of the same name. The original first season of the show ran on the El Rey Network in 2013, which had been produced by Robert Rodriguez who had originally directed the 1996 movie. Rodriguez and his team would work with Universal on both coasts to bring the house to both stateside events. "We will feature the over-the-top gore that the show does so well and our guests will come face-to-face with Robert's unique and wickedly cool take on the vampire mythos that is completely authentic to the show," said Aiello at the time. The house would be designed to reflect scenes from the first season but to also prepare guests for the second season that would debut during the event.

Entering in via the infamous 'Twister' bar façade, guests would witness various half-naked vampire sirens that would titillate and terrify in equal portions. The house was the master this year of the distraction scare, where poll dancing vampires or vampires feasting on a dead patron would distract the eye just as another more hideous version would jump out from the side.

A few days later and the SyFy show of 'Face Off' was announced with 'Face Off: In The Flesh' to be debuted at the event in the streets. Laura Tyler[4], a Universal Orlando makeup artist, who had won the fifth series of the popular show would be on hand to oversee the scarezone and bring her award winning scares to the streets of Hollywood Boulevard. "Our goal is to bring to life the macabre artistry displayed in the characters seen week after week," said Aiello[5] at the time. Over the seven seasons of the show ten iconic looks had been especially selected and then recreated for the scarezone. Each of the ten selected were then presented with their own set pieces from which they could scare and provide great photo opportunities.

This announcement was followed a few days later at the end of July by the announcement that 'The Purge' was coming to the event. The popular film franchise would feature on the streets in the New York area as 'Anarchy'. The two Universal pictures, which had been released on small budgets in both 2013 and 2014 respectively, featured a dystopia world where the new government allows one night a year where there are no laws or police/ambulances etc. available. The wildly successful movies would be both used to simulate short show sequences on the streets to make it appear that 'The Purge' was happening on the streets for real. This process would then mix characters from the movies with non-costumed scareactors (who appeared as guests), running and chasing them through the streets causing chaos and confusion in equal measures.

It was then on August 4th that 'AVP: Alien vs. Predator' would be featuring at the event in Soundstage 24. Taking what Universal had learnt the year before by seamlessly mixing puppetry with real effects enabled them to create the alien species to great effect. Marking the double celebration of the 10th anniversary of the first 'Aliens vs. Predator' movie and the 35th anniversary of the original 'Alien' film, Universal wanted to present the characters in their true and terrifying presences in a way that would delight guests by showcasing their awesome wizardry. "We're employing our full arsenal of tricks and techniques in translating the AVP: Alien vs. Predator brand into an authentic and horrific maze experience. Our guests are going to be thrown head first into this epic battle where only the strong will survive. This is truly going to be an out-of-this-world maze experience that the fans have been waiting for," said Aiello[6] at the time.

In what was probably the best house for this year, the house told the story of base LV-426 that had been setup by the marines on a far and distant planet, only to be gate-crashed by a massive swarm of aliens and various predators hot on the prowl. All of the aliens featured were puppets, designed for the scare much like the 'American Werewolf' puppets had been in the year before. These were met with huge predators over 6ft doing battle with various marines. The agreement with Fox for the use of characters enabled the creatives of the event to not tie the house to one specific time or place from any of the franchises, but would rather present various iconic scenes from the different movies. Impressive scenes such as the chest-bursting predator on a sickbay bed to the marine being pulled down through the floor by a huge alien would all culminate by guests having to bend down or crawl out via a service tunnel with aliens attacking from above and both sides. It was truly an epic house that will go down in the event's history as one of the best.

'Dracula Untold: Reign of Blood' was next to be announced in early August. The house based of the recent movie of the same name would also be located in Soundstage 24. The movie which wasn't released until October 10th would act as an 'immersive preview' that would take guests into the heart of the movie by exploring key scenes from a destroyed village, a network of caves before ending at the famous vampire's own castle[7]. The house would also be shared with Hollywood where much of the same technique will be used, with the house choosing to focus on the horrors of Dracula, while the movie will explore his origins. John Murdy, creative director of the Hollywood event, said at the time, "But there is much more to the tale than just a dark figure lurking in the shadows, drinking blood. While Dracula Untold will reveal the origin story of the man who became Dracula, our 'Halloween Horror Nights' maze will invite guests to experience the atrocities Dracula imposed on his victims in the most frightening and immersive way possible[8]." Like never before would Universal be giving guests the chance to preview a movie in this way before heading to the cinemas, a process which will likely evolve over time and become more important to the event.

The final IP house to be released for this year[9] (announced on August 28th) would be based on one of the largest movie horror franchises of all time. 'Halloween' would be presented for the first time at the Orlando event in Sprung Tent 2. "Guests will come face to face with Michael Myers as we re-create the kills committed the night he came home," said Aiello[10] at the time. The house had been presented at the Hollywood event before mixing various scenes from various movies, whereas on the east coast the house was designed to encapsulate the horrors from the first movie. "It's our holy grail of horror films. It started the slasher genre and did it so well. It has all the right pieces essential to make a great horror maze: great character, inventive kills, really great story and iconic music," said Aiello[11]. Rigidly sticking to the 1978 movie, the house would put every guest back into the scares from the iconic movie. Entering in via the house façade of the movie, the façade would feature an impressive projection of the masked murderer to the front and that appeared to show him smashing through the boarding to stare down at guests. Initially guests would see young Myers as he starts off his murderous career before witnessing all the key murder scenes from the movie through the rest of the house.

This release was followed by the final release of late August when Universal announced the final three houses to feature which would all be newly created original content for the event. These would be 'Giggles & Gore Inc.' located in the Disaster queue building. The gory house would feature a factory of evil clowns with murderous intentions. Then the next house would be 'Dollhouse of the Damned' located in the Sprung Tents. The house would feature an impressive façade of a giant doll's house with dry ice and hysterical shrieks coming from within. Inside a maniacal mix of mad people with grafted doll faces would terrorize guests throughout. The final house would be 'Roanoke: Cannibal Colony' and would be located in the Parade building which would tell the story of a recently relocated bunch of 16th Century murderous cannibals as they adjust to their new surroundings whilst looking for food. Three houses were not easy concepts to bring to life when you have to start from scratch with an original idea, tell a story and make it come to life. "That's probably the hardest step in this process, and it's also the first one so that we can really make sure that, we're delivering on the expectation of what people know from Halloween Horror Nights but also surprise them with some things," said Aiello[12] at the time.

Two further scarezones were presented this year, including 'MASKerade; Unstitched' at the Plaza of the Stars area. The scarezone featured scareactors in impressive ball gowns dancing into the night as the skin on their faces is falling off. An impressive use of makeup was used to create the concept of wax and stitches being used whilst others were rounding up victims to have their skin removed. The final scarezone would be 'Bayou of Blood' and would be located in the Central Park area. The zone would feature voodoo worshippers in a blood filled frenzy attacking others to be provided as sacrifices for their rituals.

Two popular shows returned this year, those being Bill and Ted and 'The Rocky Horror Picture Show Tribute'. The former featuring references to: 'Teenage Mutant Ninja Turtles' movie from that year, 'Guardian of the Galaxy' movie with an overall theme inspired from the movie 'Neighbors' from that year.

Notes:

[1] Orlando Sentinel June 10, 2014
[2] http://studio.florida.universalstudios.com/
[3] Orlando Sentinel Jun 20, 2014
[4] Orlando Sentinel Jul 18, 2014
[5] Ibid
[6] Orlando Sentinel Blog August 4, 2014
[7] Orlando Sentinel Aug 12, 2014
[8] Press release from Universal Orlando Aug 7, 2014
[9] Orlando Sentinel Aug 28, 2014
[10] Ibid
[11] Ibid
[12] Ibid

The Future of Halloween Horror Nights

"What we think is coming next…"

One of the most important deals that has been struck behind the scenes that will actively have a huge positive impact on the future years of the event will be Universal's partnership with Legendary Pictures. A partnership that had started in July 2013, which had weathered stormy times but has recently been cemented by the huge successful release of 2015's 'Jurassic World'.

The partnership began with Universal as the production company's partnership with Warner Bros ended. The company had made many successful movies with the former partner, including the wildly popular 'The Dark Knight' franchise, 'Pacific Rim' and "The Hangover" franchise (to name a few); though under the supposed terms of the deal, Universal would not have access to or any business with Legendary's past movies with Warner Bros[4]. Moving on to Universal, the company has found a solid partner who is keen to build on their former successes and to open their impressive back catalogue to explore exciting new creative possibilities. Universal and Legendary said at the time, "Comcast and NBCUniversal's global assets in film, television and theme parks offer Legendary unmatched breadth and opportunity to grow our business," Legendary Chief Executive Thomas Tull said in a statement. "We are delighted to be in business with this exceptional team and look forward to a successful partnership[1]."

The deal with Legendary would not only tie together the companies for the purposes of production and release of movies but it will also explore other avenues that would be mutually beneficial for both. The deal has specifically detailed the possibilities of cross-promotion that can be enabled from building haunted attractions at both of its American theme parks for Halloween Horror Nights[2]. The deal has enabled Universal to part fund Legendary's movies along with distributing and marketing them. Legendary will then co-finance some of Universal's own in-house productions and have access to their iconic back catalogue of movies and TV shows. And although the exact terms of the deal have not been released, the driving force of the deal would be to create cinematic experiences unlike anything ever released before.

From a fan's perspective we can now see from this 2013 deal (that last's five years currently, though officially started in 2014[3]), that a number of items from this partnership have already been brought to the parks for this synergy. The partnership seeks to release 'Kong: Skull Island' in 2017 with a ride of the same name coming to Islands of Adventure around the same time if not sooner. The installation of the 'Raptor Encounter' as well at Islands that ties neatly in with 'Jurassic World' and also the very first partnership house of 'Dracula Untold' at 2014's Halloween Horror Nights.

The Dracula house of that year, as discussed in the last chapter, was a house that utilized the whole Universal idea of 'immersive preview'. The idea of bringing guests into the house for a preview of a coming attraction in order to build anticipation for the movie, in a direct hope for better returns at the box-office, is something pretty new for the event, particularly when it is planned this way. Noting that in 2009 the 'Wolf Man' movie due to production issues came out after the event when it was originally planned to release during the event.

Universal with the partnership with Legendary have an impressive run of movies coming out soon that would possibly lend themselves to future houses for our event, let's consider a few of them[5]:

'Crimson Peak' to be released in 2015 was announced in July to be a haunted attraction at the Hollywood event. This is supposedly a ghostly tale with a female protagonist in a large haunted mansion.

'Krampus' likely to be released at the end of 2015, tells the tale of a demonic type Santa Claus.

'Warcraft' penciled for release in 2016 is based on the popular video game series.

'Spectral' scheduled for release in 2016, is a movie based on the concept of sending in a Special Forces team to deal with a city overrun with supernatural beings (it is rumored to be shot in 3D).

'Kong: Skull Island', which we have spoken about – could this also be a house too?

'The Great Wall', little is known about this movie other than it is likely to be a thriller and released in either late 2016 or early 2017.

Could any of these be houses for 2016, 2017 or 2018? This writer hopes that the third most financially successful movie at the box-office ever[6], 'Jurassic World', will one day become a haunt! Whatever the outcome, mixing these high-profile movies into houses by utilizing Universal's own world-renown expertise and flair for creating wholly new and exciting content will ensure us fans will never be disappointed.

This synergy of cross marketing is obviously desirable to outside production companies too who can be approached by the event's organizers to say, 'look at what we can do' and 'look at how they could help your movie's box office'. It all creates a win-win situation for all involved, that's why the future of the event cannot be safer. The event is in the hands now of some of the best creative haunt professionals in the world, they are backed up by one of the most forward-thinking can-do companies in the world – an aspect that is essential in these days of huge corporates, combined with their partnership with Legendary and the corporate friends they have made over the years with their successful handling of other IPs. That's why this award winning event will continue to grow and grow and will always stay the world's number one haunt attraction.

Notes:

[1] Los Angeles Times July 10, 2013
[2] Orlando Sentinel Aug 12, 2014
[3] Ibid
[4] Los Angeles Times July 9, 2013
[5] imdb.com Pro
[6] boxofficemojo.com

Reading/Watching List for 2015

Prepare now!

Preparation is key for enjoying Halloween Horror Nights, so-much-so we fully recommend the following movies to help prepare you for the horrors that will be coming this year. The list has been compiled from general atmospheric movies that are very detailed and have a vague resemblances to the various icons of the event, with the movies and shows for the three franchises already announced added too.

General:

- Sharknado 3: Oh Hell No: As it mixes horror and comedy right inside the very theme park that you will be attending.
- The 'It' movie from 1990 would give most guests a taste for Jack's persona.
- 'The Thing' movie from either 1982 or 2011 would be a good idea as this house was wildly popular in years past, so it could be presented again.
- 'Something Wicked This Way Comes' (1983) is good for the Caretaker.
- 'The Gingerbread Man' (2005)
- 'Jack Frost' (1997)
- 'Rumpelstiltskin' (1995)
- 'The Tooth Fairy' (2006)
- 'Snow White: A Tale of Terror' (1997)
- 'The Maze Runner' (2014)
- 'Jack the Ripper' (1988) Michael Caine version.
- 'From Hell' (2001)

The Walking Dead:

- Any of the latest seasons of the popular AMC show.

Freddy vs Jason:

- Well you need to watch the original 2003 movie of the same name at all costs!
- The original Friday 13th and Nightmare on Elm Street movies.

Insidious:

- All three of the original movies should be available online or on Blu-ray by the event, these are: Insidious (2010), Insidious: Chapter 2 (2013), and Insidious: Chapter 3 (2015).

Rex: "It's totally cool as my shift at 'Islands' finished at 7pm…"

"The people that wanna see everything in one night Touring Plan…"

Touring Plan 1 - All in one nighter

Premise: The person who wants to see everything in one night at all cost.

When: Avoid Fridays and Saturdays, Wednesdays are best, followed by Thursdays and then Sundays. The event seems to be busiest in the first weeks and the last week – so pick a week in mid-October.

Required: An express pass and a day-ticket for either the Studios or Islands Park. Note that the best location to be would be the Studios Park.

Starting point: Universal usually pens guests into two groups when the Studios Park shuts for the day. These are typically held in the New York area or Kidzone. Islands of Adventure guests can typically queue up inside the Seuss Landing area of the park and enter in via a small gate when the event opens. The best starting point used to be the New York area. Guests cannot chose which area they will be in if you are not in these areas before close, so check the time that the park closes first. Typically most fans of the event will hangout inside Finnegan's Bar and Grill waiting for the event to commence if in the New York area. On occasions the park may let guests out of the penned area before the park gates open, if they do make sure you check which houses nearby are open, as some have staggered openings to meet the footfall on busy nights. Guests in the Kidzone area can queue as early as 4pm for the houses here and are usually allowed into the houses before 5.45pm but I have excluded this for the one nighter plan as sometimes this perk can be for annual passholders only. So we must start at the New York holding area first. You will be given wristbands at both locations.

First house: Walk straight to the entrance of which ever house is located next to the Twister ride entrance near the New York Public Library façade. This way the house should empty out in Production Central.

Second House: Now in Production Central there are usually two houses that enter and exit here with a third that will exit by the Twister location. Ensure to queue for both houses that enter and exit in Production Central.

Top Tip here: Remember that your express pass is valid for one-house-per-event, so if on these first three houses if there is no queue, then do not use your express pass! You can then use your express pass later on in the evening instead when the queues build up.

Third House: As above.

Show: The first and last performances of each show are always the less crowded, this means you can see the show and then exit without losing too much time. A good tip would be to see the Bill and Ted show first. Upon exiting make your way to Sprung Tent 2.

Fourth House: Make your way into the queue for this house which should be nearby next to the Men in Black attraction. Following the queuing for this house you should be perfectly positioned in the Kidzone area.

Fifth House: You should now be near the entrance to the Parade Building, find it and queue for it.

Sixth House: You should empty back out in Kidzone, walk back up to the Men in Black area and find the queue for the Sprung Tent 1 house.

Seventh House: Walk back to New York via the Diagon Alley area and now queue for the final soundstage house. You may have to queue up a bit for this house. Note that although you have an express pass, the time to check and then scan each pass takes time. Peak night express queues can be as long as 30 minutes for the busy times.

Show: Now walk over to whichever show is in the Beetlejuice area, this should be the last show of the evening.

Eight House: You should exit right near the Disaster attraction, quickly break away from the crowds and find the nearby queue for this house.

Ninth House: If there is an eighth house it will either be next to the Shrek attraction or it will be in another soundstage. Whichever it is you can easily walk to both from this point.

Ending: With time to spare (hopefully), either enjoy the scarezones, grab a bite to eat or use your express pass on the rides. Noting that although your express pass is good for one-house-one-entry, you can go as many times as you like for the other rides and attractions. After the event closes you can usually use your event ticket to get free access to most of the night clubs in City Walk (if you are over 21) but that is if you have any energy to do so! The top tip here would be to book a room before hand with Universal at any of their resorts, so that once the event finishes you can have a short stroll back to you room. The closest resort for this is The Hardrock Hotel, which is a mere 7 minute walk from the front gates of the Studios.

Staying onsite guests:

Touring Plan 2 - Guests staying at an onsite resort

Premise: Guests who have chosen to stay onsite. Note that some guests will have free express pass for the parks, this does not work for Halloween Horror Nights, if you need it (recommended) you must buy it separately from your resort or online from Universal.

When: Avoid Fridays and Saturdays, Wednesdays are best, followed by Thursdays and then Sundays. The event seems to be busiest in the first weeks and the last week – so pick a week in mid-October.

Required: Separate event tickets

Starting Point: Assuming you are coming from your room or City Walk, guests need to head to the far right of the main arches where a separate queue for resort guests only is found. Like all guests you will have your bag checked and you will walk through an airport style scanner. Note that no weapons or costumes are allowed at the event. If you have day passes for the parks, either go to Islands and use the small entrance in Seuss Landing (where you are still scanned but it is quicker) or stay within the Studios in the New York area penned in.

Plan: Follow the steps in the 'one nighter' touring plan.

Frequent Fearers:

Touring Plan 3 - Guests who have purchased a frequent fear pass of any kind.

Premise: Guests who have either the 'Frequent Fear' pass or 'Rush of Fear' pass will likely be attending the event more than once.

When: Avoid Fridays and Saturdays, Wednesdays are best, followed by Thursdays and then Sundays. The event seems to be busiest in the first weeks and the last week – so pick a week in mid-October. 'Rush of Fear' owners can only attend on the first few nights as per your terms. Some passes exclude the weekends, please do check before heading out.

Required: Just your pass with or without express

Starting Point: Assuming you are not an annual passholder, if you are, you need to start in the park as per Touring Plan 1. If you are not you need to start at the park gates. Typically the event starts at 6.30pm with the security lines opening at 6pm. Make sure you are there either by 5.30pm or after the initial rush around 7pm – its ok, you're not missing anything as you can come back multiple days. Follow your instincts and take it easy!

Must do: The 'old' must-do for all fans of the event was a nightly ride on Jaws or 'the shark in the dark' ride, though unfortunately old Bruce is no longer with us (RIP Bruce), so instead create a new tradition. Perhaps have a meal in the Monster Café or ride The Mummy.

Exiting: To avoid a traffic jam, leave the park at least 45 minutes before closing, or continue enjoying the houses right up until the last scare. Note that using valet parking can get you ahead of the jam if you can collect your car without a wait.

"Taking ~~a chicken~~ a person who might get scared at the event..."

Touring Plan 4 - Guests travelling with a person who is scared of the event.

Premise: Guests travelling with a person who has never been before or have been and is still terrified of the prospect of attending.

When: Avoid Fridays and Saturdays, Wednesdays are best, followed by Thursdays and then Sundays. The event seems to be busiest in the first weeks and the last week – so pick a week in mid-October.

Required: Separate event tickets, though express-passes are highly recommended to cut down the anticipation or suspense felt in the queue.

Starting Point: A great starting point to help anyone with anxiety about the event is to first take them around the park during the day, either the day of or before the event, so they can familiarize themselves with the layout.

Pre-start step 1:   Next you need to take them on a day-time tour of the houses, maybe an afternoon tour after a light lunch and let them see for themselves the artistry that goes into the event without any of scareactors being present. If they can't stand that level of inclusion, then I would recommend they not attend the event. The tours are always led by several extremely knowledgeable tour guides that can extinguish any fears but showcasing the artistry and complexities that go into building every single house. If they can hack that, go to the next step.

Pre-start step 2:   Once you have done a tour, you need to be the studios park before closing and be in one of the designated areas as the park prepares for the event. Allow your guest to see the setup process and fear comfortable that it is still day-light outside. Perhaps have a snack and a drink and relax.

Assume you are in the New York area.

First house: As soon as the event opens, take your guest to one of the houses that have opened from your tour. The likelihood is that on your tour you probably visited one or more of the soundstage houses. Taking your guest to a house they are already familiar with will hopefully build confidence. If after the first house, your guest is feeling ok you can proceed to the next step.

Show: Halloween Horror Nights isn't just about the scares, it was started as a party, and party on down we shall do. Teach your guest that some of the best adult/tween orientated shows can be found during the event, so take them to see Bill and Ted.

Scarezones: Now they've seen a show and should feel more relaxed, take your guest through a couple of scarezones. Advise your guest of the following secret, 'if you make eye contact and appear not scared, the likelihood is that the scareactor will leave you alone'. And always remind them that scareactors are here to make the event enjoyable, they won't touch you or overly try and make you get scared, they want you to have fun!

Second house: Now your guest has familiarized themselves with the streets, it is now time to take them to another house. Try choosing the comedy house of the year (if there is one) or an IP house that they might be familiar with.

Show: Now walk over and see whichever show you didn't see earlier, it will probably be 'Rocky Horror', 'Beetlejuice', 'the event icon's show' or a 'magic show'.

Third house: Straight after the show walk to the closest house queue and enjoy.

Ride: End the event early with a ride on another favorite ride.

Leave: Leaving slightly earlier you should reward your guest with an ice-cream on City Walk or a drink from one of the bars. If they enjoyed themselves due to this touring plan, then you need to come back again the next day and finish off the houses and scarezones that you didn't see. If they were scared all the way round and could not possible see themselves coming back… then you need to come back solo buddy!

Top Tips:

Tickets:

1. Always buy your tickets from Universal Studios, no matter where you live in the world.

2. Purchasing your tickets ahead of time will save you having to queue up again once you have cleared security. Purchasing your tickets ahead of time can be undertaken by calling Universal, going onto their official website or attending any onsite ticket window or resort concierge before the event.

3. If you plan on attending more than once, then a Frequent Fear pass will always work out the best value.

4. Express passes have a history (though not recently) of selling out. Therefore ensure you purchase your express pass as soon as you know when you are going or upgrade your Frequent Fear pass to enable this option.

5. Universal usually does some great offers for guests wanting to spend the day in Islands of Adventure on the day of your booked event. Go to Guest Services or any park ticket window and enquire.

6. Be careful online when buying your tickets, as some guests do seem to muddle the Hollywood event with the Orlando one. Note that the tickets are non-transferable, so if you buy the tickets for the wrong coast, you will have to buy new ones.

Entry and when to go:

1. Get there as early as possible, probably enter the park during the day and 'stay and scream' as per the touring plan in this guide.

2. If you are a hotel guest ensure you keep right at the park gates, as you will have a separate entry.

3. To speed up the process at the security check area, ensure you have all your belongings out ready for inspection.

4. When to go to the event can vary each year. However a rule of thumb is to avoid any weeks that coincide with local school and college vacations. Typically the first two weeks and the last in October are the busiest, with the final week being the busiest. The third sometimes fourth weekend in October is usually referred to as 'Hell week', due to the schools that have let out combined with both local and international vacations that are all held then. The event can sometimes sell-out during this.

5. The best time to visit is within the first fortnight of the event (though the weather can be bad then) or in the middle of the month of October. Universal usually offers deals like 'Rush of Fear' tickets that enable guests to attend the event in the first two weeks at a lower cost, in an effort to push up attendance.

6. Note that parking isn't free for the event, so queues can build up at the parking garage. Therefore, ensure you leave plenty of time to park and then get through security before the event. On select nights the valet parking option also becomes congested, so don't rely on this option if you have the money to do.

7. As the event and the express passes can respectively sell out, it is always the best policy to buy your tickets early. They typically go on sale in June of every year for this very reason.

General tips:

1. Do not despair if you don't have an express pass and the queue for a certain house is over 3 hours in length, the chances are the later you stay the shorter the queue will get. Some nights, the event

224

stays open until 2am, providing enough time to see any select house.

2. The event is scary and not recommended for anyone under 13, that's exactly why they do not sell kid's tickets. So think twice before paying out for the tickets as to whether your children will actually enjoy this event.

3. Whether you have an express pass or not it is always worth attending the event more than once. Many people say that you can truly appreciate everything that is on offer at the event unless you attend at least two full nights.

4. If you see a red button inside a house – press it. It will nearly always trigger some kind of effect or scare that will be worth seeing. Look out for these buttons as they are always hidden within plain sight.

5. Not only does Universal design some unique scares every year, but they also try to come up with unique activities and food options too. In the past the unique activities have included: Fortune telling, dance parties, henna tattoos and various meet-and-greets with actual celebrities. Unique food options have include 'twisted-taters' and a 'shark attack' cocktail.

6. If you wish to drink alcohol at the event, ensure you have appropriate ID with you and register just inside the park gates.

7. Remember to have fun and not get drunk. Sheriff Deputies along with park security are stationed at every house and scarezone, so if you or your friends get too rowdy you can get expelled from the event.

8. If you are feeling unwell or too scared during a house, you can leave the house by speaking to one of the house chaperones that are stationed after every scene. They are there to direct the guests to the next scene and ensure everybody is having a good time; they typically stand in a corridor where an exit sign is located.

9. Bring plenty of money with you, as the event provides a number of unique purchasing opportunities that are only on offer during each night. Special event merchandise can include: t-shirts, hoodies, vinyl toys, fridge magnets, shot-glasses, pins and other collectibles.

House Locations at Universal Studios Orlando

Soundstage 18:

This location was originally the main production space for Nickelodeon Studios, before they relocated their productions to the West coast. It is now occupied by the Blue Man Group and has been retitled 'Sharp Aquos Theater'.

Where Evil Hides (HHN 15)

Soundstage 20:

This location has been used to film various shows for TNA Wrestling and Nickelodeon. It is one of the largest soundstages on the lot and can often house two mazes back-to-back inside.

Scream House (HHN 12)
Scream House Revisited (HHN 13)
All Nite Die-In (HHN 13)
Hellgate Prison (HHN 14)
Horror in Wax (HHN 14)
Cold Blind Terror (HHN 15)
Body Collectors: Collections of the Past (HHN 18)
Interstellar Terror (HHN 18)
Gothic (HHN 22)
Dead End (HHN 22)

Soundstage 22A:

One of the medium sized soundstages that has housed many of the haunts over the years.

Universal's Museum Of Horror (HHN 7)
Museum Of Horror: Chamber of Horrors (HHN 8)
Museum Of Horror: Unnatural History (HHN 8)
Psycho...Through the Mind of Norman Bates (HHN 9)
Insanity (HHN 9)

Anxiety (HHN 10)
Total Chaos (HHN 10)
Scary Tales (HHN 11)
Pitch Black (HHN 11)
Ghost Town (HHN 14)
Blood Ruins (HHN 15)
Psychoscareapy: Maximum Madness (HHN 16
Dead Silence: The Curse Of Mary Shaw (HHN 17)

Creatures! (HHN 18)
The Wolfman (HHN 19)
Legendary Truth: The Wyandot Estate (HHN 20)
Winter's Night: The Haunting Of Hawthorn Cemetery (HHN 21)
Silent Hill (HHN 22)
An American Werewolf In London (HHN 23)
From Dusk Till Dawn (HHN 24)

Soundstage 21:

This was formerly the main production area for TNA Wrestling   and due to this it has not been used very often for houses at the event.

The Cabin in the Woods (HHN 23)
Resident Evil: Escape From Raccoon City (HHN 23)

Soundstage 23:

One of the smallest soundstages on the lot, it has been used by various television shows over the years.

The People Under The Stairs (HHN 2)
The People Under The Stairs (HHN 3)
Universal's House of Horror (HHN 5)
Castle Vampyr (HHN 15)
Scream House: Resurrection (HHN 16)
All Nite Die-In: Take 2 (HHN 16)
A Nightmare on Elm Street: Dream Walkers (HHN 17)
Psychoscareapy: Home for the Holidays (HHN 17)
Frankenstein (HHN 19)
Dracula: Legacy in Blood (HHN 19)
Hades (HHN 20)

Psychoscareapy: Echoes of Shadybrook (HHN 20)
Nightingales: Blood Prey (HHN 21)
The Thing (HHN 21)

Soundstage 24:

One of the medium sized soundstages on the lot that has been used for the
purposes of filming for various productions including: Psycho IV, Ace
Ventura 3, Superboy (TV series), Sharknado 3 and SeaQuest 2032.
Therefore it has not been used for the purposes of this event very often.

Evil Dead (HHN 23)
Avp: Alien Vs Predator (HHN 24)
Dracula Untold: Reign of Blood (HHN 24)

Soundstage 25:

Soundstages 25 and 19 are specially constructed soundstages for the
purposes of filming TV shows due to the additional rigs and 1st floor
control room. Various Halloween Horror Nights commercials, live TV
spots and other TV shows have been recorded here. Therefore it has not
been used for the purposes of this event to until 2014. Soundstage 19
which is much larger, has never been used for Halloween Horror Nights.

The Walking Dead: End Of The Line (HHN 24) – the largest haunted
house ever constructed by the event.

Soundstage 44 (Hercules/Xena/Murder She Wrote Building):

This originally housed the 'Murder She Wrote' attraction when the park
first opened. This made way for a 'Hercules and Xena' attraction in 1997,
before it was closed down in 2000. The building was then demolished in
2012.
Horror Nights Nightmares (HHN 14)
Unknown House (HHN 2012) – was demolished before the event started
to make way for the new Transformers ride. Rumored to have been
'American Werewolf in London'.

The Parade Building (B-79):

This was originally built to house the day-time parade, it has subsequently been repurposed for Halloween Horror Nights.

Scary Tales: Once Upon A Nightmare (HHN 18)
Silver Screams (HHN 19)
Horror Nights: The Hallow'd Past (HHN 20)
The Forsaken (HHN 21)
Universal's House of Horrors (HHN 22)
The Walking Dead: No Safe Haven (HHN 23)
Roanoke: Cannibal Colony (HHN 24)

Jaws Queue:

The original haunt location that was demolished in 2012 to make way for Harry Potter phase 2.

Dungeon of Terror (Fright Nights)
Dungeon of Terror (HHN 2)
Dungeon of Terror: Retold (HHN 16)
Friday The 13th: Camp Blood (HHN 17)
Reflections of Fear (HHN 18)
Saw (HHN 19)
Orfanage: Ashes to Ashes (HHN 20)
Saws N' Steam: Into the Machine (HHN 21)

Sprung Tent 1:

Built solely for the use of Halloween Horror Nights in 2006.

Psycho Path: The Return of Norman Bates (HHN 16)
The Thing: Assimilation (HHN 17)
The Hallow (HHN 18)
Chucky: Friends till the End (HHN 19)
Catacombs: Black Death Rising (HHN 20)
The In-Between (HHN 21)
Alice Cooper: Welcome to My Nightmare (HHN 22)
Urban Legends: La Llorona (HHN 23)
Dollhouse of the Damned (HHN 24)

Sprung Tent 2:

Built solely for the use of Halloween Horror Nights in 2006.

The People Under The Stairs: Under Construction (HHN 16)
Jack's Funhouse in Clown-O-Vision (HHN 17)
Dead Exposure (HHN 18)
The Spawning (HHN 19)
Havoc: The Dogs of War (HHN 20)
Nevermore: The Madness Oo Poe (HHN 21)
Penn & Teller New(K'd) Las Vegas (HHN 22)
After Life: Death's Vengeance (HHN 23)
Halloween (HHN 24)

Nazarman's
Re-purposed as a location for Halloween Horror Nights in 1993, this location was effectively taken out of use in 2007 when the area became occupied via lease by Starbucks.

The Slaughterhouse (HHN 3)
Hell's Kitchen (HHN 4)
Terror Underground: Transit to Torment (HHN 5)
Toy Hell: Nightmare at the Scream Factory (HHN 6)
Hotel Hell (HHN 7)
Hell's High (HHN 8)
Universal's Creature Features in 3d! (HHN 9)
Superstitions (HHN 11)
Vampyr: Blood Bath (HHN 17)

Earthquake / Disaster Queue:

The outdoor queue housing for the above attraction. Most props stored within the queue have to be easily removed for the event.

Dungeon of Terror (HHN 4)
Crypt Keeper's Dungeon of Terror (HHN 5)
Crypt Keeper's Studio Tour of Terror (HHN 6)
Tombs of Terror (HHN 7)
S.S. Frightanic: Carnage Crew (HHN 8)
S.S. Frightanic: Fear In First Class (HHN 8)

The Mummy (HHN 9)
Doomsday (HHN 9)
Universal Classic Monster Mania (HHN 10)
Dark Torment (HHN 10)
The Mummy Returns: The Curse Continues (HHN 11)
Run (HHN 11)
Deadtropolis (HHN 14)
Run: Hostile Territory (HHN 16)
The Texas Chainsaw Massacre: Flesh Wounds (HHN 17)

Doomsday (HHN 18)
Leave It To Cleaver (HHN 19)
Zombiegeddon (HHN 20)
H.R. Bloodengutz: Holidays of Horror (HHN 20)
The Walking Dead: Dead Inside (HHN 22)
Havoc: Derailed (HHN 23)
Giggles & Gore Inc. (HHN 24)

The Bates Motel from 'Psycho IV':

The original sets from the 1990 movie of the same name. The motel was demolished shortly after HHN5 and then the house followed suit in 1998. These were both unfortunately located in the Kidzone area, hence their requirement to be demolished.

The Psycho Path Maze (HHN 3)
The Psycho Path Maze (HHN 4)
The Psycho Path Maze (HHN 5)

The Bone Yard:

An area in the park that used to house props and sets from previous Universal movies. The area was repurposed in 2008 to make way for the Universal Music Plaza Stage.

The Bone Yard (HHN 4)

Shrek 4-D Theater:
An attraction within the park currently.
Unknown house (HHN 25)

Islands of Adventure Theme Park Locations:

Carnage House / B285a:
A building specially erected for the event in 2012, it now serves as storage.

Maximum Carnage (HHN 12)
Disorientorium (HHN 14)
Demon Cantina (HHN 15)

Popeye and Bluto's Bilge-Rat Barges Queue Building:

The queue building from the popular water ride.

Scary Tales 2 (HHN 12)
Ship of Screams (HHN 13)

Jurassic Park Discovery Center:

The actual discovery center from the themed island.

Psychoscareapy (HHN 13)
Body Collectors (HHN 15)

Triceratops Discovery Trail:

A now defunct attraction that was in 2015 repurposed into a meet-and-greet with raptors from the Jurassic Park franchise.

Evilution (HHN 12)
Jungle of Doom (HHN 13)

Thunder Falls Terrace:

A restaurant in the Jurassic Park area of the park.
Fear Factor (HHN 12)
Funhouse of Fear (HHN 13)
The Skool (HHN 14)

Poseidon's Fury:

An attraction at the theme park.
Terror Mines (HHN 15)

Which Pass?   Save Money!

You can save money if you want to attend the event for more than one night by purchasing a Frequent Fear Pass or Rush of Fear Pass. Please see the below costs for buying these passes based on going more than one night (based on 2015 prices). All prices per person and plus tax.

General Admin - 1 night $101.99
Separate Express Pass - 1 night $69.99 - $119.99
Average Price of Express Pass $99.99

FQ F	FQ F Ex	FQ F +	FQ F Ex	Rush	No.
$94.99	$234.99	$110.99	$279.99	$83.99	1 Night
$47.49	$117.49	$55.49	$139.99	$41.99	2 Nights
$31.66	$78.33	$36.99	$93.33	$27.99	3 Nights
$23.74	$58.74	$27.74	$69.99	$20.99	4 Nights
$18.99	$46.99	$22.19	$55.99	$16.79	5 Nights
$15.83	$39.16	$18.49	$46.66	$13.99	6 Nights
$13.57	$33.57	$15.85	$39.99	$11.99	7 Nights
$11.87	$29.37	$13.87	$34.99	$10.49	8 Nights
$10.55	$26.11	$12.33	$31.11	$9.33	9 Nights
$9.49	$23.49	$11.09	$27.99	$8.39	10 Nights
$8.63	$21.36	$10.09	$25.45		11 Nights
$7.91	$19.58	$9.24	$23.33		12 Nights
$7.30	$18.07	$8.53	$21.53		13 Nights
$6.78	$16.78	$7.92	$19.99		14 Nights
$6.33	$15.66	$7.39	$18.66		15 Nights
$5.93	$14.68	$6.93	$17.49		16 Nights
$5.58	$13.82	$6.52	$16.47		17 Nights
$5.27	$13.05	$6.16	$15.55		18 Nights
		$5.84	$14.73		19 Nights
		$5.54	$13.99		20 Nights
		$5.28	$13.33		21 Nights
		$5.04	$12.72		22 Nights
		$4.82	$12.17		23 Nights
		$4.62	$11.66		24 Nights

FQ F	Frequent Fear Pass (good for 18 select nights)
FQ F Ex	Frequent Fear Pass with Express (good for 18 select nights)
FQ F +	Frequent Fear Plus Pass (good for 24 select nights)
FQ F Ex	Frequent Fear Plus Pass with Express (good for 24 select nights)
Rush	Rush of Fear Pass (good for 10 select nights early on in the event)

About the Author

Christopher Ripley was born in the UK but has been travelling to and living in the US for many years. He has been attending both Universal Studios Florida and Hollywood for over 20 years. An architect by day, his passion for architecture, construction and filmmaking has piqued his interest at Universal Studios where their dedication to design, build and performing the best Halloween attractions in the world has led him to write extensively about the subject and allowed him to write this his first book, 'Halloween Horror Nights: The Unofficial Story & Guide'.

For any comments or to purchase signed copies message us at twitter @christopherrip or facebook.com/ripleychristopher